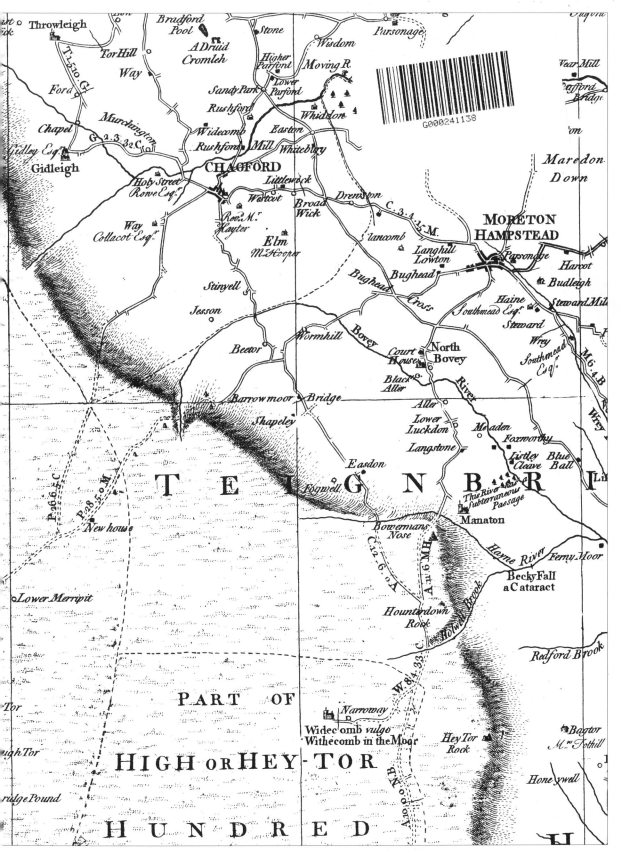

Dartmoor – from Donn's Map of Devon, 1765.

THE DISCOVERY OF
DARTMOOR

A Wild and Wondrous Region

Moorland Falls, Tavy Cleave, Ray Balkwill.

THE DISCOVERY OF
DARTMOOR

A Wild and Wondrous Region

PATRICIA MILTON

PHILLIMORE

2006

Published by
PHILLIMORE & CO. LTD
Shopwyke Manor Barn, Chichester, West Sussex, England

© Patricia Milton, 2006

ISBN 1-86077-401-6
ISBN 13 978-1-86077-401-0

Printed and bound in Great Britain by
CAMBRIDGE UNIVERSITY PRESS

Contents

List of Illustrations

Frontispiece: Moorland Falls, Tavy Cleave.

COLOUR PLATES

Colour plates are between pp.148/9.

ACKNOWLEDGEMENTS

I would like to record my gratitude to the following persons and institutions for help received: Brian Le Messurier for constant guidance and encouragement so kindly given, and use of illustrations; John Biggs of John Collins & Son Fine Art, Bideford, for providing illustrations and advice; Dave Pawley for his photographs and practical help on IT related matters; Ray Balkwill for illustrations; Maureen Attrill, Curator, at the Plymouth Museum and Art Gallery; Sue Davies of the Tavistock Museum; St John and Jack Milton for photography; Simon Dell for illustration; Andy Stevens and Forest Publications for illustrations; Mike Birch for IT back-up; Doreen and Ivan Mead for sharing moorland childhood memories; Pamela Wootton, Dr Robin Wootton, and Roger Brien of the Devon and Exeter Institution; John Smith at the Plymouth Proprietary Library; Staff at The Royal Albert Memorial Museum, Exeter; Devon Record Office (DRO), Exeter; West Devon Record Office (WDRO), Plymouth; Westcountry Studies Library, Exeter; and Plymouth Local Studies Library; Thanks for support from the The Catherine Linehan Memorial Fund.

The author and publisher are grateful to the owners and trustees of copyright for permission to publish these images: J. Collins & Son Fine Art, Bideford for the following water colours, 4, *September Heather and Gorse, Roborough Down* by J. Barrett; 7, *Ponies on Arms Tor, Near Lydford, Dartmoor* by T. Rowden; 8, *Chagford and the River Teign* by W.S. Morrish; 58, *Okehampton in 1807* attrib. to J. Farington; 69, *Tavy Cleave, Dartmoor* by E. Brittan; 72, *Evening on the River Teign, Prince and Sharipton Rocks Above Fingle Bridge, Dartmoor* by J. Barrett. Colour Plates I, *The Source of the Tavy* by J.B King (1864-1939); II, *Christmas Morn, Lydford, Devon* by W. Widgery (1826-93); IV, *Evening Sunlight, Dartmoor – The Road from Pew Tor to Vixen Tor*, by J. Barrett (fl. 1875-1900); VII, *Sheepstor, Dartmoor* by W. Widgery; VIII, *Cranmere Pool, Dartmoor* by F.J. Widgery; XI, *Taw Marsh, Dartmoor*, by G.H. Jenkins Jnr (1836-1937); XII, *Steperton Tor, Dartmoor*, by F.J. Widgery; XIII *Amicombe Hill, Dartmoor*, by F.J. Widgery; XIV, *On the Tavy at Gur Tor, Dartmoor* by E.A. Tozer, *c.*1892; Ray Balkwill: XVI and frontispiece; Simon Dell, 109; Brian Le Messurier, 18, 79, 87, 91, XV; David Pawley, 3, 6, 14, 15, 35, 49, 60-2, 74, 80, 82, 84, 95, 101, 102, 104, 110-12; Andy Stevens, 105; Dartmoor Preservation Association, 5; Devon and Cornwall Record Society, 1, 39, front and rear endpapers; The Devon and Exeter Institution, 2, 9, 10-13, 16, 17, 19, 20, 22, 28-32, 36, 37, 43-6, 48, 53, 56, 59, 63, 64, 66; 68, 70, 71, 73, 75-7, 81, 83, 85, 88, 89, 96, 97, 99, IX; Local

Studies Library, Plymouth, 33, X; Plymouth Museum and Art Gallery, 34, 51, III; Plymouth Proprietary Library, 21, 23, 38, 42, 47, 55, 57, 98; Record Office, Exeter, 25, 26, 40, 41, 54, 93, 100, 103, 108, VI; Westcountry Studies Library, Exeter, 24, 52, 107, V.

Introduction

In the 16th century, Dartmoor and its people had a dire reputation. The region was dubbed dreary; the fringe dwellers judged uncouth.

Now, each year, an estimated 10-11 million day visits are made to the moor, and local communities are well respected.

The Discovery of Dartmoor sets out to examine the various influences that brought about such profound change. The various social, political and economic developments and technological innovations that resulted in this cultural shift will be considered. A chronological approach will be followed, starting from around the late 16th century and drawing to a close soon after 1951, the year Dartmoor was designated a National Park.

In 1883 efforts to compile a bibliography of Dartmoor writings revealed just over fifty texts, most of those published in the 19th century. In 1992, when the *Dartmoor Bibliography* was published, over 7,000 books and articles were recorded – excluding the region's fiction.[1] In the years since some hundreds more books, videos, CDs, journals, postcards, television and radio programmes have been produced. And, whereas only a handful of illustrations existed prior to the mid-19th century, today the area is recognised as an inspirational subject for creative artists. Such an abundance of relatively recent material necessitates some degree of selection, so within a broad cultural context, this book will gradually focus on the ways in which water-colourists and novelists have interpreted Dartmoor.

The opening chapter will offer several definitions of Dartmoor, and provide as much information relating to its past as is necessary to make sense of later references. From then on, each chapter will begin with a brief overview of moorland developments before turning to the literature and art of the times. Chapter 2 will focus on early 17th-century descriptions of place, and persons, while Chapters 3-5 concentrate on late 18th-century developments. This was a period when the moor appealed to entrepreneurs who hoped to exploit its agricultural and industrial potential, and became of interest to a few individuals who began to appreciate the picturesque scenery fringing the region, and recognised the high moor as a relict landscape.

Chapters 6-11 reveal the dichotomy between the desires of capitalists, and those who dreamed of preserving the waste for aesthetic reasons. Concerns over the ability of Dartmorians to cope with the effects of change will be found to surface in a number of novels.

In *The Hound of the Baskervilles*,[2] the subject of Chapter 12, the social reality of late 19th-century Dartmoor will be seen as subservient to the desire of the author to conjure a particular image of the area.

On reaching the early 20th century, chapters 13-16 range over the work of popular artists and consider how topographers and novelists present 'features distinguishing the life, social relations, customs, language, dialect or other aspects of the culture of the area and its people'.[3] Attention will be drawn to how the weight of their prejudices, preferences, and ideology shapes their presentation of Dartmoor and its dwellers.

By Chapter 17, it will have become clear that perceptions of Dartmoor have shifted in response to national needs and the national mood. The once 'dreary' region is now culturally transformed into a fragile, jealously guarded environment. Representations of the population will be seen to have modified, but, as will be discussed, the region's writers are united in creating moorland dwellers who remain 'other' – different, from their urban counterparts.

1

Early Times

Devonshire, in England, is part of that stretch of land 'which shooteth out farthest into the West'. The 'Severn sea licketh with her tongue' the northern shores of the county, while 'the east part hath Somersetshire and Dorsetshire, her friendly neighbours'. Devon's south coast is 'wholly washed with the British sea', and the west is bounded from Cornwall by the river Tamar.[1] Dartmoor lies in this spacious county,

> the neer'st the Center set
> Of any place of note;
> *Poly-Olbion*, iv. 1. 290[2]

The region rises to a height of just over 2,000 feet, with many of its hills capped by piles of fissured rocks known as tors. There are various theories as to the origin of these 200 or so granite outcrops – authorities vary as to exactly how many should be regarded simply as rock piles – but, suffice it to say that chemical and physical action has contributed to the shaping of the rocks and their surrounding debris or clitter. As will become apparent, tors have proved favourite subjects for artists, and writers have set many a climatic scene on their heights.

This granite intrusion with its peaty blanket acts as a great reservoir, and is 'the mother of many rivers'.[3] The region's occasional appellation as 'the twoo forestes of Dartmoor', or 'the Dartmoors', would seem to refer to its north and south tablelands that are divided, roughly, by the lower ground between the towns of Moretonhampstead and Tavistock. From the boggy northern area, the East and West Okement rivers, and the river Taw flow northwards; while the Teign, Dart, Avon, Erme, and Yealm race towards the English channel, and the Walkham meets the Tavy, which, following the Lyd's example, joins the non-Dartmoor Tamar.

With so many rivers and their tributaries rising on the moor, it goes without saying that the rainfall is high, with an annual average of 60 inches compared with 35 inches on the South Devon coast. This was not always so, for about 7,000 years ago the region was warmer, deer, bears and the wild ox roamed, the high grounds were abundantly clothed with hazel and birch trees, while oaks flourished in the valleys. It is thought that some 3,000 years ago settlers, finding the area congenial, formed communities and gradually cleared the trees. As the climate became colder upland homes were abandoned in favour of life in the sheltered valleys. Over the centuries, the formerly tree-covered region degenerated to form

1   *Extract from Donn's Map of Devon, 1765.*

peat, a substance used by moorlanders for fuel, and by early miners as part of the tin smelting process.

Heavily waterlogged peat – of which there are many acres – presents a danger to man and beast. This is emphasised in a story in which a man, familiar with the moor, was making his way across Aune Mire, the source of the river Avon, when he saw a hat – a top hat which he kicked. A voice called out:

> 'What be you a-doin' to my 'at?'
> The man replied, 'Be there now a chap under'n?'
> 'Ess, I reckon', was the reply, 'and a hoss under me likewise.'[4]

2 *Houndter Tor and Rippon Tor, c.1845.*

Another version of this tale draws attention to the perils of the quaker or 'feather bed', signified by clumps of rushes, or a patch of a singularly green colour, a feature in many moorland illustrations. The attractive appearance belies the reality of a spot where water will have gathered beneath a thin matting of vegetation. Under any weight the surface may simply and unnervingly rock, allowing for a speedy withdrawal, or it may suddenly give way. Such treacherous places were known as 'Dartmoor Stables'.

Viewed from a distance, the looming heights of Dartmoor appear open, barren, and uninhabited. Yet, the region is neither barren nor devoid of human population and, although from a distance the moor appears unenclosed, it is a place imprisoned by boundaries, many of which are recognisable only by the cognoscenti. Nor does the term 'Dartmoor' refer only to the upland; it includes a belt of the circumambient country, a gentler area, cleft by streams, abundantly clothed with vegetation and dotted with villages, some of which grew up close to the mineral deposits typically found adjacent to granite. Exactly how much of the engirdling land should be included in the term 'Dartmoor' was, for centuries, a contentious issue.

Writing in about 1478, William of Worcester (1415-84) confined his computations to the length of Dartmoor's rivers from their source to the sea,[5] while half a century later John Leland merely described the region as 'of very

3 *Yealm Valley from Yealm Steps.*

great compace'.[6] Around 1600, John Hooker (1526-1601), Exeter's chamberlain, archivist, and probably the county's most distinguished historian, estimated, in his 'imperfect, immethodical piece',[7] that the moor extended 'some XVI myles one waye and about XII myles the other waye',[8] while Richard Pococke (1704-65), in 1750, settled on 'twenty miles long and fourteen broad'.[9]

    Estimates, from reports commissioned by the Board of Agriculture during the 1790s and early 1800s, confirm the indeterminacy of the region's extent. Robert Fraser in 1794 ventured that:

> the extent of Dartmore is not accurately known, no actual measurement, that I have heard of, having been made of it. It is in general supposed to amount to nearly 100,000 acres. I shall state it only at 80,000 acres, which, from every observation I could make, does not appear to me to be beyond the truth.[10]

William Marshall (1745-1818), in his 1796 survey on *The Rural Economy of the South West*, believed that

4   *September Heather and Gorse, Roborough Down, Dartmoor (Staple and Great Mis Tors in the distance), water colour, by John Barrett (fl. 1875-95).*

a circle of twenty miles diameter, would, perhaps, comprize the whole extent of the open lands, in this part of Devonshire; exclusively of the inclosed lands, which lie intermixed among them. Admitting this supposition to be sufficiently near the truth, to give a general idea of the extent of those open lands, we may say that they cover more than three hundred square miles of surface – amount to more than two hundred thousand acres.[11]

Charles Vancouver, yet another representative of the Board of Agriculture, in his attempt to ascertain the extent of the wastes of the Devonshire Commons around the Forest of Dartmoor, met with 'extremely vague and contradictory' replies. He dismissed the subject with a rather sour 'let their boundaries and extent be what they may, or the right of ownership in them be in whom it would'.[12] His informants were, in all probability, not being obstructive, for boundaries were in some cases a matter of custom, as commons, parish and manorial boundaries overlaid and intersected each other, often without obvious indication.

Years later, Samuel Rowe (1793-1853), one of the most respected authorities on the history and topography of the moor, suggested that the term 'Dartmoor' should include the Forest and those outlying tracts presenting the same general physical features:

[5]

Dartmoor and its adjuncts may be thus estimated, as extending about twenty miles from east to west, and 22 miles from north to south, and as containing more than 130,000 acres of land.[13]

Then, in 1879, the newly formed Dartmoor Committee of the Devonshire Association deemed that, for their purposes, Dartmoor should be regarded 'inclusively and exclusively' as consisting of 38 entire parishes,[14] but the Dartmoor Preservation Association, in 1890, recognised just 26, acknowledging only those whose common lands were contiguous with the Forest, with the addition of Tavistock.

Still the debate continued: in 1905 an index, based on the Devonshire Association's papers relating to the moor, slightly enlarged the bounds set by

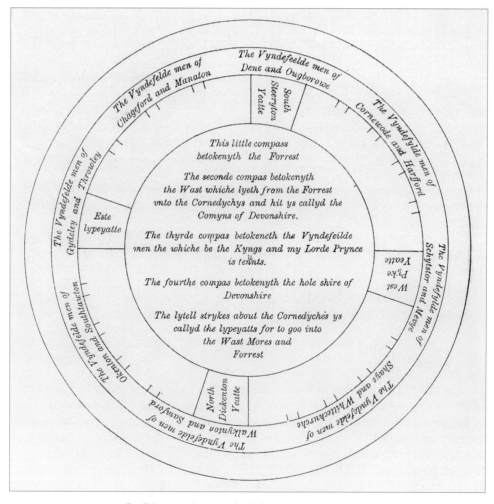

5   *Diagramatic map probably drawn in the 16th century.*

the 1879 Dartmoor Committee and redesignated the region as 'Dartmoor and its Borders'.[15] Taking a less prescriptive approach, R.H. Worth (1868-1950), after over half a century's dedicated study of the moor, opined that it should be loosely described as 'the granite area with as much of the metamorphic halo as may be necessary or convenient'.[16]

It seems, even from the few definitions of the moor presented here, that every interpretation is based on a different set of parameters, and that, essentially, the notion of Dartmoor is elusive, its centre apparent, its fringes indeterminate. However, for the purposes of this book the term 'Dartmoor' encompasses the Forest, the Commons, the encircling parishes and other settlements with close historical, social, or economic connections to the Forest and Commons. Much of this area is included within the limits of the Dartmoor National Park – designated as such in 1951. Yet, even as a National Park the region remained a shifting construct: between 1951-91 it was quoted as consisting of 365 square miles, then that estimation was adjusted, and the National Park Area now covers 368 square miles (954 sq km).

For our purposes, a diagrammatic map comprised of four concentric circles, thought to have been prepared during the reign of Henry VIII, will provide a logical means of gaining an overview of the moorland social structure.[17] Here, the innermost circle, the Forest of Dartmoor, is surrounded by the 'Comyns of Devonshire'. Beyond that, the third circle 'betokeneth the Vyndefeilde [venville] men, the King's tenants', while the outer circle includes the rest of the county.

With reference to that map, the following broad overview of early moorland demarcations will enable Dartmoor's organisation to be appreciated, starting at its heart – the Forest.

To most of us the term 'Forest' conjures up acres of trees but, properly, it refers to any tract of land, not necessarily tree-covered, preserved as the monarch's hunting ground:

> privileged for wild beasts and fowls of forest, chace and warren, to rest and abide in, in the safe protection of the King, for his princely delight and pleasure [...] of which place, together with the vert and venison, there are certain particular laws, privileges and officers belonging to the same, mete for that purpose, that are only proper for a forest.[18]

In 1204, with the exception of one area, all of Devon that had been designated as forest was disafforested. The exception was what would become the Forest of Dartmoor. To make disafforestation complete a perambulation – a form of 'beating the bounds' – was required in order to define the limits of any remaining forest.[19] The first authenticated record of a perambulation is dated 1240, marking that as the year the Forest of Dartmoor was created, when 'Kinge Henry the 3 for avoydinge of sundrye inconveniens dyd appoint sett downe and lymett the boundes of the same'.[20] The precincts fixed on by the first Perambulators, have have been subject only to minor changes since then. Of no particular consequence,

6   *Cairn at Furnum Regis or King's Oven, a Forest boundary mark.*

the features they selected are mostly still easily identifiable, and mark 'a course which any party making a tour of the Moor and resolved to get back by dinner-time would take'.[21] Perhaps this is a slight exaggeration for the twelve knights who set off on that first perambulation would have had to ride a distance of 50 miles, some of the ground over which they traversed being hard going, tussocky, and boggy.

By 1240 the Forest no longer met the qualifications to be so defined, for the same area had, legally, already become a Chase when, a year previously, its possession was ceded from the King to the Earl of Cornwall.[22] Then, in 1300, there being no heir to the Earldom of Cornwall, the area reverted to the Crown and its former status as a Forest, until in 1308 it was conferred by Edward II on his favourite companion, Piers Gaveston, who held it until 1312, when he was arrested and beheaded.[23] Edward III, in 1336, redesignated the earldom as a Duchy, for his son, Edward, the Black Prince, and included Dartmoor in the 'possessions of the Duchy of Cornwall vested in the Prince of Wales, when there was one living'.[24] This pattern has prevailed until the present, with every Duke of Cornwall's ownership of Dartmoor acknowledged in the term 'Duchy' land. It seems probable that the reason why the monarch or his heirs retained Dartmoor was that the tin mines had been, from time immemorial, regarded as an important 'Fountain of Riches'.[25]

Theoretically, whenever the Forest of Dartmoor passed into the heir's possession its status changed to that of a Chase, by custom the area continues to be known as a Forest.[26] The village of Lydford, on the moor's western fringe, embraced the whole Forest within its parish bounds and, until the 19th century, was the administrative centre for the Duchy.

There must have been clusters of homes and scattered farms in existence 'time out of mind', prior to the moor's designation as a Forest, for various parcels of land were never regarded as unlawful encroachments, nor were the inhabitants turned out.[27] The number and extent of these sites, known as Ancient Tenements, has been over the centuries a matter of dispute, though 35 seems to be the number settled on by modern local historians. The total population of tenement holders, existing by subsistence farming and stock rearing, hovered around 200 for several centuries.

To the Ancient Tenement holders, also called Forest Men, certain rights accrued. They were entitled to pasture all commonable beasts in the Forest and on the surrounding commons; to dig peat for fuel; to remove stone and sand to mend their homes and land; and to take heath for thatching, and probably, for use as animal litter. A 'fines villarum' or 'venville', in other words a rent, would be payable for these rights, sometimes known as 'venville rights', or 'Commoners' rights'. A further right, attached solely to the Ancient Tenements, was that of 'newtake', of increasing the holding by up to eight acres of land when a new tenant took over, providing the farm had been held successively by the two previous generations. It was customary to interpret the privilege as eight acres excluding rock and bog, which, considering the nature of the terrain, could amount to far more than the prescribed limit. The practice was open to abuse, and rescinded in 1796.

Living 'in venville' imposed certain duties: persons were bound to respect their venville agreement; to assist at the three annual Dartmoor drifts – when stock was rounded up and any unclaimed animals impounded, and to attend court at Lydford when summonsed, where local problems might be resolved. Tenants seem to have lived relatively peaceably, records indicating occasional lapses such as attempts at illegal enclosure, poaching, or stealing each other's stock – as happened in 1512, when a group of moorlanders 'unlawfully and riotously, in the manner of an insurrection' took 40 oxen and steers, and 10 geldings from Brattor, near Lydford.[28] Echoes of one complaint – against the moorlander who kept 'a certain suspicious dog where of right he ought not', – would resound down the years, culminating in a work of fiction – *The Hound of the Baskervilles* – that, for many people over many years, would define Dartmoor.

Forest dwellers were expected to attend their parish church at Lydford, a long and often difficult journey from the eastern bounds, especially when bearing a coffin along the Lich – or corpse – Path. Fortunately, in 1260, Bishop Walter Bronescombe granted the inhabitants of two Ancient Tenements, Babeny and

7   *Ponies on Arms Tor, near Lydford, Dartmoor, watercolour by Thomas Rowden (1842-1926).*

Pizwell, permission to attend services at St Pancras, Widecombe-in-the-Moor, which must have been a great relief. On Dartmeet Hill, two blocks of granite known as the Coffin Stone are a reminder of the time when a cortège on its way to St Pancras would set down the coffin and rest. One day, so the story goes, when a particularly evil character's body was lowered, the single block of granite was, as can still be seen, rent apart by lightning.

The Second Circle boundary established by this 1240 perambulation, between the Forest of Dartmoor and the Commons, did not, in a material sense, exist, for Venville rights extended over both the Forest and the Commons. The Commons, while in theory assigned to the various moorland parishes, were, in practice, one great common girdling the Forest where animals could roam at will.

The Third Circle related to inhabitants of parishes whose common land was at some point contiguous with the Forest. On payment of a small fee or rent, they would be considered as being 'in venville', entitled to enjoy the same rights as the Forest Men.[29] Parishes contiguous to the Moor, but not paying their dues, were considered on a par with the remainder of Devonians, as 'strangers', that is, able to claim rights of common on a different scale of fees from the venville tenants. To complicate matters, there were also certain parishes in venville whose boundaries did not adjoin the Forest,[30] and certain other parcels of land beyond the Forest, in and out of venville according to whether or not rents had been paid to the Duchy.

Lydford village was not in venville until the 1890s, a curious situation considering that the Forest was part of the parish.[31]

Ancient Tenement holders and other holders of venville rights enjoyed what amounted to valuable privileges and they seemed, from the point of view of the excluded moorlanders, to belong to a separate, closed community. But, in venville or not, dwellers in the remote settlements and on the periphery of the moor were routinely despised by all the rest of the world and, whenever possible, the waste itself was a place to be assiduously avoided by outsiders.

Except for persons residing in Totnes or Barnstaple, the Fourth Circle embraced all Devon residents who, holding the right of pasturage on the commons, might, on payment of a fee, graze their beasts within the Forest.

Four market towns, all on the moorland borders – Ashburton, Chagford, Tavistock, and Plympton – were designated as Stannary towns, where tin from the whole of the county was received.[32]

Chagford, a prosperous little wool town, high on the river Teign, had its moment of fame in 1643. During a Civil War skirmish the young Royalist, Sidney Godolphin, was shot and died in the porch of the *Three Crowns Inn*, thus devolving 'the misfortune of his death upon a place which could never otherwise have had a mention in this world'.[33]

Tavistock, again a stannary town, famed as the birthplace of Sir Francis Drake, of circumnavigation and Armada fame, owes its initial expansion to the Benedictine monks who settled there around 960, and built an abbey, razed by the Danes in 977. Undeterred they rebuilt a splendid foundation famed as a centre of learning and printing, for it was here that the second printing press in the country was installed. Dissolved in the 1530s, only fragments of the Abbey remain.

8   *Chagford and the River Teign, watercolour by W.S. Morrish (1844-1917).*

[11]

9 *The South East Prospect of Ye Town of Tavistock in Ye County of Devon, engraved by R. Parr after C. Delafontaine, 1741.*

10 *The Market Place, Ashburton, engraving by W. Deeble after T.M. Baynes, 1829.*

11 *Plympton, Devon, birthplace of Sir Joshua Reynolds, by E. Finden after W. Westall, 1829.*

On the main route between Exeter, the county capital, and the port of Plymouth, Ashburton's wealth, like that of the other Stannary towns, fluctuated with the state of the tin trade, though it maintained its economic health through cloth mills set up along the banks of the Ashburn, a tributary of the Dart.

Plympton, on the eastern bank of Plym estuary, the latest of the Stannary towns, was included on account of its proximity to the sea. The settlement, dominated by its early 12th-century castle and its priory, created its wealth through tanning, wool-combing and brewing.

These towns held the privilege of selecting representatives to meet in a general Session of Parliament held 'at Crockern Tor, a high hill in the middle of Dartmore'.[34]

With some knowledge of the physical setting and social structure of Dartmoor, focus can now shift towards the people, and specific locations.

2

'A Scythia within England'

Now that a kind of social map of the moor has been established, Lydford's role as the centre from which Duchy affairs and the mining industry were regulated can be touched on. Mention will be made in this chapter of methods of tin mining, the activity that has so profoundly shaped the moorland environment, and the chapter will close with a consideration of early writers' reports on the place and its people.

Besides receiving officials in its capacity as an administrative centre, Lydford village was visited by topographers during their surveys around the South West. As well as updating previous surveys of the district, noting changes in land ownership and keeping track of the pedigrees of gentlemen and their families, topographers sometimes recorded their reaction to locations they considered worthy of note.

'Lydford', announced Devon country gentleman Tristram Risdon (c1580-1640), is a place 'where no nice nation would have made choice'. It might once, he said, have been a fine town, but by the 17th century,

> hath neither market nor fair to comfort it, and little fruitful land; and the only privilege it enjoyeth now, is the custody of the prince's prisoners.[1]

Devonian Thomas Westcote (1567-1639/1644?), who had been on one Sir Francis Drake's expeditions, and now turned topographer, believed that Lydford's decline could be traced back to 977 when it was 'grievously spoiled by the inhuman Danes', since when the passage of time and 'the furious force of storms' had contributed to its ruinous state.[2] The town's misfortune was also attributed to an earlier time when, if tradition is to be believed, Julius Caesar found entertainment there during his second expedition to England:

> to boast of this, must be making a virtue of necessity, as we may conceive in what manner, and how obsequiously, the favour of a conqueror must be conciliated – by the anticipation of every want, and a passive submission to every order.[3]

The place made a dismal impression on William Browne (1591-1643), of Tavistock, who as poet/narrator utters, at the conclusion of 'Lydford Journey',[4] his determination to avoid further visits to a place 'so wide and ope'. Yet, the town had been important as one of the four Saxon mints in the county, its great earth ramparts thrown up as part of the line of defences against Viking incursions – admittedly not successfully. According to Domesday Book the place had once

12 *Lydford, Devon, etching by Miss Hawksworth, after S. Prout, 1810.*

been rated in the same manner as London, but '40 houses have been laid waste there since King William has had England'.[5] Maybe the opprobrium with which Lydford was regarded stemmed from the evil reputation of its second castle.

There are indications that the first castle at Lydford, standing on a tree covered promontory above the river, was built soon after 1066, with its soon-to-be-hated replacement, a sturdy square keep built nearby just over a century later. Venville tenants brought before the Forest Court – when the land was in the monarch's remit, or by the Courts of the Forest when the Forest was in the heir's possession – and found guilty were imprisoned at this castle, where the Court of Justice Seat, responsible for sentencing, convened just once every three years. Rather than hold prisoners for any length of time it was the gaolers' customary practice to anticipate the death sentence by summarily executing prisoners,[6] a practice famously described in the opening lines of verses ascribed to Browne[7]

> I oft have heard of Lydford law,
> How in the morn they hang and draw
> And sit in judgment after.
>
> 'Lydford Journey', verse 1

13 *Crockern Tor, etching by P.H. Rogers, 1826.*

Besides those alleged to have contravened whatever set of Forest Laws were prevailing at the time, tin miners who offended a stringent set of regulations, known as the Stannary Laws, were also liable to incarceration at Lydford Castle.

Stannary Law was administered by 24 stannators from each of the four towns, who formed the Stannary Parliament. They would gather at Crockern Tor and, presided over by a Duchy representative seated in his granite chair, would gather around a granite table to consider stannary matters and mete out justice. First recorded in 1494, meetings continued to be convened at Crockern until the middle of the 18th century, although by that time the main agenda would be discussed at Tavistock. Miners convicted of contravening stannary statutes would, like offenders against the Forest Laws, be confined in Lydford Castle, a place of dreadful repute.

Mining was a sporadic industry, and tinners were not necessarily indigenous to the region, but itinerants, willing to endure temporary discomfort in the hope of making a fortune. They might well have been from the poorer classes, for at times, in an early example of positive discrimination, claims were granted only on condition that very little landed property was possessed by the prospector.[7] But, in practice it seems that the tinners did not always remain self-employed, for many, borrowing against their prospects fell prey to exploitation and remained impoverished wage-earners. Miners were recognised as a rough, tough breed, and 'strangers to comforts', for, as Tristram Risdon observes,

14   *Former tin workings, Chaw Gully, near Birch Tor.*

there is no labourer in hardness of life to be compared; for his apparel is coarse, his diet slender, his lodging hard, his drink water, and for lack of a cup he commonly drinketh out of his spade or shovel, or some such thing.[8]

The early method of searching for tin was by 'streaming', or separating out by washing, the oxide of tin particles that had percolated from the mineral lodes into the surface gravels of the streams. As the tinners worked they threw the sifted waste along the stream banks to form the mounds of rubble, a defining moorland characteristic.

As the stream-beds became less productive open cast excavation developed; miners began to dig for ore stone, scooping out 'gerts' or gullies as they followed the tin-bearing lodes. Their efforts, according to Sabine Baring-Gould (1834-1924), have left the sides of hills 'marked as with confluent smallpox'.[9] But, I would suggest, with all due respect to Baring-Gould, whose contribution to Dartmoor's discovery will be considered later, that the connotations in his remark are ignored, and the great gullies should now be looked at in a rather different way. Looked at afresh, the once stark outlines now greened over, may be perceived as landscape art. Like the leats, the mortar-stones, and the mould-stones, the gurts bear mute witness to the men who toiled in this land, buoyed up by their belief that it was 'richer in its bowels than in the face thereof'.[10]

As early as the mid-17th century, shaft mining had begun for, as Westcote notes, to reach the ore, miners are like moles working below ground, where the earth is 'propped, posted, crossed traversed, and supported with divers great beams of timber'.[11]

Particles retrieved from streams were far easier to process than the lumps of ore stone that had to be crushed, usually by water-powered stamps, then passed through a series of buddles – circular ponds – where the tin would gradually fall to the bottom to be gathered up for smelting.

By the mid-14th century the smelting process would take place in a purpose-built – granite, naturally – 'blowing house', of which numerous ruins of many are still to be seen. A leat would be constructed to carry water alongside the blowing house to activate a water-wheel. The power thus generated would be transmitted to two pieces of equipment: to 'stamps' which would crush the stone, and to work a pair of bellows to raise the temperature in the peat- or charcoal-fuelled furnace until the tin oxide in the crushed material would melt. This method of smelting prevailed until ousted, in the late 18th century, by the coal-fed reverberatory

15   *Double mortar stone at Black Tor Falls.*

furnace. Whatever method prevailed would result in molten tin, which could be ladled into moulds. When cooled the ingots would be removed and taken to a Stannary town for weighing, stamping, and the payment of duty. Legend has it that at times grains of gold would be gathered and kept by the finder in a goose quill, until quietly sold as one of the perks of the job.

A decision made at a Crockern parliament was sorely tested in Henry VIII's reign, when, in 1512, Richard Strode, Member of Parliament for Plympton, was imprisoned in Lydford Castle, by then notorious as 'one of the most annoyous, contagious and detestable places' in the country.[12] Strode had infuriated Dartmoor tin miners when, in the London parliament, he proposed a bill to prevent tin miners from silting up Devon harbours through their practice of putting discarded material back into streams. Because mining took place on Strode's lands tinners were able to have him summonsed to Crockern Tor to explain his anti-miners' action. Failing to turn up on the day appointed, he was apprehended, fined and confined at Lydford Castle in 'a depe pitte under the grounde'.[13] On his release he successfully presented a bill that, in effect, granted him and members of future parliaments the privilege to raise any matter in the House without fear of punishment. Thus, from a local spat in this remote moorland region, a basic principle of democratic government may have been established.[14] But, there was a downside for the tinners when the London parliament passed an Act condemning the Stannary Court's behaviour towards Strode. This Act, coinciding with one of the periodic downturns in mining, contributed both to the curtailment of tinners' privileges and the powers of the Stannary organisation.[15]

By 1650 a parliamentary survey noted that Lydford Castle, for so long the embodiment of draconian power, was in a state of decay 'the chiefest beames being fallen to the ground and all the rest is following'.[16] William Browne agreed:

> They have a castle on a Hill
> I took it for an old Windmill
> The Vanes blown off by Weather
>   'Lydford Journey', verse 2

Apart from tinners, farmers, traders and the occasional Duchy official there was no cause for travellers to venture on to the waste. The main route to the far South-West skirted the northern moorland border, passing through Okehampton, while the Exeter-Plymouth road traversed the gentler terrain of the South Hams and, to the east, the north-south route, now part of the Mariners' Way, passed through Chagford and Widecombe-in-the-Moor.[17] Any pre-18th-century references to the moor are cursory and usually derogatory. William of Malmesbury (d.1143?) described Dartmoor as 'of barren Soil and of little else but for the harbouring of wild and savage Beasts; hardly yielding any Corn but Oats and Pulse',[18] while John Leland (1506?-52) merely noted that 'Dartmore is muche a wilde Morish and forest Ground'.[19] William Camden (1551-1623) observed that the Dart ran through 'squallida Montana Dertmore';[20] 'squallida' unfortunately being translated by Bishop Gibson, in 1695, as 'dirty'.[21] Topographer Thomas

16   *Entrance to Wistman's Wood, sketch by Mrs Prior, c.1870.*

Read reinforced the unenviable adjective in 1746, remarking that 'the river Dart forces its Passage thro' dirty Places'.[22] Not until the publication of Richard Gough's translation of Camden's *Britannia* in 1789 was some reparation made, when Gough demurring over the word 'dirty' explains that

> Bishop Gibson translates squallida, dirty, and seems to derive the name from the tract thence, whereas it is from the river Dert. Mr Camden would not have been guilty of such a pun.[23]

Gough writes instead of the 'river Dert, which, rising in the heart of the country, rushes through the dreary mountainous tract called from it Dertmore', and for a long time hereafter 'dreary'[24] becomes a key word in the Dartmoor writers' vocabulary. John Hooker concentrates on the inhospitable climate of the region, finding 'coldenes continuall stormes and wetness of the grounde' not confined to winter:

> and this one thinge is to be observed that all the yere through out commonly it rayneth or it is fowle wether in that more or desert.[25]

Acknowledging the rain-sodden moor as 'our daily supplier and nursery of Rivers',[26] Westcote asserts that the moor is best avoided on account of the peril of deep tin works, steep tors, high mountains, low valleys, bogs, plains, being neither in any hazard or fear of danger, without wetting your foot in the many meers, or fouling your shoes in the many mires.[27]

Skimming over the details of the difficulties in traversing the 'heathy and rocky'[28] moorland terrain, Risdon sums up any problems that might be encountered with his comment that the distance to Lydford Church from some of the Ancient Tenements might be 'eight miles in fair, and fifteen in foul weather',[29] a phrase that would be incorporated into numerous future guide books, and still in use, as succinctly conveying the circuitous routes necessary during rainy periods. William Browne expresses the same sentiment:

> Of fourscore miles scarce one foot's good
> And hills are wholly bogs.
>
> 'Lydford Journey', v. 10

In spite of generally negative assessments of the region made before the mid-18th century, a few locations were held worthy of notice. In a phrase that seems to have been coined by Risdon in his 1630 *Survey*, and which would be endlessly repeated, 'three remarkable things'[30] were to be found on the moor. Roughly at its heart, and close to each other, were Crockern Tor, Childe's Tomb and Wistman's Wood.[31] Along the left bank of the West Dart above Two Bridges, Wistman's Wood flourished amid the clitter from the Littaford tors. The three separate copses of dwarf oaks appeared

> as if the Trees had sunk away by some Earthquake, leaving only their scrubby Heads and a small part of the trunks above ground, for many of them are only 3 or 4 feet in diameter, yet scarce 2 feet high.[32]

That description is just as highly poetical as the claim that the wood consisted of 500 trees 500 feet high – meaning that each tree attained the height of precisely one foot. In fact the Wistman oaks, gnarled and hung about with lichen, are on average ten feet tall, and the centre grove, damaged by fire in 1886, happily soon recovered. Less accessible than Wistman's Wood, two other ancient groves survive – Piles Copse, where the trees are less stunted than at Wistman's, and Black Tor Copse on the West Okement where dwarf oaks flourish in a spectacular setting.

Childe's Tomb reputedly marked the spot where a huntsman died. In a saucer-like depression, on the edge of the notorious Fox Tor Mire and

17 *Child's [Childe's] Tomb, etching by P.H. Rogers, 1826.*

18   Great storm at Widecombe Church, woodcut, c.1638.

its several streams, and with little shelter, it is a cheerless place where a traveller could easily become disoriented.

Both Risdon and Westcote provide similar versions of the tale,[33] explaining that Childe, while out hunting, became separated from his companions before losing his way.[34] To protect himself from the elements, he killed and disembowelled his horse, but in spite of creeping into its belly for warmth he was frozen to death, although not until, using his horse's blood as a medium, he had written a will leaving his lands and possessions to the parish in which he was buried.

Men from Tavistock and Plympton vied over the removal of his body, the Tavonians, by guile, proving successful.[35] Risdon's recollection of a similar tale relating to a Bishop of Winchester would seem to move the story of Childe into the realm of myth; but William of Malmesbury tells of two incidents closer to home – to Tavistock – in which wanderers are isolated in some way, die a lonely death, their possessions devolving to Tavistock Abbey, thus raising the possibility that there might have been a germ of truth in the incident.[36]

According to Risdon a verse was inscribed on Childe's tomb near Fox Tor:

> They fyrste that fyndes and bringes mee to my grave,
> The priorie of Plimstoke they shall have.[37]

By 1701, as John Prince (1760-1811) reported, although the supposed site of Childe's demise was remembered, the inscribed tomb either no longer existed or could not be located.[38] But, around the beginning of the 20th century, pieces of the monument were discovered and the ancient relic remains as a moorland landmark. Childe's story is typical of moorland tales that emerge over the years, generally tinged with melancholy or tragedy.

Further sites mentioned by Risdon, which travellers might seek out, were the bold outcrop of Blackstone, 'magnifying god for the founder thereof and not man', and a similar formation at nearby Whitstone, on the skirts of the forest near Moretonhampstead.[39]

Prior to the late 18th century the only other place the curious traveller might visit was the church of St Pancras at Widecombe-in-the-Moor. Built in the 14th century, possibly replacing an older foundation, and enlarged during the late 15th and early 16th centuries, the church is often referred to as the 'cathedral of the moors' on account of its 120-feet tall and graceful tower. In the roof of the nave is a boss showing three rabbits sharing three ears that form a triangle.

19   *Bren Tor and Church, Devonshire, engraved by J. Storer after S. Prout, 1804.*

It is thought that this boss, with its connotations of alchemy, may point to a connection between the church and the Dartmoor tin miners.

Widecombe-in-the-Moor is a village that, ever since 21 October 1638, has capitalised on its Great Storm. While a service was in progress, a lightning strike on the church left four persons dead and 62 injured. As Richard Polwhele's (1769-1811) various accounts of inclement weather reveal, several other moorland communities experienced similar events at various times, but none was so devastating as at Widecombe, nor commemorated in such detail.[40]

A vertical rent left in the otherwise restored fabric of the north side of the church tower, and verses displayed on a wooden tablet inside the church, acted as a reminder of the tragedy. Two accounts published soon after the catastrophe described in detail the horrid effects of 'God's visible judgments and terrible remonstrances',[41] and the salutary tale became a staple of Dartmoor history, granting Widecombe a notoriety that would draw tourists to the area long before it became a subject for fiction and before the ballad 'Widecombe Fair' became widely known.[42]

Between Lydford and Tavistock two locations noticed by early topographers would later become the subject of numerous prints and paintings. Brent Tor, visible for miles beyond the moor and said to serve as a mark for sailors making

20 *A view of the river Lid, etching by T. Bowen, 1755.*

for Plymouth, is a rocky outcrop, once fortified and since 1319 topped by a votive church, 'weather beaten, all alone, as it were forsaken'.[43] It was, so the story goes, intended to build the church at the base of the hill, but the evil one invariably moved stones placed by the builders for the next day's work to the top of the hill until the builders decided to let the devil have his way. Not far away, just on the outskirts of Lydford village, travellers were recommended to pause and peer over the bridge where, 70 feet below, the waters of the river Lyd

> gathereth into such a straight by the fretting of the earth between the rocks, that it seemeth to cavern itself, as loath to see the desolation of the place. It maketh such an hideous noise, that being only heard, and not seen, it causeth a kind of fear to

the passengers, seeming to them that look down to it, a deep abyss, and may be numbered amongst the wonders of this Kingdom.[44]

The valley below this bridge was reputed to be the stronghold of a local group whose reputation was dire. Famously described by Thomas Fuller (1608-61) the gang is established as a separate, dysfunctional and dissident sub-group:

> The Gubbings. So now I dare call them (secured by distance), which one of more valour durst not do to their face, for fear their fury fall upon him. Yet hitherto have I met with none who could render a reason of their name. We call the Slaverings of Fish (which are little worth) Gubbings; and sure it is they are sensible that the Word importeth shame and disgrace. [...]
>
> I have read of an England beyond Wales;[45] but the Gubbings-Land is a Scythia within England, and they pure Heathens therein.[46] It lyeth nigh Brent-Tor, in the edge of Dartmore. It is reported, that, some two hundred years since, two Strumpets being with child, fled hither to hide themselves, to whom certain lewd Fellows resorted, and this was their first original. They are a Peculiar of their own making, exempt from Bishop, Archdeacon, and all Authority either Ecclesiastical or Civil. They live in Cotts (rather Holes than Houses) like Swine, having all in common, multiplied without marriage into many hundreds. Their language is the drosse of the dregs of the vulgar Devonian; and the more learned a man is the worse he can understand them. During our Civil Wars, no Souldiers were quartered amongst them, for fear of being quartered amongst them. Their wealth consisteth in other men's goods, and they live by stealing the Sheep on the Moore; and vain it is for any to search their Houses, being a work beneath the pains of a Sheriff, and above the power of any Constable. Such their fleetnesse, they will outrun many horses; vivaciousnesse, they outlive most men; living in the ignorance of luxury, the extinguisher of life. They hold together like Burrs; offend one, and all will revenge his quarrel.
>
> But now I am informed, they begin to be civilized, and tender their Children to Baptisme, and return to be men, yea Christians again.[47]

Edmund Gibson, in 1695, endeavours to retrieve the reputation of the Gubbins, explaining that near Brent Tor 'there is a village nam'd the Gubbins, the inhabitants whereof are by mistake represented by Fuller [...] as a lawless, Scythian sort of people'.[48] This remark is, in substance, repeated by Thomas Cox, in 1700, who states, unequivocally, that the portrayal of the inhabitants of a 'village named Gubbins' as a 'barbarous sort of People, rude and lawless' was based on false information supplied to Fuller by an informant with a grudge against the villagers.[49] Cox was mistaken in believing in the existence of an actual village named 'Gubbins' in the vicinity of Brent Tor, but the possibility of an anti-social tribe living somewhere in the area provided a modicum of interest and excitement for many writers searching for local 'colour' in a place devoid – until well into the 19th century – of much of a store of written folk tales.

Probably the most familiar description of the Gubbins is attributed to Browne but it should be noted that while his 'Lydford Journey' was supposedly composed prior to 1643, these following verses in which the Gubbins are described do not appear in versions of the poem until 1774:

> Now hereto's the Gubbins Cave;
> A people who no knowledge have
> Of law, or God, or men
> Whom Caesar never yet subdued;
> Who've lawless liv'd; of manners rude;
> All savage in their den.
>
> By whom, – if any pass that way,
> He dares not the least time to stay,
> For presently they howl;
> Upon which signal they do muster
> Their naked forces in a cluster,
> Led forth by Roger Rowle.
>
> 'Lydford Journey', v.11-12[50]

In this version of the ballad, the name Roger Rowle encapsulates the characteristics of the group. Vulgarly, 'roger' referred to a goose, and 'to goose' or 'to roger' is to make an unsolicited sexual pass, while 'to row' or 'rouse' suggests the noisy uncontrolled behaviour associated with the Gubbins. The verses, described as witty, humorous, satirical and 'commonly sung by many a fidler',[51] together with Thomas Fuller's description of the same group, will prove to be germane in respect of the representation of Dartmorian characteristics in a range of writings.

Drawing on the 12th-century French poet Johannes De Hauvilla's *Archi-trenius*, Westcote argues that 'no nice, neat effeminate fellows' would have settled in the borough of Lydford, a place where

> giants whilsome dwelt yclad with skins of beasts,
> Whose drink was blood; whose cups; to serve for use of feasts,
> Were made of hollow wood; whose beds were bushy thorns,
> and lodgings, rocky caves, to shelter them from storms;
> Their closets, hollow rocks; their hunting found them meat:
> To ravish and to kill was to them pleasure great
> Their violence was rule. With rage and fury led
> They rushed into the fight, and fought hand over head.
> Their bodies were interr'd behind some bush or brake;
> To bear such monstrous weights the earth did groan and ache.[52]

Robert Herrick, incumbent of Dean Prior, a border parish situated below the southern slopes of the moor on a main route between Exeter and Plymouth, draws a less than positive parallel between his parishioners and the Dean Burn running though the village:

Rockie thou art, and rockie we discover
Thy men, and rockie are thy ways all over,
O men, O manners; Now, and ever knowne
To be *A Rockie Generation!*
A people currish; churlish as the seas;
And rude (almost) as rudest Salvages.
　　　'To Deane-bourn, A Rude River in Devon,
　　　By Which Sometimes He Lived', 70[53]

There was, as in 1701 John Prince, vicar of Berry Pomeroy in South Devon, points out, a general tendency to disparage those who lived in outlying districts:

> Our Country being then, somewhat Mountainous and Rocky, some perhaps may take occasion hence, to censure or condemn the natives, as less docile and disposed unto various Achievements. Monsieur Bodin, a learned French author, takes occasion, as we find, to condemn all mountainous People as Blockish and Barbarous.[54]

Exonian newspaper proprietor, Andrew Brice, confirms the French author's opinion, dismissing the high moorlanders as 'inhabitants of the wild part, who are by the circumjacent People called Moor-men', judging them 'the most ignorant and rustick People in the West of England, Strangers indeed to Luxury and Excess, but as much to Good Manners'.[55] Later, in his *Grand Gazetteer*, he returns to the attack, focusing on the fringe dwellers:

> About the skirts of Ex-moor, on Dartmoor and some other of the wilder Parts, the ordinary People may be truly enough said to be born Clowns, their Carriage being very rustic and ungainly, and their Speech so coarse, corrupt, and uncouth, as to be scarcely intelligible to strangers.[56]

The term 'clown' carries a layer of meanings similar to that of 'savage', implying a contrast between the refined emotions experienced by the cultivated person of taste, and the supposed insensitivities of the rustics. It is, Brice intimates, the confined social conditions in which Dartmorians exist that affect them rather than their station in life, since:

> tradesmen, Shopkeepers, Clothiers, Dyers, fullers, and other Artificers, having better Education and better conversation, are not a whit very many of 'em, in Good-Manners, Good-Works, Good-Nature, Good-Behaviour, or Good-language, inferior to the Gentry.[57]

　　Prior to the Roman conquest, Cambro-British tribes had colonised what would become Wales, while other British groups, the Danmonii or, as they are now known, the Dumnonii, inhabited areas of the south-west of England, including the present counties of Cornwall and Devon. Then, towards the close of the seventh century, after the death of King Cadwallader around 689, Wales ceded from Danmonia. The south-west Danmonii retained their own rulers, until about 936, when under renewed pressure from the Anglo-Saxon King Athelstan they were mostly driven across the river Tamar. Whether a rump of Danmonii had managed to remain on the waste of Dartmoor after the newcomers established their rule is a matter of ongoing, inconclusive debate but Dartmorians were – still are, dare I say – regarded as 'different' from other Devonians.

Such scathing imputations seen here in respect of the indigenous Dartmorians would be confirmed and restated in all manner of writings over the following centuries. Contained within their appraisals is both the notion that the location in which a person chooses to settle corresponds with his existing character traits, and the idea that the environment in which any individual lives determines his personality. Considering the generally held bleak opinion of the moor, it goes without saying that the moorlanders will not be favourably presented.

As is becoming evident, material relating to the moor was written from the point of view of the 'outsider'; therefore, the place and the cultural practices of its dwellers were being constructed relative to the world beyond the moor, resulting in the creation of an *idea* of Dartmoor that stood in opposition to England and its cultured society. Dartmoor is treated as an alien region, beyond England, these early writings placing heavy emphasis on the inhospitable terrain and the savagery of the 'native' inhabitants who, in reality, simply went about their business of subsistence farming and stock rearing.

3

SURVEYORS AND ENTREPRENEURS

With business concerns in the port of Plymouth, and aware of the town's need for a reliable water supply, the Mayor, Sir Francis Drake of Armada fame, supported a plan for the first long-distance extraction of water from the moor, by means of a leat – an artificial conduit – from near the source of the river Meavy to Plymouth. Tinners, well-acquainted with the local terrain and the making of such channels, were co-opted as part of the labour force for this massive task which would make such a significant incision on the waste. The course of the leat, remarked Westcote,

> from the head is seven miles, but by indenting and circling through hills, dales, and waste bogs, but with the greatest labour and cost through a mighty rock generally supposed impossible to be pierced, at least thirty.[1]

Completed in 1594 the Plymouth or Dock Leat, in reality somewhat over 18 miles long, created a physical link, a kind of umbilical cord, that the town – now a city – continues to celebrate through the annual Fyshynge Feaste. Gradually, too, the story of the great day metamorphosed into a popular myth passed down the generations, and a telling of the time when Sir Francis, responding to the town dwellers' urgent need for water, had raced out to the moor and, on finding a bubbling spring had uttered an incantation, wheeled his horse round and galloped back towards the town. As he raced home, so the spring, now formed into a channel of water, followed in his wake. The busy and colourful oil painting *Drake Building the Plymouth Leat at Burrator*, by Samuel Cook (1806-59), gives some idea of the immensity of the task.

For nearly two hundred years after the leat contoured away from the Meavy, the moor's landscape and its age-old customary practices hardly altered. Then, within the space of a generation, new technologies and methods of work, and the cultivation of different crops, changed the appearance of great swathes of the region, while fresh ways of responding to wild and rugged places, and to the monuments left by ancient civilisations, would lend another layer of value to the region. In this and the following two chapters, the various ways in which Dartmoor began to be interpreted and represented in the late 18th century will be examined in some detail.

In 1794, Robert Fraser, one of the Board of Agriculture officials, visiting Dartmoor to assess the possibility of cultivating the waste, seemed to feel he had left civilisation behind, when he reported that this part of Devonshire has long been considered as an inhospitable desert. Strangers were anxiously warned to avoid passing over it, and a thousand stories told of people being pillaged and murdered, and of others perishing in the floods and the snow.[2]

In fact, Gibbet Hill, near Lydford, taking its name from the eponymous erection on which the bodies of miscreants were left hanging as a salutary reminder, was supposedly a haunt of highwaymen. Tales were also told of malcontents 'being confined there in an iron cage and left to die, as a punishment for their crimes on the highway'.[3]

However, entrepreneurs managed to stifle any reservations as to their safety, and within the space of 35 years, between 1770 and 1805, the spirit of the Enlightenment began to impinge on the moor, and draw it into the national consciousness. Suddenly, various disparate voices began to be heard debating the value of the region to the nation. Economically, evidence of the debate was reflected through the influence of agricultural surveyors and the efforts of newcomers in their endeavours to make the land profitable. Culturally, there was a new appreciation of the region's scenic qualities and a growing recognition of its importance as a stronghold of the British past, with both features evident in a growing body of writing and images relating to the place. These facets of interest developed in tandem with national road improvements and, locally, in response to the construction of a turnpike road to replace the notoriously difficult east–west moorland crossing.

Devonshire roads in Hooker's day – the late 16th century – had been 'very paynefull for man or horse to travell',[4] and remained so for years, and topographer William Chapple (1718-81) found, even a century later, that strangers would take Devon roads to be 'watery Ditches' rather than public highways.[5] A *Gentleman's Magazine* correspondent noted, in 1752, that the state of the roads was so bad that anyone travelling to 'terra incognita', west of Dorset, 'dwells constantly on the horrible strip of dirty earth under his nose'.[6] For 'all that was known of the far South-West,' he mused, mapmakers might 'fill the vacuities of Devon and Cornwall with forests, sands, elephants or savages'.[7]

There was no need for mapmakers to exercise their ingenuity in respect of the indigenous Dartmorian for, as those familiar with their immediate environs knew, the moor provided as many indications of location as does any great city, and was webbed with numerous byways and paths. There were local lanes giving passage from settlements to grazing grounds or peat cuttings, paths trodden by Ancient Tenement holders travelling to Lydford or Widecombe for secular or sacred duties. There were tracks formed by tinners, and a network of trans-moor routes linking towns, villages, and – until the Dissolution – the several religious houses. Many of the early bridges around the periphery of the moor were sturdy arched structures while, from about the 13th century, on the higher terrain clapper bridges were erected to ease the problem of river crossings. A number of these clapper or 'cyclopean' bridges, composed of large granite slabs laid on piers, still survive.

21   *The Clapper Bridge, a 'cyclopean bridge' at Postbridge, c.1880.*

Granite crosses mark a number of moorland tracks, the first reference to such a signpost dating from the Perambulation record of 1240, when the 'crucem Sywardi' assumed its role as a Forest boundary marker. Re-erected towards the close of the 19th century, Siward's or Nun's Cross standing at the junction of several routes remains a comforting landmark for walkers. Between 1699-1700, soon after an Act of Parliament granted authority for the placing of wayside markers, the Plymouth accounts indicate that there was enough traffic across the moor to warrant expenditure:

> Towards defraying the charges of putting vpp Moorestones on Dartmoor in the
> way leading from Plymouth towards Exon for guidance of
> Travellers passing that way the sume of £2 0 0.[8]

But, it will be remembered, Dartmoor is notorious for its high rainfall, since its tracks, lanes, byways, and paths were often difficult enough for pedestrians, riders, pack-horse trains, and sleds to negotiate, the use of wheeled vehicles was impracticable.

A map of Devonshire published in 1765[9] by Benjamin Donn (1729-98), indicates that both the southern route from Exeter to Cornwall skirting the moor near Ashburton, and the northern route that passed through Okehampton, were already mostly turnpiked, leaving the old trans-moor crossing between Moretonhampstead and Tavistock disadvantaged for any mode of long-distance travel between counties.

Dartmorians might have been content with the prevailing situation, and in any case were far too poor to do anything about it, but, in the summer of 1771, moves

22   *Siward or Nun's Cross, sketch by W. Crossing (1847-1928), c.1880.*

[31]

23 *A pack horse, sketch, c.1880.*

were initiated to improve the east–west trans-moor crossing. Mr Turner, steward to one of the greatest local landowners, the Duke of Bedford, whose eastward boundaries marched with the Dartmoor commons, gave notice of a public meeting to press for a sound road across the moor.[10] While this action may have been in the best interests of the Duke of Bedford it would also open the region to venture capitalists eager to exploit the area's agricultural and economic potential.

The proposal for a turnpike road generated enough support for a petition to be presented to Parliament and in spite of opposition from Okehampton, whose inhabitants feared loss of trade through the upgrading of the moorland track, permission was granted in 1772 for a toll road to link Tavistock and Moretonhampstead. A new and less steep route was constructed between Tavistock and Moorshop where it joined and followed the line of the former track, passing near the clusters of ancient tenement on the East Dart and onwards to Moretonhampstead.

Construction seems to have been somewhat protracted, neither the Tavistock-Moreton road nor the Ashburton turnpike, which merged with the east-west route at Two Bridges, reaching completion until 1798. But, the knowledge that road building was in progress proved an incentive to venture capitalists to whom the barren waste now seemed a reproach, a visual indictment of Man's failure to dominate and conquer. Dartmoor was the unproductive virgin womb, and the possibility of coaxing or forcing that body into gestation seemed to be a financially attractive enterprise. Lured by the possibility of reaping a fortune, speculators snapped up parcels of the best land abutting onto the new roads, and so began a brief, intense period when the waste seemed set to 'blossom as the rose'.

Sometime manager of the Duke of Bedford's Devonshire estate, Edward Bray, of whose family more will be heard, took the opportunity to acquire ground at Bair Down, near Two Bridges, and invested in developing plantations. In 1780 improvements were commenced at the ancient tenement of Prince Hall, on the Ashburton road, though little land was enclosed there until Judge Francis Buller (1746–99) bought the estate in 1790 and extended it to 2,000 acres. Convinced that a totally new approach to the organisation of moorland agriculture was imperative, he raised a petition that the forest should be wholly enclosed and ceded from Lydford to form a separate parish. This plan would necessitate the termination of customary practices and the redistribution of land.[11] It seems that Buller's intentions were to initiate changes similar to those taking place over a great swathe of central England where land owners, in a perfectly legal manner,

TURNPIKE-ROAD,

Over DART-MOOR.

THE Proposal for making a ROAD from the *Exeter* Turnpike, through *Moretonhamp-stead*, over the Forest of *Dartmoor*, towards *Plymouth*, and *Tavistock*, &c. having met with the greatest Approbation; and several Members of Parliament having engaged their Services to carry it into Execution, the Committee, who were appointed at the last General Meeting, met this Day and ordered it to be advertised in the EXETER and SHERBORNE PAPERS, that there will be another GE-NERAL MEETING, at the SCHOOL-HOUSE, in *Moretonhampstead* aforesaid, on THURSDAY the 25th Day of this Instant July, at Three o'Clock in the After-noon; and that Plans of the intended Roads, taken from an actual Survey, will then be produced, on Purpose to give every Person who shall please to attend, an Opportu-nity to be acquainted with the whole Design, and to pro-pose, any Thing for its Improvement; the Promoters being determined to adopt that Scheme, which, upon this Exa-mination, shall be proved to be the most preferable.

JULY 1, 1771.

24 *Proposal for a road across Dartmoor,* Flying Post, *1 July 1771.*

were appropriating wastes to their exclusive use, with the result that commoners, railing to no avail, found themselves deprived of traditional rights. The Dartmoor tenants and commoners' protest against Buller's wishes might also have passed unheeded, but the Duchy's representatives joined in to argue successfully against the petition and in favour of the maintenance of venville rights.

The Duchy would not always prove so protective of ancient rights, for, in future years, numerous leases would be granted for agricultural and industrial development in the Forest, with the result that gradually and stealthily the acreage over which commoners' stock might roam gradually diminished. This would prove a double blow since the most fertile grazing stretches would be contained within the new enclosures.[12]

Of the entrepreneurs, the most successful and public-spirited was Thomas Tyrwhitt (1762–1833), at various times Secretary to the Prince of Wales, Lord Warden of the Stannaries, and Member of Parliament, representing Okehampton and, later, Plymouth.[13] In 1785 he obtained land just within the boundary of the Forest, close to Justice Buller's acres, six miles from Tavistock, and conveniently

25 *[Tor Royal], Sir Thomas Tyrwhitt's residence, from particulars of sale, c.1828.*

near the turnpike from which, at the Rundlestone, he had an access road made to his Tor Royal estate. He was also involved in improving passage from Dousland, on the south-west of the Forest, to Two Bridges, the road intersecting with his Tor Royal–Rundlestone road.

Across his 2,500 acres Tyrwhitt instigated a programme of agricultural trials, his results, particularly with flax, auguring well. For many years his secure financial base cushioned him against losses in bad times, unlike the moorland agricultural workers for whom, he realised, there needed to be alternative means of wealth creation to see them through the lean periods. In 1805 he pounced on an opportunity to fulfil his ambitions for a diversified moorland economy. He promoted the idea of a war prison on the moor, and successfully pressed for its construction on land adjacent to the link road he had laid out. This move, as will be discussed, would prove to be an action that, quite literally, altered the face of the moor.

During the 1790s and the following two decades, while the entrepreneurs were striving to change the face of the moor, teams of Surveyors, known also as Improvers, and already briefly mentioned, traversed the county as part of a nationwide project for the Board of Agriculture, their remit being to report on agricultural conditions and to identify and suggest ways land utilisation and work practices could be bettered. Everyone engaged in any form of agriculture would be encouraged to contribute ideas, and the Board of Agriculture would encourage experimental husbandry. This determination to make farming efficient seems in accord with Adam Smith's premise that

> the complete improvement and cultivation of the country be, as it most certainly is, the greatest of all public advantages.[14]

There was an alternative view: that agrarian reform, far from being driven by the government's concern over maintaining food supplies for an increasing population, was in reality spurred on by exploitative landowners seizing on opportunities to increase their profits. That may have been true, but Britain had begun to import wheat by the late 18th century, and when trade was disrupted – by war with the

American colonies and France – it became imperative to maximise both the home acreage and potential crop yield in order to feed the population.

Robert Fraser, the first Board of Agriculture Surveyor to visit Dartmoor, in 1794, stated that the total Duchy revenue, of £43 a year, indicated 'a most unprofitable species of management'.[15] With proper preparation and encouragement he felt convinced that economic and social change could be effected to provide 'an additional source of wealth and force to the nation'.[16] In his opinion, persons of rank and determination should spearhead change, and he identified Judge Francis Buller, whose Prince Hall estate was 'a constant resort of men of enterprize and experience in agriculture', as just such a role model.[17] The judge's programme of land fertilisation, experiments at improving the quality of sheep and cattle and the large-scale planting of conifers was promoted as an example of best practice.[18] His efforts in reclaiming the waste had not proved easy, as witnessed by the fact that most of the 40,000 newly planted trees soon perished. However, as the Surveyor noted, 'the great expense and miscarriages experienced in the first attempts to improvement, are as worthy of notice as those which are successful'.[19]

The Surveyors felt that by judicious clearance of the natural growth, the draining of excess water and intensive application of fertilisers 'the brown heath on Dartmore would soon turn into verdant green'.[20] Not everyone agreed with such proposals. In his account of a three-days moorland excursion undertaken in the late 1780s and published over several issues between May 1795 and September 1796 in *The Gentleman's Magazine*, Devon attorney John Laskey observed that, in respect of moorland farming, the limits had been reached, 'the rage for improvement of poor lands seems of late to have been carried too far'.[21] He was evidently upset by the rate of moorland enclosure, arguing that 'some things, though strictly private property, should, in certain degree, be enjoyed in common, and conduce to the accommodation of mankind in general'.[22] Setting aside ancient rights in the interest of capitalism, he maintained, might be strictly lawful, but would result in 'palpable injustice to some' and be, in a wider context,

> greatly to the diminution of the pleasure and convenience (not to say the health-fulness) of a large and populous town (Plymouth Dock).[23]

'As an open space', he continued, the moor provided a place for urban dwellers to 'walk abroad and recreate themselves'.[24] This comment is much along the lines of William Wordsworth's 1819 proposal for a national property open for all to enjoy, for which the poet received much credit, although he had, certainly, been pre-empted by Laskey.[25]

John Henry Southcote, a local farmer, made swingeing comments on the work of Fraser and his colleagues, echoing Laskey's belief that land unsuitable for cultivation was being put to the plough. He argued that partial information had been applied to the whole area. 'If facts', he wrote,

> had been collected from many Principal farmers, how different would the information then have been [...] they would have given the most ample and convincing proofs

> [of the land's utility]. Why have not applications been made to persons of this
> Description who reside upon their own estates adjoining or very near the Forest?[26]

'Improvements', Southcote continued, should be 'not for the advantage of a few individuals to the exclusion of many'.

The time was not apposite for either Southcote's or Laskey's perspicacious comments to be acted on, but their words mark the stirrings of a tension that would slowly gather force over the following one and a half centuries and, while some matters have been satisfactorily resolved with the implementation of the Right to Roam legislation in 2005, there remain areas of concern and simmering discontent, which will be touched on in the final chapter.

There seems no doubt that the Surveyors and entrepreneurs envisaged modifications to, or the setting aside of, the moorlanders' ancient rights, not only as a necessary concomitant of agricultural improvement, but also as a means of social control. Wild uncultivated country, it was still assumed, bred unsocial humans whose natural propensity was to live in a primitive fashion and display a sullen attitude to authority. Such casual classification of upland dwellers as rude savages was part of the general zeitgeist of the times. For instance, while enjoying the 'savage rudeness' of the Alps, Thomas Gray had observed that 'the creatures that inhabit them are, in all respects, below humanity',[27] and Dr Johnson found that the inhabitants at Glensheals exhibited 'a very savage wildness of aspect and manner'.[28] Similarly, such opinions were reflected in the jaundiced view of the Dartmorians presented by travellers and Surveyors. George Lipscomb (1773-1846), skirting the moor, described a poverty-stricken area, where, in some places,

> the villagers' pronunciation differs so much from all the world besides, and they seem
> to have an idiom so peculiarly their own, that strangers find it almost impossible to
> understand them.[29]

Their 'corrupt' dialect induced in him a sense of unfamiliarity: 'Every enquiry which we made upon the spot,' he noted, 'only served to bewilder us with uncertainty or confuse us with error'.[30] His report of the moorlanders' lack, or pretended lack, of topographical knowledge concurs with John Swete's surprise at finding the people apparently 'ignorant of the roads even by which they were surrounded'.[31]

John Swete (1752-1821), having inherited a large fortune, had the leisure to improve his mansion and travel extensively around the county, from 1789-1800.[32] Records of his wanderings extend over 20 journals and include nearly 700 illustrations. A late 19th-century plea to publish this valuable historical resource passed unheeded until between 1997-2000 when 17 of the journals appeared in four volumes, the three others being destroyed in the Second World War. It is a pity that most of his Dartmoor observations were among the destroyed material, but fortunately he crossed the moor a number of times, and, with his insatiable curiosity, never missed a chance of noticing and recording what he saw.

According to writer and artist Thomas Hewitt Williams (fl. 1800-30), living just a few miles from the moor, the environment exerted a detrimental influence

26   *Tin mines on Dartmoor, water colour by J. Swete, 1797.*

on the dwellers, whose minds 'appear to be coloured by the country they inhabit, which is dreary in the extreme'.[33] On their visits to Plymouth, Williams asserted, the Dartmoor dwellers can be distinguished by 'their peculiar manners and habit', and by the fact that 'some of them possess a degree of roughness quite terrifying', though he added that the 'moormen' do not always live up to their dubious reputation.[34]

Surveyor Robert Fraser believed that many of the local farmers were 'inclined, from aversion to new experiments, from indolence of temper and from ignorance, the source of all prejudices, to treat every proposition of improvement as the airy vision of a sanguine projector'.[35] There was general consensus between the visiting officials that the introduction of new practices, new land tenure agreements in place of venville rights, together with an influx of settlers would have a beneficial effect on the social and moral behaviour of the cotiers (cottagers). But Charles Vancouver expressed some doubt as to the value of providing formal schooling for the young, believing that a peasant 'should never be inspired with a desire to amend his circumstances by the quitting of his cast'. Education, he stressed, might lead to unrest if the peasant believed that

27   *View of the Brideston (Bridestowe) model cottages, c.1800.*

penury had 'grown upon him by oppression, and in a manner incompatible with the rights of man!'.[36] This, in his superior William Marshall's opinion, was going too far. 'Good Heavens!' he expostulated, calling Vancouver's remarks 'a barbarian doctrine', amazed that he had 'nerve enough' to make such comments. He was, however, mollified by Vancouver's conclusion that peasants should be encouraged 'to excel in all their avocations, even to those of breaking stones for a lime kiln, or for repairing the highways', responding with 'Hear! Hear! – this is English.'[37]

Land reform, which all the surveyors agreed was necessary, would entail the development of new villages with homes with allotments and grazing grounds rented out to 'industrious people, on moderate terms'.[38] This utopian view of a moorland future, with all its ramifications, would prove to be a contentious issue never quite resolved.

4

TOURISM AND TASTE

In the preface to his first tour, published in the 1720s, Daniel Defoe noted that in travelling through Britain,

> a luxuriance of objects presents it self to our view. Where-ever we come, and which way soever we look we see something new, something significant, something well worth the traveller's stay.[1]

Defoe is referring not to scenery but to evidence of human endeavour, in particular to methods of manufacturing. Although he is always aware of the terrain over which he passes, of the 'frightful' chasm in the Mendips, the 'pleasant and beautiful valleys' and the 'horrid mountains' of South Wales, his journeys are always an adjunct to an objective, a necessary evil to be borne. For him, as was customary, the journey is a means to an end.

Nathaniel and Samuel Buck's various travels around England and Wales were, too, made as a means to an end, when the drawings of antiquities and venerable remains, amassed by the brothers, were published in five volumes between 1726-52.[2] Of the 400 illustrations, four are of buildings on the skirts of the moor: the remains of Buckfastleigh Abbey, once a Cistercian foundation, on the river Dart; and of the abbey at Buckland Monachorum, much of which had been incorporated into a fine mansion once owned by Sir Francis Drake. The walls left standing after King Henry VIII's order that Okehampton Castle should be destroyed are illustrated, as is a view of Tavistock Abbey. The engravings of these four locations soon attracted other artists' attention; a number would simply repeat the Bucks' work, while others would gaze at those borderland sites with fresh eyes.

By 1789, consequent on the general upgrading of roads, 'travelling about Britain' had become 'so contagious, that every man who can write or read makes a Pocket Britannia for himself',[3] with many of those 'pocket Britannias' compiled by a new breed of traveller, one who toured for pleasure, whose journey was an end in itself, and whose peregrinations included a certain way of interpreting landscape. Such words as Defoe had used – 'frightful', 'beautiful', and 'horrid' – had, by the middle of the 18th century, been captured as part of the theory of Taste, in which debate raged over the formulation of a set of standards against which animate or inanimate objects or persons could be measured.

An early key work, Edmund Burke's (1729-97) *A Philosophical Enquiry into Our Ideas of the Sublime and Beautiful*, 1756, is based on the premise that aesthetic

28   *Buckland Abbey, Devonshire, the seat of T.T.F. Elliott Drake Esq., engraving by H. Wallis after S. Condy, 1833.*

judgment is stable.[4] There are, he states, certain characteristics which, when possessed by anything animate or inanimate, would elicit the same intuitive emotional response from all persons. Any deviation from the general response would be caused by some defect within the observer.

Small, smooth, bright, and rounded, nicely proportioned objects were beautiful and should elicit feelings of pleasure and tenderness from the beholder. Objects possessing antithetical properties, suggesting vastness, infinity, power, and obscurity should induce sublime feelings, of terror, awe, and astonishment, until the terror subsides and feelings of 'delight' suffuse the individual. For a civilised individual, Burke believes, the sublime experience acts as a safety valve, as a conduit through which barbarous human passions are dissipated, the feeling of 'delight' following the passing of the climatic moment being a kind of catharsis.

A key point in such a theory as Burke – and others – were propounding is that the aesthetic experience was not a concomitant of religious doctrine. He was writing at a time when ideas that had long held the human mind in theological thrall began to weaken, allowing other possibilities to be pursued. When, for example, concepts of time, and of the age of the Earth, began to be pondered anew, mountains no longer need be dismissed as 'the rubbish of the earth', but open to re-evaluation, as awe-inducing, majestic reminders of the convolutions through which the Earth had passed during countless aeons. Thus rugged mountains and hills culturally metamorphosed into places inspiring inward, personal reflection that might lead to a moment of sublimity. Writing from Lyons, Thomas Gray, who would later enthuse over the hills of the Lake District, writes of his delight at encountering in the Alps 'the most solemn, the most romantic, and the most astonishing scenes' he had ever beheld.[5] On the road to Glensheals, in 1773, Samuel Johnson is affected by 'regions mountainous', pausing to reflect how the imagination is 'excited by the view of an unknown and untravelled wilderness'. Surrounded by mountains, he muses how a traveller, confronted 'with his own weakness', realises 'how little he can sustain, and how little he can perform'.[6]

Over the years the theory of Taste constantly evolved and, by the last two decades of the 18th century, it was acknowledged that the viewed object itself possessed no intrinsic qualities; an individual's reaction to a particular kind of visual stimulation derived from that person's own experiences. Taste, in other words, was recognised as a cultural concept: it was learned. It was realised that any individual's response to certain types of scenery was subject to change for, invariably, perception was influenced by the vagaries of fashion.

With improved roads at home and tension in France, it became the custom for travellers to search for locations in Britain that might fulfil the requirements of current Taste. The Lake District in particular, the Scottish Highlands and the Welsh Mountains, all previously shunned, were included as essential locations in the British itinerary by the close of the 18th century. Dartmoor would never match these places as venues for aesthetic appreciation, but from the 1780s certain viewpoints around its fringes were regarded with favour as fulfilling the criteria for the beautiful and, occasionally, for the sublime, and as matching the requirements necessary for a location to be considered as picturesque.

The basis on which scenes are judged to be 'picturesque' relates to their conformity to criteria quantified by William Gilpin in his *Observations on the River Wye*. Arbiter of taste and promoter of the picturesque, William Gilpin (1724-1804), vicar of a New Forest parish, proposed:

> a new object of pursuit; that of not barely examining the face of a county; but of examining it by the rules of picturesque beauty; that of not merely describing; but of adapting the description of natural scenery to the principles of artificial landscape; and of opening the sources of those pleasures which are derived from the comparison.[7]

The truly picturesque scene would be composed of two 'side-screens', and the immediate foreground and the background would complement the main area of the picture. The contrast and combination of 'all the ingredients of landscape', of

29 *Lydford Bridge, Devonshire, etching by and after G. Beck, 1785.*

light and shade, colouring and texture, were essential elements of the scene.[8] But picturesque beauty, Gilpin insisted, was simply 'one species'[9] of beauty, and scenery should not 'be examined only by the rules of painting'. He had simply intended to make a distinction between 'beautiful, amusing, or otherwise pleasing' scenes,[10] and those conforming to painterly principles – those that were 'picturesque'. In effect, Gilpin was straddling the neo-classical and what would become labelled 'Romantic': the compositional demands of the 'truly picturesque' are very much in the neo-classical tradition – prescriptive and balanced – but in acknowledging the virtue of 'other scenes' he was freeing himself and his adherents to enjoy a wider spectrum of views.

Gilpin's notions are evident in William Chapple's 1785 moorland description:

> the more open and less fertile Parts afford a Variety of Objects worth a Traveller's Attention; [...] as near the Forest of Dartmoor, the Herds of Cattle feeding among scatter'd Rocks become agreeable Contrasts to some more lively Spot within reach of the Eye: Nor may the many Torrs in that Forest be omitted, of which some may be seen at 20 or 30 miles distant; exalting their heads towards the Clouds; and appearing on a nearer View, like so many exhausted volcanoes.[11]

Chapple is among the first visitors to assess the moorland scene in a painterly manner, finding 'agreeable contrasts', an essential element of the fashion for 'the picturesque', on the lower slopes of the moor, against a background of distant hills.

Also in 1785, an engraving of Lydford Bridge and another of the waterfall into the Lyd, both accompanied by unsigned articles, appeared in *The European and London Review*. The short pieces offered new departures in respect of the Dartmoor fringe, for notice of the place rather than being confined to the pages of topographical histories was aimed at a wider readership, to persons interested in the art of drawing, who might find the environs of the river Lyd a suitable location to visit for leisure and pleasure. Lydford Gorge, directly below the bridge conformed to the necessary criteria of fashionable taste:

> The river Lyd, taking its rise near the small village of Lidford, in Devonshire, scoops itself a very deep channel in the solid rock. Its banks are romantically broke, some variegated with herbage, some rude and bare, projecting in a tremendous manner. Some good majestic trees would make its wild beauties vie with those of any river that can be mentioned. It is curious to see how small a stream finds and wears away its seemingly imperishable bed. The road from Tavistock to Launceston crosses this river over a bridge, from whence looking down you have a dreadful prospect of a deep gulph, where rude walls, supporting the bridge, are rendered just visible by sparry gems, depending from every fissure, and by the silver-glimmering streamlet, about seventy feet below, whose murmurs are just heard.[13]

Picturesque detail, with melancholy and romantic overtones, is present for the culturally aware, and there is a hint of the sublime in the evocation of aeons

30 *Lydford Waterfall, Devon, engraved by H. Wallis after W.H. Bartlett, 1832.*

of time during which the gorge was channelled out. In addition, a local anecdote is included, of a Captain Williams, an Exeter gentleman who, failing to persuade his horse to jump across the river, 'dismounted, and took a fatal leap himself'.[14] This story, together with other similar incidents, would, within a decade, be embellished by other writers to evoke further 'the horror that broods around' the chasm.[15] Traveller John Swete was sceptical at the notion of anyone riding 30 miles to jump in Lydford Gorge, when, as he muses, 'by a little arsenic from the Druggist's, or amid the waters of the Exe that flowed by his doors, he might at once have compassed his end'.[16]

Lydford waterfall did not entirely conform to the demands of the picturesque, the trees appearing 'mean' and 'ungrouped', obscuring the 'bare rocky precipices'. But, as a writer explained, 'to a mind blest with poetic conceptions and the power to realize (and even improve)', the deficiencies of the scene might be made good, and on this premise a number of imaginative interpretations of a not entirely natural cascade were published.[17]

William Gilpin was not overly impressed with Dartmoor, possibly because the wet and misty weather blotted out its heights and even when he visited the Lydford area his expectations of 'a very grand scene'[18] visible from the bridge over the Lyd were dashed, on account of the narrowness of the sides of the gorge. He was somewhat mollified when, about a mile upstream, he found a location that matched the requirements of the picturesque, where the river descends through two side-screens 'beautifully adorned with wood and rock'.[19] That spot, Kitt's Steps (there are several variant spellings) would soon become the subject of numerous illustrations. When Gilpin concluded his visit with the observation that 'no part of this magnificent scenery would be a disgrace to the wildest and most picturesque country',[20] he was using the term 'picturesque' in a rather general manner, as referring to scenery in which some, but not all, of the elements of the picturesque are present. It is in this looser sense that the term

31   *Kate's Fall above Lydford Bridge, etching by and after T.H. Williams, 1804.*

'picturesque' is used today, the word having become part of our common cultural capital.

Like Gilpin, artist, teacher and writer T.H. Williams found the Dartmoor hills unappealing, causing 'every object' he explained in 1804 'to be viewed through a gloomy medium'.[21] Over the years he modifies his opinion of the high moor but, for the present, he advises his readers to shun the heights and discover the pleasures of moorland fringes for themselves – armed with his guidebook, *Picturesque Excursions*. Here he describes three journeys starting from Plymouth with the objective of assisting visitors to admire 'the picturesque treasures' of the locality. Claiming the 'greatest correctness in the Views',[22] his guidebook – instruction manual – produced in a size 'adapted for the pocket', was intended to enable tourists to compare his etchings with the actual scene.

Directing his readers to peer over Lydford Bridge, where Gilpin's hopes of the grand scene had been dashed, Williams directs their attention to features of the sublime. Light is excluded, there are jet black pools, the 'confidence of security diminishes as the eye explores the terrifying scene'.[23] Following in Gilpin's footsteps, at Kitt's Steps, Williams draws attention to qualities that belong to the picturesque; to the colour imparted to the Lyd by its granite bed, to the variety, colour, and form of the vegetation; the straggling branches of copse-wood; and the textures of lichens and mosses that should be contrasted with 'beautiful loose grass fantastically overhanging the water'.[24]

Joseph Farington (1747-1821), founder member and sometime secretary of the Royal Academy, did not hold Williams' work, exhibited at the Academy between 1801 and 1814, in high esteem. During a stay at Exeter Farington confided to his diary that

> a *good drawing master* is now wanted at Exeter. Such a one would find employment in the town and neighbourhood. At present an Artist of the name of Williams resides here for that purpose but is not considered to be very well qualified.[25]

Well, that may be so, but Williams's various illustrated guidebooks – for which he produced etchings from his paintings – probably gave a heightened awareness of scenic pleasures to a wider section of the public than ever were privileged to gaze on the works of the great masters.

Several new locations on the skirts of the moor began to be promoted by travellers as providing particularly agreeable sights. Agricultural Surveyor William Marshall waxed with enthusiasm as he identified facets of the picturesque at Okehampton Castle,

> whose ruins still occupy a peninsular hillock that faces this bold woody steep; being divided from it by the Western branch of the Oke. The Scenery is truly alpine.[26]

William Maton expressed similar sentiments: 'Nothing', he declared, 'can be more pleasing than the whole scenery, which with the ivy-clad ruins of the Castle, its mouldering turrets, and crumbling walls, conspires to form a most picturesque landscape'.[27] By the time Maton and Marshall were waxing enthusiastic the castle,

32 *The South View of Okehampton Castle in the County of Devon, engraved by and after S. and N. Buck, 1734.*

in a pleasant rural setting just a short stroll from the town, itself on the main road into Cornwall, had already become an almost obligatory subject for any artist in the locality, one of the earliest prints, a copper engraving, appearing in 1734, while John Inigo Richards' (1731-1810) oil of Okehampton Castle was exhibited at the Royal Academy in 1770. Richard Wilson RA (1713?-1782). Francis Towne (1740-1816) produced his pen, ink, pencil and watercolour of Okehampton Castle in 1794 and, in 1800, William Payne's (1760-1830) watercolour 'Oakhampton Castle & Town from the Park' viewed the castle looking towards rather than from the town side.

Employed by the Board of Ordnance as a draughtsman, Payne was deployed from London to Plymouth in 1782, until around 1790 when he returned to the capital and set up as a drawing master. Among his numerous topographical watercolours made during his formative years in the West are picturesque scenes of the Dartmoor borderlands, such as his Meavy and Sheepstor 1788-9, where labourers are moving beyond the side screen of trees, cattle are drinking, the church is in the middle distance and the tor dominates the background. In what seems to the first study of a moorland industrial location, *A Slate Quarry on Dartmoor, Devon*, exhibited at the Royal Academy in 1788, trees frame a great hole encompassing the middle ground, the predominant colour is grey.[28] Payne introduced a number of new techniques – detractors would say 'tricks' – that

33 *Thaugh [Shaugh] Bridge, Devonshire, aquatint, anon after William Payne, 1803.*

would serve him well in future years as a sought-after teacher, as he explored the possibilities latent in improved art-paper: 'dragging' a dryish brush over a surface to achieve highlights, 'scumbling' a dampened surface to flatten colour, and splitting his brush to give his foliage added form and texture. Above all, his name is associated with 'Payne's grey', when 'for foreground shadows he used Indian ink, and sometimes lampblack, toning these colours into the distance by the lavish use of his grey'.[29]

'Enveloped by mountains', Bickleigh Vale, through which the river Plym flowed in 'a very picturesque manner,' was judged 'truly romantic';[30] the river Teign near Fingle Bridge and the river Taw at Sticklepath were, also, considered to be of especial worth. At the latter spot there were all the ingredients sought after by artistic excursionists: a ruined chapel, 'mean and humble' with a straw roof, where 'over its unwhitened walls, many a patch of ivy had crept'. In parson, topographer and antiquarian John Swete's opinion this derelict building, 'with its rural and wild concomitants', provided an excellent example of picturesque beauty.[31]

Swete's erstwhile friend and travelling companion Richard Polwhele is full of admiration for Becky Fall, near Bovey Tracey, on the eastern side of the moor, 'often visited by gentlemen, who admired it', where the little river, winding its way over a rough and stony bottom, at one time foams along, as if ready to force its passage through the obtruding rocks, [...]; till, at length, rushing full into view, and reaching a precipice of high-piled moorstone, it tumbles from the summit in one collected mass, with a roar that almost stuns the ear; while the foam of the waters [...] envelopes the whole scenery in a sort of magic obscurity. After this magnificent interruption, the river pursues its course through a gloomy valley that exactly accords with the genius of the cataract – sometimes gently distilling from the moss-grown rock, yet more frequently smoothing by its violence the immense bodies of stone thrown about on every side, into globular appearances or polishing them into planes.[32]

Not everyone was prepared to set aside the exigencies of a moorland journey and enjoy the romantic scenery. 'I have never', bemoaned William Maton,

seen a more dreary tract than that over which we passed from the tin mines towards Lidford. The soil is exceedingly swampy and moist, and covered with bogmoss, through which our horses' legs penetrated knee-deep at every step [...]. If we had not been accompanied by the captain of the mines, who seemed to be well acquainted with the country, we should have been in unceasing apprehension of sinking deeper than our heads.[33]

34 *Buckfastleigh Abbey, Devonshire, watercolour, J.M.W. Turner, c.1826.*

35 *Waterfall on the East Dart.*

Differences in perception were not solely due to climatic conditions. The view of privileged excursionists enthusing over picturesque scenery, in this case by the river Dart, near Ashburton, compared with the heart-felt reaction of their local female guide, is neatly encapsulated in a letter in the *Gentleman's Magazine*,[34] when the correspondent describes how the guide,

> upon my friend's observing how beautifully picturesque the river was at that moment, said, 'Ay, you may call it beautiful if you will, but I know it carried away a rick of hay for me last year. Beautiful indeed! Let everyone speak as they find.'

The conclusion of the letter – 'We laughed at her idea of picturesque beauty' – serves to highlight the great cultural gulf between visitors' and locals' viewpoints. It is a simple example of how a whole range of social and economic factors may determine perception and that no common human response to a situation should be assumed.

Williams also warns excursionists to be aware of making facile judgements when viewing an apparently idyllic and picturesque rustic cottage. Knowledge of the inhabitants' incessant struggle to survive, he writes,

> embitters every rural walk, renders as fabulous all the delightful visions of country life imbibed in youth, and reduces to fictions, extravagant as Arabian tales, the descriptions of poets.[35]

In spite of Williams' reservations a number of artists could not resist the exterior delights of the Dartmoor cottage and, in direct opposition to Williams' remarks, Nathaniel Howard, teacher and linguist, member of the coterie of Plymouth artists and writers, muses on the positive attributes of cottage life as he saunters through Bickleigh Vale, by the river Plym.

John Bidlake may not be remembered as an effective Head Master of Plymouth Grammar School between 1779-1810, for during his regime attendance declined, on account, it was thought, of his dedication to young persons who showed literary or artistic aptitude at the expense of other pupils. But of the boys who came under his influence, Samuel Prout (1783-1852), and Philip Hutchins Rogers (1794-1853) would become well-known painters, and the above mentioned Nathaniel Howard, were part of this group, and all would include Dartmoor as part of their repertoire. T.H. Williams, already mentioned, and Ambrose Bowden Johns (1766-1858) would help and advise the aspiring young men, as would Henry Woollcombe (1777-1846), a Plymouth solicitor with a keen interest in the arts and Dartmoor.

Benjamin Haydon, another of Bidlake's pupils and a painter, not of the moor, tells, in his autobiography, how the master would take his pupils to Bickleigh Vale hoping to instil in them an appreciation of nature.[36] Maybe that is why Nathaniel Howard set out from his Plymouth home in reflective mood for a day's walk from the estuary of the Plym along its course through Bickleigh Vale to its confluence with the Meavy at Shaugh Bridge. The transforming effects of light are evident as he looks along the valley and notices

> The woods and distant hills, that change their shapes,
> As Smile new tints, or vagrant mists involve.
>
> 'Bickleigh Vale', 121[37]

Happening on a cottage, the poet finds his romantic sensibilities stirred as he muses on the idyllic quality of life in such a place compared with existence in towns. As he meanders further into the valley he becomes both increasingly introspective, and acutely responsive to the power of the river and

> Streams
> Bright-bursting headlong from the dusky cliffs!
> Whilst opening on the skies the mighty roar
> Of rough cascades deafens the listening ear.
> and swells the grandeur of the rugged scene.
>
> 'Bickleigh Vale'

[51]

36 *Dewerstone Rocks, etching by and after T.H. Williams, 1804.*

His enjoyment of picturesque scenery changes to feelings of terror and awe when, at the head of the valley, he reaches the 'cliffs sublime' – the Dewerstone. With a storm imminent, he calls on Horror to lead him towards the tumult, and keep him safe, allowing him a period of inward speculation, to

> give the awful hour to solemn thought;
> Secure, whilst all the raging torrent-rains
> Rush ponderous down the mountain's murky sides.
>   'Bickleigh Vale', 497

With the passing of the storm emotional tension dissipates and the poet concludes his walk in a mood of quiet calm.[38] From the time of the poem's publication, the possibility that visitors might find themselves caught in a moorland storm was presented by compilers of guidebooks as both an opportunity for tourists to experience a sublime moment and a useful climatic device for future novelists. One of the two illustrations in 'Bickleigh Vale' is after Samuel Prout – of whom more later – the second, by H.I. Johns, is of Dewerstone Rocks, a 120-foot pile rising sheer from the river Plym. In T.H. Williams' interpretation of the massy

37   *[Moorland excursion] Vignette, etching by and after T.H. Williams, 1804.*

Dewerstone outcrop, the artist is looking downstream towards Shaugh Bridge, recently painted by William Payne.

The frontispiece of Williams' *Picturesque Excursions* suggests that the combination of better access, the rise of the coastal resorts as holiday spots, the fashion for personally experiencing the beauties of nature is encouraging leisured women to visit beauty spots. However, at this stage he is not expecting his readers to venture far from the road; both the Dewerstone rocks and Lydford gorge were but short distances from enclosed roads in 1804.

Both Lydford and the Plym gorges have retained their popularity. For much of the time still today a stroll along the Bickleigh Vale to the Dewerstone offers the same experience as Howard and his artist friends enjoyed, but there are days when a different atmosphere prevails for, noted for its graded climbing routes, the rocks have become one of the most popular moorland venues for outdoor activities' groups.

Lydford Gorge, now owned by the National Trust, received 67,000 visitors in 2005. It is not simply to see the narrow chasm and the waterfall, but to enjoy the one-and-a-half-mile-long walk along the valley of the Lyd. Downstream from the Gorge the bed of the stream widens and the actual meagreness of the river's flow becomes apparent, and it becomes a pretty, though undistinguished valley, but that its scenery is still viewed with approbation reflects a long-lasting shift in Taste. This aspect of our present-day culture was expounded in the preface to the 1802 edition of *Lyrical Ballads*, its preface rejecting contrived and convoluted language, and the strict metrical formality of poetry. As poetry became more direct and seemingly spontaneous, so the Classical tradition in painting was giving way to realistic representations of the English landscape and, when natural scenery began to be enjoyed, tourists could discard their Claude glass,[39] and other places on Dartmoor, apart from the few of which Fashion had approved, would gradually be included on the tourists' itinerary.

While the various activities touched on in this chapter contributed to a growing appreciation of the unique beauty of moorland scenery, there were, concurrently, a number of enthusiasts venturing on to the high moor discovering other, sometimes darker, pleasures.

5

A Relict Landscape

In the late 1780s, at the time when entrepreneurs were setting up their ventures, John Laskey who, as we have seen in a previous chapter, believed in freedom to roam, recorded his impressions of a moorland excursion made purely for pleasure.[1] His three days' ramble is seen, in retrospect, to have set a number of precedents, besides raising issues that remain subjects of contention today.

The journey of discovery had begun at Sacker's Bridge near Modbury, in the South Hams, where Laskey, armed with 'a compass, a sketch from Donn's map, [...] pen, ink, and pencil', joins John Andrews (1750-1824), a solicitor, their friend Bennicke, and a serving man. While the group ride across the South Hams we will have time to pause over the relatively new map on which they will rely.

The friends were using a map completed in 1765 by John Donn (1729-98). Born in Bideford, north Devon, Donn showed early promise in maths and natural philosophy, became a teacher at his father's private school, and writer. Besides books on mathematics his contributions to *The Gentleman's Magazine* indicate his general interest in topographical matters, and in 1759 he was accepted as a candidate for a premium offered by the Society for the Encouragement of Arts, Manufactures and Commerce for a county survey. After close on six years' work he received a £100 award, which even with his subscribers' support would hardly have covered his costs. Engraved by Thomas Jefferys, Dartmoor dominates two of the map's 12 one-inch-to-the-mile sections. In comparison with the busy circumambient lands, the moor, dotted with what appears to be exhausted volcanoes, seems largely uninhabited, flat and wild.

Laskey, having been riding steadily towards the southern heights, is less than impressed with the scene, finding 'nature here having apparently denied every benefit which in general she lavishly bestows', and the moor seeming to be 'the fag-end of her work'.[2] As he grows accustomed to the rough terrain and responds to the physical challenge he begins to enjoy himself, before reaching Tavistock, and finding 'the busy hum and bustle of crowded streets, noisy children, and lamps just lighted' a great contrast to the quiet moor.[3] After a night's lodging at Tavistock he sets out for Lydford, pausing at Brent Tor on the way. Here we detect signs of Enlightenment thinking: he is endlessly curious and enthusiastic, seeks for scientific explanations, and will not accept received opinions unquestionably. He pokes about among the rocks collecting samples, puzzled that instead of the expected granite the rocks were black, hard and heavy, with pores here and there as if worm-eaten [ ] Some pieces were found more porous, even resembling a cinder or a piece of burnt bread, and very light.[4]

Drawing on Brydon's description, in *A Tour through Sicily*, he concludes that the tor is 'the effect or remains of some long-ago extinguished volcano'. A thoroughly modern man, he is unencumbered with the religious restraints of earlier times in his appraisal of the church, commenting that

the whim for building a church in such an elevated position is a matter rather unaccountable. Possibly in the days of superstition, they might think it peculiarly meritorious to take extraordinary pains to serve God.[5]

Even though almost unbelievably exaggerated and reminiscent of St Michael's Mount in Cornwall, a watercolour of Brent Tor by William Payne (1766-1830) supports Laskey's opinion as to the site's volcanic origins.

After getting somewhat confused in the lanes, Laskey and friends reward a young girl with an extraordinarily large tip – half-a-crown – for leading them to the Lydford cataract. They listen to local stories and then, leaving their horses, they embark for their afternoon excursion to Cranmere Pool. This would prove to be an injudicious, but quite understandable decision. On Donn's map, the

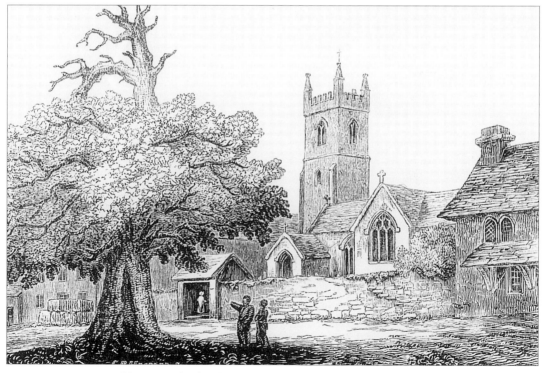

38 *Meavy Church and oak, wood engraving by G.P. Hearder after N.M. Condy, 1833-6.*

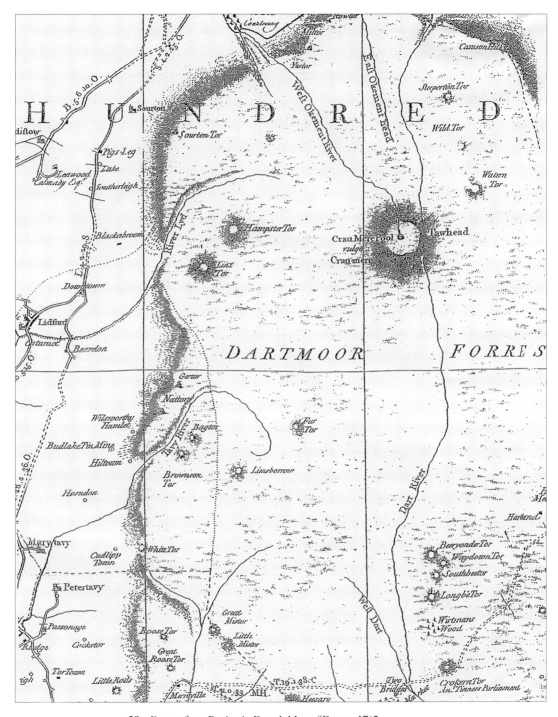

39 Extract from Benjamin Donn's Map of Devon, 1765.

40 *Exploring Dartmoor, sketch, attributed to J. Cranch, c.1789.*

best available to Laskey, there is no question but that the Pool's location would have looked appealing to young men intent on exploring the moor. But, some weary hours later the inaccuracies of the map have become apparent: unexpected rivers have been encountered, as have tors not shown and the terrain, 'black and spongy, full of bare and moist channels resembling gutters', definitely defies their expectations. The expedition is abandoned, the exhausted ramblers returning to Lydford late in the evening to pick up their horses and trail back to Tavistock. Reflecting on the aborted journey Laskey cautions his readers that 'the distance of places on the Moor appear to lie considerably greater than we supposed from measuring on the map in a straight line', and there are 'many tors and brooks not noticed on the map'.[6]

On the third morning the friends, somewhat fatigued from the previous day's exertions, stroll around Tavistock, looking at the abbey ruins and the church. It was along the banks of the Tavy that the Benedictines had founded an abbey around 974. Razed in 997 by marauding Danes it was soon rebuilt, surviving as a noted centre of learning – the second printing press in England was set up there – until, in 1539, it surrendered to Henry VIII. Besides the Bucks' previously mentioned illustration, R. Parr's 1741 engraving provides a fine panorama of the town.

Sightseeing over, the group set out for home, meandering towards 'Crockern Tor, and other remarkable places on the moor'. They fail to locate the stone seat and table for which they search. No wonder, for, as Laskey later realises, they had been on the wrong tor. In spite of the lack of granite furniture, spirits high, they settle down for a picnic, passing round their 'frugal store of exhilarating sherry pretty brisk',[7] before corking up messages in the sherry bottle 'for the next honest finder, breathing a wish that he might be as happy as we', and placing it under 'the projecting edge of a massy rock',[8] before setting out for home. With their action of leaving a message for others to find, Laskey's group are initiating a practice that would be increasingly refined until today, at any one time, there are thousands of letterboxes hidden in moorland recesses.

Happy conclusions to the friends' first excursion came to light during the Second World War. Waste paper was collected as part of the war effort during that conflict. At Modbury a sharp-eyed helper noticed and set aside an assortment of documents likely to be of historical interest. Among the rescued papers John Andrews' account of his moorland expeditions came to light, and this jolly little unsigned sketch 'Exploring Dartmoor', 1788. Historian, R. Hansford Worth (1868-1950), who began the task of collating Andrews' papers, thinks it probable to have been drawn by another of the diarist's friends, Devon-born John Cranch (1757-1821). Having showed promise in drawing, Cranch settled for a while in London, coming to the notice of Sir Joshua Reynolds, also from south Devon. A letter from Cranch to Andrews is revealing in respect of the attitude of the metropolitan man to former companions, as mirroring the attitude of travellers towards the Dartmorians. In a rather condescending manner Cranch finds Andrews' general pronunciation of common words 'barbarously provincial', adding that he had rectified such errors in himself.

Andrews includes in his notes a sketch of the supposed Crockern 'Chair' still in situ, stating that,

> at the Southern End of the Tor its Summit is formed into a kind of Chair, consisting of 4 high Steps like a Lifting Sock, adjoining to the upright part of the Rock, like a one-sided Elbow chair.[9]

Confusing the issue, Laskey had mentioned in his articles how he had heard that most of the Crockern furniture had been removed, possibly to the Prince Hall estate by its 'late proprietor, a Mr Gullett'.[10] But John Andrews, referring to Prince Hall in his 1794 notes, claims 'no chair or table brought there from Crockern tor'. Whatever the truth of the matter, a hare had been started, and the chase to ascertain the location of the stone furniture would continue for many years and be the subject of endless speculation.

The group of friends finally reached Cranmere on 11 August 1789.[11] They rode out from Chagford and, after leaving their horses with the guide – whose fee for the day amounted to two shillings – at the point where the ground is exceptionally boggy, came across a man cutting peat, 'who tho' he had never been at the Pool, shewed us to it', and received sixpence. Cranmere had been discovered. By leading the companions to the site 'with no water in it, but moist', that unnamed moorlander had created a centre for the moor, which, before long, every rambler would aspire to reach.

During the 1789 excursion Andrews and his party visited the Spinster's Stone at Drewsteignton, a monument beginning to attract the antiquarians' attention. Today it is hardly likely that any moorland wanderer could remain unaware of the number and variety of prehistoric monuments, mute witnesses to some 5,000 years of human activity, but in the late 18th century many had been removed and put to some practical use, or were prone beneath the herbage. Some, however, still stood proud. In 1740, the antiquary William Stukeley (1687-1765), had begun to re-ignite interest in Stonehenge, postulating a connection with Druidism, and 40 years later – ideas trickled down quite slowly to Dartmoor – William Chapple[12] accredited similar new and rich meanings to a strange, man-made structure, known as a cromlech, near Drewsteignton. Known locally as the Spinster's or Spinner's rock, the monument at Drewsteignton was, according to Chapple, unique in the county and 'truly remarkable though hitherto little regarded'.[13] It lay, he calculated, 'within two and a half miles of the centre of Devon',[14] and conformed to the description of a cromlech as defined by William Borlase:

> a large flat Stone, in a horizontal Position (or near it) supported by other flat Stones fix'd on their Edges, and fasten'd in the Ground, on purpose, to bear the Weight of that Stone, which rests upon, and overshadows them.[15]

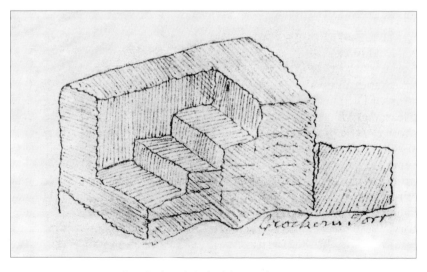

41 *Crockern chair, sketch by J. Andrews, 1789.*

42   *Cranmere Pool, etching by A. Dawson after J.Ll.W. Page.*

The site began to excite attention and draw visitors and artists into the moor's interior. In 1800 one of those visitors, Richard Warner, who had made several excursions around Britain, found the cromlech a 'vast natural acervation of granite rock, naked and rugged, [...] an apt spot for the exhibition of priestcraft and the celebration of Druidical rite'.[16]

At least eight illustrations of the cromlech were published between 1800 and 1810, most of which convey the strangeness and power the artists felt inherent in the monument, while Williams' etching giving an idea of the cromlech's truly quite human scale. But, with the growing craze for druids and mystery, the reality of Dartmoor's relics was subsumed in place of words and images conveying a sense of the arcane and terrifying.

William Chapple, convinced that the cromlech had served as 'an astronomical laboratory',[17] added, with prescience, that his conclusions would stand only 'till another subverts the inchanted Castle of his Predecessor, and erects another of his own'.[18] How right he was, for only 20 years later Richard Polwhele did, indeed, erect his own 'inchanted castle', in the pages of his *History of Devonshire*. Nowhere

43 *Cromlech at Drewsteignton, engraving by J.C. Smith after S. Prout, 1807.*

are the 'Druidical' monuments and the strange rock formations on Dartmoor more colourfully associated with generally horrid religious rituals than through the imaginative conjectures in which he melds ancient history and the sublime, and it is probably due to his work that so many artists illustrated the monuments soon after his book was published.

Born in 1760 of Cornish extraction, Polwhele took Holy Orders in 1782 and, after a short incumbency in his native county, settled at Kenton near Exeter and publicised a plan for a history of Devonshire.[19] Perhaps as a result of his peers' ambivalence in respect of his ability to produce a county history, Polwhele gave assurances that he did not intend to go into 'deep scientifical disquisition', but would have an eye to 'popular information and amusement', and present his findings with 'clearness, simplicity and elegance'.[20] Keen antiquarian John Swete would often accompany Polwhele on his expeditions, until, that is, there was a serious falling out when Swete published an essay on some of the antiquities they had visited together, but, despite the quarrels and bitterness attending its protracted birth, *The History of Devonshire* eventually appeared piecemeal between 1793 and 1806.[21]

Among his references to Dartmoor, Polwhele includes Parson Lyle's account of the great storm at Widecombe in 1638, anecdotal information from a variety of contributors among them John Laskey, and miscellaneous snippets disregarded by previous historical topographers. But it was his portrayal of the region as a

44 *Cromlech at Drewsteignton, etching by and after T.H. Williams, 1804.*

relict landscape that would exercise an influence on the imagination of visitors and writers.

Dartmoor's terrain appears to Polwhele as the aftermath of some great cataclysm. He was not the first to recognise the disturbed nature of the moorland terrain, for William Browne had observed of Dartmoor that:

> Thereon a goodly plaine (by time throwne downe)
> Lyes buryed in his dust some ancient Towne;
> [...] Here stands a Mountaine, where was once a Dale;
> There where a Mountaine stood is now a Vale.[22]
>
> *Britannia's Pastorals*, Book i, Song 2

Polwhele, in essence saying the same as Browne, couches his views in more sonorous language. Devonshire, he states, is an 'irregular', 'fractured county', its topographical centre, Dartmoor, particularly tumultuous. Over this high tract are scattered 'enormous masses of granite', 'massy and misshapen'.[23]

Up until now the moor's ancient monuments had been of little concern to travellers or topographers, the stone avenues, circles, and burial chambers having been erected, according to local folklore, in far distant times, 'when winged serpents frequented the hills, and wolves inhabited the valleys'.[24] Polwhele would change that way of thinking.

45 *Stone Avenue, on the North Teign, lithograph by P. Gauci after C.F. Williams, 1848.*

Among the natural, tumbled chaos of Dartmoor he identifies man-made stone circles and stone avenues as signs of a people who both venerated and feared a landscape that inspired 'even the cultivated mind with a sort of religious terror'. The whole tone of Polwhele's description of the moor carries intimations of the sublime, and of a deep organic bond between the moor and its people – a theme that permeates Dartmoor fiction. His speculations and descriptions would exert an influence on writings relating to the moor, particularly in the poetry of the 1820s, and in 19th- and 20th-century travel and tourist writings. The key to that influence lay in the writer's poetic skill and emotional evocation of specific moorland locations and hints of pagan ceremonial. Guided by his descriptions, future visitors would seek out sites he believed to be of special significance.

In his remarks on the abundance of such relics on Dartmoor a tone of gentle levity amounting to scepticism, bound to upset some adherents to Druidic theories, creeps into his remarks:

Nature has exhibited her wild scenery in so many places, that we know not whither to divert our first attention. [...] We are afraid to fix on a Druid-Idol, lest the neighbouring mass should have the same pretentions to adoration; and all the stones upon the hills and in the vallies should start up into divinities. If Bowerman's Nose, for instance, in the vicinity of Dartmoor, be considered as a rock-idol of the Druids, there is scarcely a torr on the forest, or its environs, but may claim the same distinction. [...] If we bow down to this granitical god, we shall meet deities at every step, [...]. Thus Dartmoor would be one wide Druid temple, and its dark wastes, now consecrated ground, would breathe a browner horror.[25]

However, although Polwhele *appears* at that point to be intent on consigning Druidism to the realms of fancy, he changes course, to present a possible Druidical past, generally offering fanciful conjectures that compilers of tourist guides and popular histories of the district would, for many years, offer as facts.

According to Polwhele, at the time of the Roman invasion the influence of the Danmonii extended over the whole of what is now Devon and Cornwall. The region, he believes, was divided into administrative 'cantreds', each with its own seat of judicature with several cantreds forming a kingdom. There were, in

46 *Bowerman's Nose, lithograph by P. Gauci after C.F. Williams, 1848.*

47   *Grimspound, etching by A. Dawson after J. Ll. W. Page, 1889.*

Polwhele's estimation, two such courts on Dartmoor: at Crockern Tor, the site of the tinners' parliament, which he reckons was a continuation in modified form of the Druidical court, and at Grimspound. Located just south of the junction of the toll road and the track to Widecombe, the clusters of small walled circles enclosed by a roughly circular stone wall at Grimspound are perceived by Polwhele as a spot likely to have been 'one of the principal temples of the Druids'.[26]

Like Chapple, Polwhele is convinced that the Drewsteignton cromlech was of greatest significance, the centre where annual ceremonies for the whole of Dumnonia had been held. Throwing caution to the winds, on taking note of the rudimentary line of stones leading moorwards, Polwhele does not scruple to assert

> that this *Druid Way*, beginning on the environs of the Cromlech, was intended to inspire those who were approaching the monument from Dartmoor with greater awe and reverence; where, probably, on a solemn anniversary, the druid priests might have met the attendant people, and commenced the procession.[27]

A little later this processional passage becomes 'the Druid Way or *via sacra*', and by this appellation it would be promoted by the tourist industry, even until this present time.

48   *Logan Stone near Drewsteignton, Devonshire, engraving by W.B. Cooke after S. Prout, 1806.*

Moorland logan stones – boulders so delicately poised that they would rock at a touch – were, in Polwhele's estimation, tools through which priests exercised control over the local population. He believed, though not all his fellow antiquarians concurred, that such stones were formed naturally. The approach to the logan in the river Teign (below Hunter's Tor), through scenery of 'uncommon grandeur', was calculated, he said, to induce powerful emotions:

> the ignorant multitude were struck with astonishment at the fearful magnificence of every object, whether they turned their eyes up the steep where the rocks frowned over them, or whether they looked onward through the valley where foamed the waters of the Teign; [...]. Amid such a scene, therefore, the Logan-stone, which doubtless acquired a more than common degree of sanctity from its position in the very channel of the river, must have been an admirable engine of priestcraft, and operated on the multitude precisely as the Druids wished.[28]

Of other monuments used in Druidical rites, none raised the antiquarian spleen more than the Rock Basin.[29] Conceding that many of these shallow, roughly circular bowl-like indentations on flattish rocks at the tops of tors were natural formations, Polwhele adds that 'there are, surely, Rock-basons that are not owing to such attrition'. 'I think', he continues, 'we may easily conjecture,

49 *Rock Basin on Gutter Tor.*

that they were contrived by the Druids, as receptacles of water, for the purpose of external purifications by washing and sprinkling.' He creates a dramatic picture of such a ceremony taking place on the south side of the moor, where

> there is a flight of steps, regularly cut out, in Heytor-rock, by which the Druids might ascend to the basin on the top, and perform the accustomed ceremonies, whilst the multitude were assembled below.[30]

By the conclusion of his remarks on Dartmoor, Polwhele has strengthened the link between the moor and the sublime. His work is suffused with words and phrases conducive to rousing awe and terror. Confronting the reader with images of 'fearful magnificence', a 'magnitude of stone' and 'rude grandeur', he turns the whole moor into a relict landscape.[31] He vividly presents high moorland scenery as varied and grand, unlike the manner in which it had been customarily described. Before long, Hay Tor and Grimspound would become sites of interest for serious antiquarians, and for the tourist whose imagination had been whetted by the prospect of communion with a pagan past.

At the time when Polwhele was writing his county history, a coalescing of various factors – better roads, interest in landscape, the effects of proto-industrialisation, war with France and the consequent restrictions on European travel – seems to have helped bring about an increasing awareness of the influence of the past on the construction of national identity. In John Swete's opinion, a retrospective view 'tended to the amusement if not to the enlargement of the human mind',[32] and a statement in the short-lived journal *The Topographer* urged an appreciation of the distant past: 'If history be useful, antiquities which are the basis of history must be so too'.[33] Such influences are evident in Polwhele's appraisal of Dartmoor's monuments and, just as William Camden had begun the process of restoring 'Britain to its Antiquities and its Antiquities to Britain', so Polwhele might be judged as having restored Dartmoor to its antiquities and its antiquities to the nation.[34]

6

A Great Work

For two hundred years Plymouth's water supply had sufficed but, by the 1780s, could barely cope with the additional demands made by Plymouth Dock, a relatively new and rapidly expanding town that had sprung up near the naval base on the banks of the Tamar. The upstart town, remembering how Plymouth had solved its problem, turned to spongy Dartmoor and obtained permission for the construction of a leat, completed in stages between 1794-97. Water extracted from the Cowsic, the Blackabrook and the West Dart entered a 648-yards-long tunnel near to Nun's Cross, cascaded down Raddick Hill, across the Meavy by aqueduct and contoured over 20 miles (34.2km) from its most remote take-off point, to supply the town and naval base, busy with preparations for war with France.

Besides the Devonport leat sweeping across the south west of the moor, signs of the escalating intrusion of the world – the turnpike road, recently enclosed fields, and the sight of thousands of saplings, were reinforced with the development of a new town roughly half way between Moretonhampstead and Tavistock.

For some years, along the length of the trans-moor turnpike, only

> a solitary hut was to be seen to cheer the lonesome traveller in a dreary ride of a dozen miles, and that inhabited by a family as uncouth as the region they dwelt in.[1]

T.H. Williams warned potential visitors that they would find the high moor 'dreary in the extreme', presenting 'nothing of consequence'.[2] 'An increase of building', he believed, could only improve the appearance of the waste.[3]

In fact, by the time Williams's work was published in 1804, changes were under way. At Judge Buller's behest, an inn, now the *Two Bridges Hotel*, and a few cottages had been erected between Crockern Tor and the West Dart, adjacent to the turnpike, while Thomas Tyrwhitt funded another inn, the *Plume of Feathers*, and a scattering of cottages on a ridge to the south, not far from his Tor Royal estate. While Williams was only dreaming of buildings interrupting the moorland skyline, the shattering of the Peace of Amiens in 1803 brought about renewed hostilities with France, and provided Thomas Tyrwhitt with an opportunity actively to promote a project that would result in the construction of an edifice that would become a famous moorland landmark.

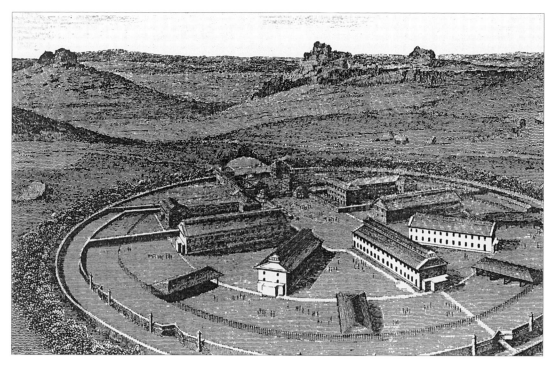

50   *Perspective view of the War Prison near Tor Royal upon Dartmoor, by and after S. Prout, c.1806.*

Motivated by his determination to create a wealth-generating base for the moorland population, and concerned over the desperate plight of prisoners of war crammed into hulks at Plymouth, Tyrwhitt, by now knighted and Member of Parliament for Plymouth, successfully petitioned members of the Admiralty Transport Board to recommend a site near his new hostelry on which to build a war prison. The place would be described by Sir George Macgrath, who took up his post as medical officer in 1814, as a 'great tomb of the living, embosomed as it is in a desert and desolate waste of wild and, in the winter time, desolate scenery'.[4]

In March 1806, a few hundred yards to the west of the *Plume of Feathers*, the laying of a foundation stone for the 'depot at Dartmoor' signified the raising of a 'great work' within walking distance of Risdon's 'three remarkable things'. Designed by Daniel Alexander, and using a workforce comprised largely of Cornish masons, by May 1809 the granite prison, that 'very much altered the face of the country',[5] was ready to receive its first complement of French captives.[6] A month later there were 5,000 inmates. Building work continued, with prisoners co-opted as a paid labour force, until the concentric compound extending over 30 acres could accommodate 10,000 men who would pass beneath a gate on which was inscribed, 'Parcere Subjectis'.[7]

Fortunately, one young artist, Plymouth-born Samuel Prout (1783-1852), ventured on to the prison's building site during 1807 to capture work in progress in a series of wash drawings. Sometime earlier, Prout's work had been drawn to John Britton's attention when he visited Dr Bidlake's school. Britton then invited Prout to accompany him to Cornwall with the object of making drawings in preparation for Britton's *Beauties of England*. Prout found the work difficult, but persevered, pursuing his studies in London where he lodged with Britton, and in 1803 exhibited at the Royal Academy. Suffering from indifferent health, Prout returned to the Plymouth area for three years and, while recuperating, produced illustrations of South Zeal, exhibited in 1813, Lydford, Okehampton, Ivybridge and, besides detailed images of the prison, provided a perspective view published in Charles Vancouver's *General View of the Agriculture of the County of Devon*. In 1820 he became a member of the Water-colour Society, travelled on the continent besides teaching and publishing manuals on drawing techniques, and receiving recognition as 'painter in watercolours' to both King George IV and Queen Victoria. As a specialist in vernacular architecture, he was noted for his 'decomposing composition', achieved through his 'broken line' technique, and for capturing the interplay of light and shade, such work lending itself to mass production as prints. Dartmoor cottages and villages, in his work, appear charmingly picturesque, the hills in 'South Zeal' (1806) tamed and managed, while the cottage in his 1819 'On Dartmoor' seems to be an outpost of civilisation, with the great tor dominating the background.

To return to the prison, where some captives were granted a subsistence allowance with permission to live beyond the prison confines, the terms of their parole enabling them to travel one mile in any direction along the turnpike, with

51   *Construction of the War Prison near Tor Royal upon Dartmoor, by and after S. Prout, c.1805.*

the proviso that they should return to their lodgings each evening. Officers found accommodation as far afield as Ashburton and Chagford.

Just beyond the prison, quarters were built for guards, mostly militiamen commanded by regular officers, and dwellings were erected for a considerable number of persons who had moved to the area to provide ancillary services for the prison, including the 'proprietors of the public bake-houses, slaughter-houses, and the brewery'.[8] Possibly in honour of the Prince of Wales, who had granted land for the construction of the prison, the expanding settlement became known as Prince Town or Princetown.[9] In 1801 an estimated 200 persons had inhabited the 53,000 acres of the Forest;[10] by 1811 the lure of business with the prison had attracted over 500 newcomers to the area. It would seem that, as well as fulfilling Tyrwhitt's ambition, the Surveyors' hopes that a fresh population might be attracted to the area had also been met. The building of the prison and creation of the boom-town, complete with its church, St Michael and All Angels – built by French prisoners, its interior fitted out by American captives – resulted in a complete regional demographic realignment, with Princetown gradually ousting Lydford as the moorland 'capital'.

Developments at Princetown were not wholly applauded. During 1811 a diatribe in *The Independent Whig* claimed that the prison was simply a 'speculative project', existing for the town's convenience.[11] Disregarding the fact that the comment was probably politically motivated, the truth of the remark cannot be denied. The prison was, most certainly, a means of boosting local wealth for, besides necessary victualling and maintenance, thriving businesses had developed through direct contact with the captives, many of whom, having access to funds from London banks, and remittances from home, could patronise the market,

> held in the prison from nine o'clock in the morning till twelve on every day except Sunday, that such prisoners as have the means may be enabled to purchase such articles or clothes as they may wish for.[12]

John Pike Jones (1793–1857), vicar of North Bovey, provides a rare eye-witness account of an excursion to Princetown made during the time the war prison was operative. Published in the *Devon Freeholder* Jones describes the place, without a hint of irony considering its austere setting, as 'well-aired, abundantly supplied with fresh water'.[13] His expedition party, setting a precedent for future tourists, was openly curious as to the inmates' lives. Easily gaining admission to the outer court, they climbed the inner wall 'to observe the activities within', and discovered that prisoners had set up shop and were engaging in brisk trade, selling artefacts such as straw bonnets, hair bracelets and bone models they had manufactured, to the 'numerous visitors continually arriving at the Prison'.[14] Just as this interchange of commodities led to friendly fraternisation between locals and captives, so a good rapport was established between a number of the prisoners and their guards. The administrators, aware that militia men as well as locals were often complicit in the numerous escapes, insisted that a tour of duty at the prison should last for only two months.

Jones's comments on the prison market concur with the regulations mentioned above, and suggest a rather relaxed regime. Up to a point this may have been accurate, but Basil Thomson, governor of the prison during the first decade of the 20th century, in compiling a history of the prison, revealed that there was a darker side to the place already dubbed 'a sepulchre' in a 'Siberian desert'.[15] Apart from such problems as overcrowding and frequent outbreaks of disease, a class of intractable misfits, known as the Romans, or Romains, existed in a state of utter degradation in the 'cock-loft', until they were removed to a prison hulk moored off Plymouth.[16]

Warm sympathy for the French and American captives surfaces in two poems written in the 1820s. Felicia Hemans recalls how:

> 'twas then the captives of Britannia's war,
> Here for their lovely southern climes afar
> In bondage pined[17]
>
> verse 6

and Nicholas Carrington reflects that in Dartmoor prison

> green youth
> lost all its freshness, manhood all its prime
> and age sank to the tomb, ere peace her trump
> Exulting blew.[18]
>
> verse 32

Twenty years later Rachel Evans from Tavistock imagines the frustration of incarceration with her poem's melancholy opening:

> Oh set me free,
> I am young in years;
> And my heart repines,
> Though I shed no tears:
> My spirit was formed for joy and glee;
> It still is buoyant; – 'Oh set me free.'[19]

When epidemics rage obsequies may be hasty, and so it proved at Dartmoor prison, as around 1,500 dead were laid in shallow graves in the gashouse field and ignored for years. Evans finds a sorry situation as she observes that

> without the walls of the prison, on the eastern side, is the burial place of the
> unfortunate captives, which has been sadly neglected; the horses and cattle have
> broken up the soil, and left the bones of the dead to whiten in the sun.[20]

So the situation remained until, in 1865, pigs rooting in the field began to expose coffin lids together with more bones. Only then was an attempt made to exhume as many remains as possible, divide them arbitrarily for reburial in either the American or French cemetery, each marked with a granite obelisk.

But the wars and the dead had not been forgotten as testified by both French and American former inmates who, for posterity, provided graphic descriptions of their period in captivity. The links with the Princetown church their forebears had helped to build remain evident in the memorial window presented by the Daughters of America in 1910, and in the memorial plaque set up in 1928, which reads, 'to the Glory of God and in loving memory of 218 American sailors of the war 1812 who died there'.[21]

Moorland prosperity was short-lived. Following the cessation of hostilities with America in 1814, and France in 1815, repatriation was completed by February 1816, and the prison was deserted.[22] With the departure of the prisoners Tyrwhitt became, in effect, the victim of his so-recent success. Deprived of its economic base, the town was not viable and quickly fell into recession, presenting, by 1818, 'a melancholy aspect, many of the inhabitants having left it'.[23] To stave off economic collapse Tyrwhitt suggested commissioning the prison as a penal institute,[24] and the Prince of Wales endorsed a plan to establish a colony for underprivileged young persons in moral danger, but no such action was initiated.

It was not only Princetown that was in decline. Near Postbridge, Jones explained, while a superficial glance still posited a thriving settlement, on closer inspection it could be seen that estates had been abandoned, 'houses were shut up and falling to decay [...], and Dartmoor was fast hastening back to its original

52 *Hollwell-Tor Granite Quarry, High Tor, etching by T.H. Williams, 1829.*

53   *Hey Tor, lithograph by and after W. Spreat, 1845.*

uncultivated state'.[25] The reason he gave was that the improvements had been too grandiose, embarked on by men who, 'without respect for local conditions or local knowledge, and little versed in agriculture', had forced the land into 'unusual produce'.[26]

In typical Dartmoor fashion, while the Princetown area was suffering economically, two pockets of the moor were prospering. Mines around the Mary Tavy area had reopened in 1796, to cover about thirty acres, although in reality their impact extended for miles, with water extracted from the Tavy by a five-mile-long leat, and peat carried from the heights near the source of the river Walkham. Horse-drawn transportation of mostly copper ore through Tavistock to Morwellham on the Tamar had proved a tedious business, so there was general celebration when, on 24 June 1817, John Taylor's canal link opened. Mineral ores could then be horse-drawn on the downhill stage of the journey to Tavistock, transferred on to barges for the journey to Morwellham, and lowered down an incline plane to the Tamar, for onward shipment.[27]

There was also activity on the eastern side of the moor, where George Templer, inheritor of the family estate, Stover Park, in the Bovey basin, initiated a large-scale commercial project that intruded onto the heights of the moor. During the second decade of the 19th century Templer decided to diversify his business interests by exercising his rights to a granite quarry on the slopes below Hay Tor.[28] Permission was granted for a tramway about eight miles long, to connect the quarry with an existing canal at Ventiford, near Teigngrace. It was an admirable achievement, the line falling more than 1,300 feet in a seven-mile stretch. There was public jubilation and press attention when the line was opened in 1820, the occasion being marked by a fête at Hay Tor Down where the line commenced. A contract already signed for the extraction of granite to expedite the London building boom increased the sense of optimism. For the first few years several thousand tons of granite was dispatched annually by tramway to the canal and loaded onto barges for the short journey to the mouth of the Teign where it was removed onto a coaster bound for London.

Fortunately a few illustrations of the quarries around Hay Tor quarry exist, certainly two by J. Cartwright, and two by T.H. Williams, which seem to have been planned as part of his 1828 two-volume *Devonshire*.

In an attempt to revitalise the Princetown area Tyrwhitt, guided by Taylor and Templer's initiatives, decided it was imperative for Princetown and Plymouth to be linked by an efficient transport system. He made a statement to Plymouth Chamber of Commerce in November 1818, proposing a tramway that would be of value to both communities. With Plymouth as an assured market for produce, he planned:

> to reclaim and clothe with grain and grasses a spacious tract of land, now lying barren, desolate and neglected; to fill the unoccupied region with an industrious and hardy population; to create a profitable interchange of useful commodities between an improvable and extensive line of back country and a commercial seaport.[29]

Lime and sand for fertilisation, together with all provisions and building materials would be the prime imports from Plymouth, while granite and agricultural produce would be exported from the moor.

'Public tranquillity', said Tyrwhitt, depended on the provision of 'a comfortable constant subsistence'.[30] A tramway would open up such a large market for goods that the dispirited, indigent, and unemployed would grasp their opportunities and, therefore, not only would Princetown's future be assured but also other settlements would develop. Enough subscriptions were raised as a result of Tyrwhitt's overtures to enable the formation of the Plymouth and Dartmoor Railway Company.[31] Construction of the line met with a hiatus when the planned gradient proved too steep. Innovative engineering solved the problem, when a tunnel – only the second railway tunnel in the country – 567 yards long and, at its lowest point, 33 yards below ground, was constructed.

54 *Wharf on Roborough Down, from particulars of sale, c.1828.*

On 26 September 1823 the line opened to great enthusiasm and public interest. To mark the occasion Sir Thomas Tyrwhitt 'invited many hundreds of respectable persons ... to partake of a public breakfast' at Roborough Wharf, where three marquees had been erected, and afterwards proceed to the terminus. The South Devon Band played as the tram entered Leigham tunnel, when 'unaccustomed to such dark and dreary passes, the poor horses in some instances refused obedience to their intrepid drivers'. There was much merriment when the procession was halted by a donkey lying down and 'dancing all fours to his harmonious yell'. Eventually the animal was dragged away, the procession emerging from the tunnel to be met by 'thousands of waiting spectators who rent the air with hearty good wishes for the success of the Dartmoor Rail-road Company'. The day concluded with a subscription dinner for 50 gentlemen.[32]

The building of the tramway had attracted immigrant and itinerant workers with their families to formerly remote communities. For example, in 1821 the vicar of Bickleigh and Sheepstor[33] reported that, of 48 families, 25, consisting of 105 persons, were temporary residents, moving on as the railroad progressed.[34] The land lease for the railway included a granite quarry near Princetown which, remaining in production for most of the 19th century, would prove a fragile economic lifeline for the district,[35] at times employing as many as 600 workers.

In effect, the moorland developments were realising the objectives of the Surveyor: the waste was shrinking and new settlements peopled by incomers had been established. Tyrwhitt died in 1833 some years after his estate had been sold, a short obituary commenting that

> his name has been made the lay of the poet, and the memorials of his existence are almost as imperishable – from the works which his fostering hand (even to the interruption of his personal comfort) were mainly instrumental in producing – which the War Prison, the Plymouth and Dartmoor Railway, and the population and cultivation of Dartmoor attest.[36]

55 *'Tunnel of the Dartmoor Rail-Way', wood engraving by P. Hearder, 1833-6.*

With the colonisation of moor around Princetown, its 'great work' visible for many miles, any sense that Risdon's 'three remarkable sites' were in the heart of the moor had eroded. Crockern Tor, sloping down to the turnpike at Two Bridges, was just a short stroll from the inn and cottages, and Wistman's Wood, hardly out of sight of the new house at Bair Down, could be reached by strolling along above the banks of the West Dart. To reach even the most remote of the locations, Childe's Tomb, the Devonport Leat could be followed until sight of the ruined monument was gained, thus enabling visitors to avoid the dangerous Fox Tor Mire. By the early 19th century a new 'heart' was needed for the moor, a place that could be invested with a sense of mystery. The site that emerged to fill this position was Cranmere Pool, which lay near the centre of the north moor.

William of Worcester had stated that 'the source of the river of Okehampton [which] runs by the before-mentioned castle, begins at Cranmere in Dartmoor';[37] then, in 1765, Cranmere makes its dramatic appearance in Donn's map. In 1793 Polwhele had mentioned the place in his *Historical Views of Devon*, explaining that 'the Dart has its rise in a bog called Cranmeer-pool, in a direct line between Okehampton and Crockern tor'.[38]

Polwhele recommends making for 'a small neck or isthmus of dry solid ground, by which a person may proceed on horseback to Cranmeer pool from the north or north-west',[39] and Thomas Brice, in 1802, assures his readers that

Cranmere is the source of the West Okement, rather than, as was sometimes assumed, the Dart which rose some three miles to the south.[40] A year or so before Brice, Edward Atkyns Bray of Tavistock and Bair Down also located the pool, accompanied by companions and a guide.[41] About a mile from the source of the Dart, in the midst of a 'bog of considerable extent', Bray reaches his destination – 'not as represented in the map on the top of a hill, but in a low part of the bog'. As most visitors in the future would do, Bray finds the pool dry. The guide informs the party that 'spirits are here condemned to suffer', this proving to be the germ of stories that would be routinely included in guidebooks. Benjamin Gayer, a former mayor of Okehampton, is the subject of both. Said to have haunted the pool in the shape of a dwarf, his unquiet spirit found peace only after he had emptied Cranmere. For years Benjie laboured using a sieve until, utilising a sheepskin, he completed his task. The water raced towards Okehampton, overwhelmed the town and carried its population away. Although Benjie was released from his onerous task it might be possible to come across him, for, according to another tale, he still haunts the surroundings of Cranmere in the shape of a black colt:

> The spirit of 'Benjie Gear', as the townsfolk called him, from some cause troubled the inhabitants to such an extent that the aid of the archdeacon was called in, and the clergy were assembled in order that the troubled spirit might be 'laid', and cease to trouble them. There were twenty-three of the clergy that invoked him in various classic languages, but the insubordinate spirit refused to listen to their request. At length one, more learned than the rest, addressed him in Arabic, to which he was forced to succumb, saying – 'Now thou art come, I must be gone.' He was then compelled to take the form of a colt; a new bridle and bit, which had never been used, were procured, with a rider, to whom the Holy Sacrament of the Church was administered. The man was directed to ride the colt to Cranmere Pool on Dartmoor, the following instructions being given him;–He was to prevent the colt from turning its head towards the town until they were out of the park, and then make straight for the Pool, and when he got to the slope, to slip from the colt's back, pull the bridle off, and let him go. All this was dextrously performed, and the impetus thus gained by the animal with intention of throwing the rider over its head into the Pool, accomplished its fate. Lastly, an impossible task – that of making trusses of sand and binding them with ropes of the same, until the Day of Judgment – was imposed on the spirit, and so, tradition says, the matter remains unto this day.[42]

When, in the mid-17th century, Risdon mentioned those 'three remarkable things' as sites of especial significance, their very inaccessibility had invested rather unremarkable spots with a certain mystique, for taken together they seem to encapsulate aspects of the human condition. Crockern Tor represents the political and social life; Wistman's Wood, humankind's spiritual aspirations; while Childe's Tomb was a reminder of human vulnerability in the face of Nature and of Man's cupidity. But, with the opening of the road that passed quite close to these sites, they were no longer isolated and the cultural demand for heightened experience, engendered through wild and bleak landscapes, would be met by the long trek across the moorland bog to Cranmere Pool.

While John Pike Jones found himself defeated by the pool's 'obscure situation',[43] his friend furnished a fanciful eye-witness account of the site for Jones's guidebook, explaining that the pool 'cannot be approached with horses on account of the quaking bogs', and that water 'gushes from a bed of gravel beneath the stratum of peat bog'.[44] From the early 19th century, a visit to Cranmere was being presented as a challenge for the sturdy, offering desolation, disorientation and perils that would incline the emotions toward the sublime. Striving to reach 'the urn of Cranmere'[45] seemed to symbolise the human quest for spiritual enlightenment, while success in attaining the spot would bring catharsis and peace.[46] On a more practical level, reaching the pool that is not a pool meant a wearying journey back across the bogs.

7

'WILD SCENES AND ABUNDANT CURIOSITIES'

During the 1820s, three poets reiterated fervent echoes of the Surveyors' hopes – that much of the waste could be put to the plough, and the moorland population develop some agreeable characteristics. Felicia Hemans, Joseph Cottle, and Nicholas Carrington. Hemans' and Cottle's brief interest in the moor as a literary subject was probably generated by the Royal Literary Society's offer, in 1820, of a £50 prize for the best poem on the subject of Dartmoor. Carrington, while aware of the prize on offer, had already made the moor a subject of his work.

Felicia Hemans (1793-1835) emerged as the recipient of the prize.[1] Born in Liverpool, she spent most of her life in the hills around Conway, moving to Daventry in connection with her husband's military duties for about a year, before returning to Conway around 1815. She was self-taught, an avid reader with an eclectic mind. Her acquaintance with the Welsh bard Edwards, the Harpist of Conway, had stimulated her passion for ancient history. At the time the poetry prize was on offer she was toying with the idea of a piece that would contrast 'the spirit and tenets of paganism with those of Christianity'.[2] While she abandoned the plan for a major piece on that theme, it seems to be the frame on which her prize-winning poem was based, the work mentioning Dartmoor – indeed, any moorland location – but once. There is no record that she actually visited the area.

The moor, in Hemans's opinion, suffers from 'a curse of barrenness' (i. 14), a barrenness that embraces both the infertility of the soil and the fact that no oral tradition had been maintained:

> vain the warrior's pride
> The chieftain's power – they had no bard and died.
>
> 'Dartmoor', iv. 5

From the few remaining signs of early occupation Hemans extrapolates a moorland past, imagining a Druidical ritual in which a human victim is 'bound on the shrine of sacrifice' and killed (v. 9). Then, turning to the future, she envisages a scene that would have gladdened the hearts of the Surveyors:

> Yet shall thou smile, by busy culture drest
> And the rich harvest wave upon thy breast
> Yet shall thy cottage smoke at dewy morn
> Rise, in blue wreaths above the flowering thorn,

And, mid thy hamlet shades the embosom'd spire
Catch from deep-kindling heavens their earliest fire.
'Dartmoor', xviii. 11

The poem closes as she imagines 'social mirth' and 'peasant songs' mingling with 'Merry England's voice', as the new era is ushered in (xix. 3, 5, 6).

Joseph Cottle (1770-1853), a Bristol bookseller and publisher,[3] visited the moor on two occasions at least. A runner-up in the Royal Literary Society's Dartmoor competition, his poem, 'Dartmoor', was published in 1823.[4] His moor is a rugged, barren island of 'mouldering crags'.[5] He is conscious of the 'otherness of the region': can, he ponders, such a stretch of land 'belong to thee, my native isle?'[6] Through a series of cameos, his imagined history of the area includes terrible scenes from the Druidical past, though the poet avers that

deform'd prostrations of the mind
Have to oblivion's gulf been long consigned.
'Dartmoor', line 336

Saxon invaders abandon the moor to the race of simple folk who live quiet, hard lives, but their present successors, Cottle predicts, will live in happy prosperity:

I view the smiling hamlet lift her head
Expanded meads, in vast luxuriant spread;
Trees flourish where so late huge tors were found
And many a church casts sanctity around.
'Dartmoor', line 545

In 1826 a poem to rival Mrs Hemans' 'Dartmoor' was published. Nicholas Carrington (1777-1830), schoolmaster at Devonport – recently Plymouth Dock – had, according to his son, Henry, composed the work[7] with the intention of submitting it for the offered prize, but 'the premium was awarded several months before he became aware that the time for presenting it had gone by'.[8] The piece eventually came to the notice of William Burt, secretary of the Plymouth Chamber of Commerce and a great admirer and supporter of Thomas Tyrwhitt. Burt encouraged Carrington to publish the piece and agreed to provide an introduction and commentary.[9] Burt's contribution proved such an authoritative overview of the moor that it has become one of the most valued documents relating to the area, in spite of the fact that, for the second edition of Carrington's 'Dartmoor', the introduction was scrapped in favour of a shorter, less scholarly piece.

There seems little doubt that Carrington felt impelled to write what he thought would be well received, for he was under considerable pressure. Expressing his hopes for a favourable review, he revealed his anxieties in a letter to the editor of the *British Review*, confessing that he found himself in 'a fearful situation'. As a result of the sudden proliferation of subscription schools there was a worrying possibility that he would lose his livelihood, since his Classical and Commercial School, which provided the sole means of support for his wife and eight children, was under threat of closure.[10] Reviewers were invariably at pains to mention Carrington's 'humble' status, and certain of his readers were keen to humiliate him: 'How am I crucified by the upstarts [...]. One subscriber sends me back my book because esquire is not added to his name, another because MD is not attached', he complains.[11] The composition of poetry, such reaction seems to suggest, should remain the preserve of the wealthy, leisured class.

Artist and Devonian James Northcote remarked that the author 'had shown his genius in creating beauties where there were none, and in exhibiting enthusiasm for rocks and quagmires',[12] and imputations of too close an adherence to the work of a predecessor led to the dubbing of Carrington as 'the Thomson of Dartmoor',[13] and his poem as 'Carrington's craze'. General consensus allowed that it was 'plainly his own soul that prompts, but he borrows another's tongue to give its own promptings utterance'.[14] In spite of the critics' reservations, the public enjoyed the work, a second edition being prepared within two months, amid calls for the poet to be granted a pension in order that his talent should not be squandered through mundane activity. No award was made, fortunately in one respect, since he had admitted it was diurnal pressure that prompted his nocturnal muse.[15]

Following an opening salutation to Devon, the focus of 'Dartmoor' gradually shifts from the cultivated lands of the county to the moorland fringes and then to the uplands, 'a wild and wondrous region' (iv. 37), where the narrator/author recalls he has often listened to the 'speech of the half-savage peasant' (iv. 42). In contrast to Hemans, Carrington maintains that the oral tradition is still surviving though in a parlous condition. Through his poem he is, by the transference of oral history to a printed medium, helping to ensure that the moorlanders' traditional tales will survive.

Dartmoor is the poet's spiritual home:

> where'er I wander'd – still, my wayward eye
> Rested on thee!
>
> 'Dartmoor', verse 4

He finds pleasure in the solitude:

> I love to tread
> Thy central waste when not a sound intrudes
> Upon the ear, but rush of wing, or leap
> Of the hoarse waterfall.
>
> 'Dartmoor', verse 12

Following his outpouring of pleasure in the scenery there is a quite extraordinary change of tone, as he envisages a time when:

> the dauntless grasp
> Of industry assails you mighty Tors
> Of the dread wilderness, and soon they lift

> Their awful heads no more. Ye rose sublime –
> Ye monuments of the past world, ye rose
> Sublimely on the view, but fate has struck
> The inexorable hour.
>
> 'Dartmoor', verse 7

Already 'the Railway', the tramway between Princetown and Plymouth, 'leads its mazy track' (vii, 9) and the

> peasant views
> Amazed, the masses of the wild moor move
> Swift to the destined port.
>
> 'Dartmoor', verse 8

The poem certainly does describe the unique beauty of the area, graphically delineating 'every spot of beauty – every form of grandeur'.[16] But, there is no doubt that Carrington, like Hemans and Cottle, was projecting, with equanimity, the homeland state's 'politically correct' vision of a future when the moor would be entirely cultivated:

> Yet how great
> The toil, if Labour from the tor-crown'd hills
> Collect within his nervous grasp the rocks
> That baffled the eternal winds, and bid
> The cheerful sward upspring [...]
> And Ceres reign, where silence deep as death,
> And stern sterility, from age to age,
> Held unrelenting sway!
>
> 'Dartmoor', verse 7

For Carrington, 'on Fancy's gaze delicious visions rise' (ix, 2) of a future moorland:

> A thousand cots, fair sprinkled o'er the sward,
> The smoke upcurls between the trees; – the fields,
> High cultured spread around
>
> 'Dartmoor', verse 9[17]

His prognostications match Cottle's 'visions before me burst',[18] and Hemans' 'light of prophecy'.[19] These poets project a thoroughly conservative construct of an agriculture-based community, symbolically clustered around the established church, a microcosm of English life, much as the Surveyors had anticipated. But this was, even in the 1820s, a nostalgic view, antithetical to reality. As a percentage of the national economy, farming was diminishing in importance, and it was unlikely that whole areas of waste would ever be put to the plough. For the future, national wealth creation lay in manufacturing industries centred on the coalfields and their agglomerations of expanding towns. Following the national trend, the

56 *Meavy Vale, etching by P.H. Rogers, 1826. The managed lands where 'smoke up curls between the trees'.*

source of prosperity on Dartmoor was by the 1820s beginning to accrue from industry, for, if there was no coal, there was tin and copper and granite. For a few years, new and, it would often prove, short-lived little settlements sprang up, creating a shifting population moving in response to work opportunities in the mines and quarries.[20]

Philip Hutchins Rogers (1794-1853) produced 12 delicate etchings, four of which are vignettes, specifically for Carrington's 'Dartmoor'. These illustrations, quite unlike his robust landscapes and marine views in oil, represent his major foray into moorland subjects before he left Plymouth and settled on the Continent. Nicholas Carrington remained a 'sport' in a town not noted for its interest in literary matters, and it was left to supporters elsewhere, including John Pike Jones and a number of Devon gentry, to give the poet encouragement and support during the final months of his life. Three years after his death a monument suggestive of a cromlech was proposed; after all the planning and designing, nothing materialised except a plaque in the church of St Edward, King and Martyr at Shaugh Prior, and the poet's name and dates inscribed on Dewerstone's summit. Even while the

57   *Proposed Monument to Carrington, c.1835.*

erection of Carrington's memorial was under discussion, 'the wand of industry' had been waved to great effect over the Dewerstone's slopes, just as he claimed he hoped would happen across the moor. There, granite quarries were opened up, served by tramways linked by an inclined plane, but the venture was short-lived, and today the tramways are green paths, and tree-cover softens the hillside's scars.

Over the years J.M.W. Turner (1775-1851) made a number of visits to Devon, enjoying the company of local artists, including Ambrose Bowden Johns (1766-1858) in whose cottage at North Hill, then on the borders of Plymouth, he stayed for a time. Greatly influenced by his eminent friend's style, a certain frisson developed when one of Johns's pieces was engraved and published as Turner's work – an enormous compliment to the highly embarrassed Johns. Apparently Turner did picnic and paint at Shaugh Bridge, and in his sketchbooks makes references to other moorland visits. He exhibited a view of Ivybridge Mill at the Royal Academy in 1812, of the area around Lustleigh Cleave in 1832, and of Holne Chase in 1840. Here, his work is represented by an engraving of Okehampton Castle and a watercolour, *Buckfastleigh*, executed in 1826, in which the still standing walls of the abbey dominate the picture's centre while, marking the passage of the Dart, a series of interlocking spurs melt into the horizon and the plateau of the high moor.

Of the early excursionists, Sophie Dixon (d.1855), who lived at Billacombe, near Plymouth, and later at Princetown, published the most comprehensive accounts of the region.[21] She had, from childhood, felt an affinity with the moor:

> I claim thee as mine own – and I may well
> From early right, and long attachment claim [...]
> Mine infant eyes gazed on thy peaks so oft,
> Till I became its own unfettered Child.
> 'Stanzas Written on Dartmoor', line 77[22]

After a long search for 'the miraculous pool' at Cranmere the reality does not meet expectations. It disappoints on account of 'its insignificant dimensions, and the total absence of any kind of sublimity or mountain wildness in the adjacent portion of the hills'.[23] 'In no case', Dixon briskly notes,

> can it be entitled to the attention it usually attracts from those whose object it is to penetrate into the wild scenes and abundant curiosities of these uncultured regions.[24]

A number of poems in her collection *Castalian Hours* explore the spiritual benefit she gains from the wilderness, in places unfrequented by tourists. Such inward reflections are replaced by robust observations in her journals of 1830 when, recently recovered from personal tragedy, she tackles moorland walks of over twenty miles a day, revealing her knowledge of and empathy with the region.

Any surviving accounts of moorland expeditions in the early 19th century hold a certain interest, if only because of their rarity; but Dixon's reports, the first published Dartmoor descriptions by a woman, make a positive contribution to the appreciation of the region. The two journals describe several days' walking and exploring Dartmoor and its immediate environs between May and July 1830. The objectives of her party were to approach the area in the spirit of 'adventurous discoverers',[25] and to find and enjoy 'sublime and beautiful scenes'.[26] The group booked lodgings in advance and worked to a carefully planned itinerary.

The first excursion starts and terminates at Princetown. Rather than complying with received opinion, deferring to the opinions of her predecessors,

58 *Okehampton in 1807, watercolour attributed to J. Farington (1747-1821).*

as might be expected from a woman writing of an area that had been the preserve of male commentators she presents her own judgments with confidence and equanimity.

She notices how the people of Okehampton cling on to civic pride during a period of economic decline. The town's misery, in sharp contrast to the affluence apparent at Chagford, with its woollen manufactory in a buoyant phase, acts as a caution against making generalisations on the economic state of the moorland region.

Dixon finds 'wildness and grandeur', at Becky Fall,[27] although her contemporary Henry Woollcombe found the spot 'not deserving of any great journey'.[28] Contradictory impressions were, I suggest, the result of weather conditions preceding any particular visit. A characteristic of the moorland streams is the rapidity with which they rise in response to rainfall, and a phenomenon known locally as a 'freshet' occurs when, after a period of drought with the ground hard, a sudden burst of rain causes a rapid run-off into streams resulting in a brief and spectacular surge.

Until now the moor had been generally regarded as a looming, distant presence into which the writer intruded, but Dixon presents an alternative view: that of *from*, as opposed to looking *towards*, the heights of the waste. As her gaze sweeps from the distant perspective to the close range she sees the panorama of managed acres stretching across the Tamar Valley as providing a 'singular contrast' with the 'rugged majesty of untamed nature' where she stood.[29]

That consciousness of the moor in relation to the distant horizons might be accounted for by her avowed determination to explore those distant hills that she could see, rising to the north, from her childhood home. As an adult she chose to settle for a time at Princetown, where she would be entirely within the moor's confines.

When Dixon shifts her attention from the panorama of the managed lands to her immediate vicinity, she reveals the waste as a unique bio-region in comparison with the circumjacent country. The flora of the moor had been exhaustively categorised, catalogued, and appended in various editions of Carrington's and Jones's works, but the general vegetative covering had not previously formed part of the pedestrian experience. She observes the ground beneath her feet with the kind of empathy possessed by the moorlanders. She illustrates the need to look at and interpret the moor through understanding the signs conveyed by its covering growth. Where other writers had stressed the dreadful hazards of water-logged morasses, Dixon notices how 'some declivities are wholly covered with grass, [...] while the opposite hill may be an entire peat-bog, or else shagged with heath and rushes, having swampy intervals of bog moss'.[30] Armed with knowledge and respect, she maintains that a visit to the moor could be of positive spiritual benefit, a place 'to wonder, to admire'.[31]

Moorlanders who 'always exaggerate tremendously the difficulties of approach, and often refuse any sort of information as to the precise situation or means of access' fostered, in Dixon's opinion, the reluctance of visitors to venture onto the waste.[32] The fact that the locals were inclined to withhold knowledge and attempted to dissuade strangers from penetrating the area might be regarded as the outward expression of an underlying, perhaps unconscious, territorial strategy. Lack of knowledge would engender fear of the waste and keep the potential intruders at bay. On the other hand, as revealed by the fact that Dixon finds comfortable lodgings around the moor, there was among some of the locals a willingness to cater for visitors. There certainly was a need for guest accommodation, as evidenced in Jones' tracts, published as a guide for

> the numerous visitors, who during the summer months are continually exploring the vicinity of Moretonhampstead, but from the want of some assistance, scarcely know in what direction to turn their attention.[33]

However well meaning and informative, Jones's guides tend to reflect what he and his friends had seen and where they had been, rather than providing details enabling others to follow the same route. But, A Devonian's *Devonshire Scenery; or Directions for Visiting the Most Picturesque Spots*, published in 1826, did just that. The guide seems to be aimed at visitors staying along the south Devon coastal resorts, who might care to enjoy a moorland excursion spread over two days, making circular expeditions from recommended 'temporary headquarters'.[34] It is evident that visitors were not expected to be too energetic:

> Before arriving at the bridge on the Becky, and at the entrance of the common from Manaton, it may be necessary to walk to the summit of the hill on the left, whence the fine part of the vale of the West Teign to Lustleigh cliffs and North Bovey is to be seen, bounded by torrs. It is *possible* for a car or gig to pass from Manaton to South Bovey, but horses, particularly those of a small hardy breed, accustomed to the part, would ensure safety, even in such a descent as from this point to Becky Bridge.[35]

This is the area captured by F. Stevens (1781-1822/3) in his oil painting Lustleigh Cleave, the first large-scale moorland panorama. The Cleave is a narrow valley a mile or so long, through which the river Bovey flows. One side is thickly wooded, while on the Lustleigh village, or east, side the steep slope, rising 400 feet from the river, is comparatively open. Among the ferns and bushes is a scattering of enormous boulders, one of which is the famed logan stone known as the Nutcrackers.

In 1820, the artist presented the piece, which had probably been exhibited at the Royal Academy, to The Devon and Exeter Institution. Besides working in both oils and watercolours, Stevens produced etchings from his own paintings and undertook commissions from other artists. A drawing master in Exeter from around 1817, he died suddenly, 'having fallen down in apoplexy at the door of the Devon and Exeter Institution', where 'Lustleigh Cleave' still hangs.[36]

Following the recognition of the moorland fringes as exhibiting culturally fashionable qualities, the scenic features of the high moor which Chapple had remarked on in the 1780s also excited John Swete, who rejoiced in the

> cloud-capt Tors, which either rear their craggy summits aloft into the air, or fractured into huge blocks spread themselves around the Parent Rock, which not infrequently assumes the air of an Ancient Castle, and frowns a Ruin over the dilapidated fragments.[37]

In the first decade of the 19th century the high moor received an accolade in *The Beauties of England and Wales*:

> on approaching this tract from the south and south-east, the eye is bewildered by an extensive waste, exhibiting gigantic tors, large surfaces covered with vast masses of scattered granite and immense rocks [...]. These huge fragments, spread in wild confusion over the ground, have been compared to the ponderous masses ejected by volcanoes, to the enormous ruins of formidable castles, and to the wrecks of mountains torn to pieces by the raging elements.[38]

59   *Vixen Tor, 'The Sphinx of Dartmoor', above the river Walkham.*

This shift in attitude is apparent in Williams' guidebooks. While he had, in his early work, dubbed the moorland heights as 'unprepossessing',[39] by 1828 he is encouraging tourists to quit the road to roam a region that 'combines the forms and impressions of wildness, desolation and sublimity'.[40] He eulogises over the appearance of the tors, directing attention to 'Vixen rocks rising like a vast ruined castle'.[41] Likewise, Plymothian Henry Carrington's 1828 guide to the moor is punctuated with images of ruins: the rocks on the high tors 'wear the appearance of ruined fortifications'; isolated piles are so

> regularly piled on each other that the spectator can with difficulty persuade himself
> that he is not gazing on the architectural remains of other years; the poet will muse
> amid fallen columns and shattered arches; the antiquarian will imagine ruined castles
> lifting high their tottering turrets.[42]

Cottle had recently cogitated in similar fashion:

> In silence I survey the prospect round [...]
> Imposing structures glisten in the Sun,
> Completed often, oftener just begun,
> Base, architrave, and outstretch'd columns fair,
> Promiscuous cast, and whitening in the air.
>
> 'Dartmoor', line 27

[91]

60 *Hen Tor, castle-like formations.*

And the cleric John Pike Jones sees Hounter Tor (Hound Tor) as

> a magnificent group of rocks, like the remains of some ruined castle, rising in the
> horizon with its beetling front from the dreary plain, its toppling crags having the
> appearance of pinnacles, which the hand of time had loosened.[43]

The motif of tors as castle-like ruins belongs to the currency of the gothic and romantic. Appreciation of Dartmoor's tors as formidable, massy ruins dominating the high skylines was within that part of the gothic discourse concerned with 'political liberty and constitutional rights'.[44] That the crumbling tors should be imagined as decaying castles is wholly in keeping with the region as a place where the common man's rights were held dear: those claimed by the holders of ancient tenements, by persons in venville, and those enshrined in the Crockern Tor stannary parliaments. Castle ruins in a peaceable land suggest an absence of draconian rule, the dissolution of absolute power, and a liberated population. In another manifestation of the gothic where conceptual thought is subordinate to the sensate life, the castle motif evokes the kind of terror associated with the gothic novel.

Besides the tors, the general terrain of the high moor began to be appreciated as a location suggestive of the sublime. Samuel Stokes, who lived at Tavistock in the 1820s,[45] hails the moor as a place of 'gaping chasms' and 'peaks that heavenward start' (i. 4. 6):

> Where seems the Beautiful for aye exiled,
> And the Sublime, eternal rule to hold
> 'Mid all that is romantic, strange, and wild,
> Rough, rude, tremendous, stubborn, stark and bold.
> 'The Lay of the Desert', i. 4. 1

Although disappointed with Cranmere, Dixon finds that other aspects of moorland scenery could evoke sublime moments. When sunshine emerges from banks of cloud and the hills are 'clothed with a splendour of hue', the whole scene is transformed, and she feels that 'encountering a tempest to behold this scene, would have cheaply bought the pleasure of that sublime recollection which it left behind'.[46] The East Okement, too, provides an experience of the sublime, at a point where the scenery 'so frequently changes on the eye as to surprize by its variety, as well as deeply to occupy and interest the mind by its sublimity'. The 'beauty and grandeur' of a moorland storm leaves 'sublime recollection' in its wake. The difference between Nathaniel Howard in 'Bickleigh Vale' and Dixon's interpretation of the sublime illustrates a cultural development. Howard's emotional catharsis was achieved because the conjunction of scenery and weather matched his pre-determined parameters. Dixon and her contemporaries use the word 'sublime' in a looser way, to denote the effect of any powerful sensory experience. But, as she points out, any response to the visual aspects of the landscape, and any heightened spiritual awareness, are dependent on whether an individual's mind is open or whether 'his own perversity keeps his mind shut fast'.[47]

There seemed to be but a few local stories, connected with the moor,[48] so, undeterred Dartmoor writers begin to follow Richard Polwhele's example and dally with supposition, John Johns among them.

The site for Plymouth-born Unitarian minister John Johns's invented 'historical' episode was Clazey Well Pool, to the south of Princetown.[49] There he imagines King Edward II's favourite, Gaveston, in contemplative mood:[50]

> The wanderer there
> Had stood too near an English throne –
> Had breathed too long in princely air:
> He was the banished Gaveston.
> 'Gaveston on Dartmoor', verse 25

Piers Gaveston did have some connection with the moor, the Forest having been conferred on him in 1308 by Edward II, but the action of the poem is located in the 'dark area' of history, where neither the events nor the sentiments expressed impinge on any known happening. Having fallen from favour, Gaveston takes refuge from his enemies, and waits by the pool for a sign from a local witch. A mist rises, encircles the pool and words appear on its smooth surface:

'Fear not, thou favourite of a king,
That humbled head shall soon be high'
'Gaveston on Dartmoor', 83

61 *Crazy well Pool, an old mine working said to be bottomless.*

Misinterpreting the verse Gaveston leaves the forest, and the poem concludes with his capture and execution, and the displaying of his head high on the wall of Warwick Castle. The tale would seem to fit nicely with the few other moorland tragedies, but guidebooks generally ignored it in favour of presenting Crazy Well as a bottomless pool.[51]

Johns's verses did contain a grain of truth, but the decision of Edward Atkyns Bray (1778-1857), vicar of Tavistock and husband of prolific novelist Anna Bray, to embellish moorland history was devoid of any historical foundation. Bray initiated a literary project that would also leave traces on the land. He selected Bair-down, bounded by the Cowsic river[52] to the west and the West Dart and Wistman's Wood to the east, as an appropriate location,[53] for, he reasoned, it was probable that when the ancient Britons 'retired' into Wales and Cornwall during the Roman occupation,

> a colony might still be permitted to exist, either from their insignificance or their insulated position, and this colony might be called by the other inhabitants Welchmen.[54]

Wistman's Wood, so Bray reasoned, might well have once been 'the wood of wisemen' or Welchman's Wood, while the adjacent Bair-down, with its commanding position and 'sacred circles', was probably known as Bard Down in former times, a place of special Bardic significance.[55] Determined that poetic associations concomitant with the word 'bard' should be commemorated, Bray decided to consecrate certain granite boulders on Bair Down to particular poets, tracing out names that were incised by a local workman, confident that sight of the name 'could not fail to communicate to a poetical mind a train of pleasing associations'. In such a solitary place the words were intended to indicate that the 'hand of man has been here', a fact that should have seemed obvious from the abundance of antiquities in the area.[56]

Bray then conceived a plan to address the 'divinities of the rock', in a series of verses, in Bardic characters.[57] The site for these verses would be a tiny island on the Cowsic that he renamed the 'Isle of Mona'.[58] In order for visitors to decipher the verses carved on the boulders two 'diviner's wands', hidden in 'Merlin's Cave' marked by a rock designated and inscribed as 'Merlin's tomb', would provide the magic key. Unlike similar inferences with other moorland sites that would during the 19th century acquire a spurious history, Bray's efforts seemed to come to naught, for just over three decades later, when his project was brought to public attention, many of the inscriptions were moss-covered and difficult to locate.[59]

It is, I think, fair to say that by the close of the 1820s battle lines had been drawn up in respect of the moor's future. On one side were the proponents of clearing the waste and reducing the tors to dust, while on the other side stood those who were beginning to raise concerns over the deleterious effects on the landscape of various industrial and commercial incursions.

Soon after John Laskey had mentioned his general reservations over enclosures, Richard Warner voiced his displeasure at 'the destructive havock' of the owner of Gidleigh Park, who with 'most Vandal-like want of taste' was despoiling a beautiful spot by cutting down oak trees.[60] In the river Lyd Sophie Dixon found evidence of serious pollution, the water 'much discoloured by the refuse of the lead mine [...] and many dead trouts lying by the water'.[61] Cate's Fall (Kitt's Steps), also on the Lyd, highly recommended as a spot to visit, no longer existed, for the river had been diverted to serve the wheel for the nearby lead mine.[62]

By the 1830s, Edward Bray's reaction to quarrying adjacent to the tramway between Walkhampton and Princetown is one of utter dismay. His description provides a rare contemporary account of work in progress, and amply justifies the concerns expressed by activist Samuel Rowe.

62   *Swell Tor, ravaged for its granite.*

The railroad, 'of a very monotonous character',[63] was the means through which Bray believed incalculable damage was being wrought on the moor. The use of gunpowder to loosen granite was producing great raw scars on the hills, making 'mole-hills of mountains'.[64] Passing under some machinery suspended over his head, he explains,

> I ascended an inclined plane of great breadth, on which were massy chains running on rollers, [...]. Another huge mass of machinery [...] was connected with two immense cranes.[65]

Saddened at what he sees, he lamented over the violation of a picturesque area, convinced that his reaction would not be generally shared:

> perhaps I may be laughed at, if not censured, for lamenting what I consider the destruction of such magnificent structures, erected by the hand of Nature.[66]

'It may be hoped', he continued, 'they will leave at least one tor in all the rude magnificence of nature.'[67] Neither laughed at nor censured, his lament was simply ignored, and over the next decade industrial activity escalated as never before. With employment prospects on Dartmoor at a premium there was a need for more than isolated voices to point out the benefits of preserving the area. With industrial activity on the west of the moor, and continuing at Hay Tor, as etchings by Williams reveal, a pincer movement seems to be in operation, encroaching on the fastnesses of the moor.

Around the time Dixon was making her long expeditions and Bray was feeling appalled at the inroads of industry, members of the Plymouth Institute, including Plymouth cleric Samuel Rowe (1793-1853), were embarking on an ambitious moorland project that would have far-reaching consequences. Rowe had presented his observations on moorland depredations to the Institute in 1828.[68] Historians and topographers, he said, had ignored Dartmoor with some justification, but the cause of the antiquarians' neglect was not that the relics were of less intrinsic value than elsewhere, but the remoteness of their location. As events turned out, the very cause of neglect had proved to be a boon. Nationally, he believed, the burgeoning population and increasing commercial speculations involving land clearance had 'resulted in large numbers of monuments over the country being lost to the nation', while those on remote Dartmoor had remained relatively untouched.[69]

Rowe pleaded that the unique qualities of the area should be recognised and cherished. Moorland antiquities, he believed, were vestiges of ancient settlements whose inhabitants had retained their identity during a period when much of the country had succumbed to invaders and assumed the victor's culture. Now, though, as neither wildness nor remoteness presented insuperable barriers against the inexorable tide of present commercial progress, the relics were 'in hourly danger of spoliation'.[70] As well as the need to preserve 'Druidical' monuments, he argued, signs etched into the landscape through centuries of use should be protected. Trackways, tracklines, boundaries, and dwellings might, he felt, through careful study, reveal much about the more mundane social aspects of life in ancient times. The presentation was well received. Rowe was asked to continue the work, and with the assistance of Henry Woollcombe and various friends began to map and collate evidence of early man's use of the moor; the results of their long deliberations will be considered in due course. Perhaps the fears felt by Rowe and his supporters are best expressed in one of Carrington's short lyrics, where he realised that as a result of human intrusion,

> Nought is heard
> Now, in the leafy world, but earthly strains
> 'The Pixies of Devon', 6[71]

8

ENCROACHMENTS

By 1830 Samuel Rowe had formulated a plan for his proposed book: the moorland relics would be revealed through 15 excursions following the route prescribed by the 1240 perambulators. Finally published in 1848, the work received unequivocal praise, as enhancing 'our interest in such a region, to associate each spot now desolate with the lives, the passions, cares, and joys, of men like ourselves'.[1] The work was illustrated with 11 lithographs by the highly regarded, London-based Paul Gauci, after C.F. Williams, a drawing master at Exeter. Lithography, developed at the close of the 18th century and beginning to supersede engraving by the 1850s, was a simple and effective means of reproduction.

Early testimony to the power of *A Perambulation* appeared in the *Flying Post*, from a correspondent who had used Rowe's work as an expedition guide:

> My indignation has been roused to witness the Destruction of many of these interesting relics of bygone days by the ruthless hand of idle curiosity – miscalled antiquarian research – by the so-called agricultural improvements – by the demands of commerce – all tending to obliterate the time-honoured relics of our ancestors.

This excursionist was further outraged to find how, at Hay Tor, 'a commodious flight of steps has been formed to enable some ponderous and pinguidinous subject of patrician indolence to ascend its summit comfortably'.[2] (The steps were already there in the 1700s.)

While Rowe and his friends were engaged in their perambulations, industry was making further encroachments onto the waste. Scattered around the region there were over sixty mines, producing chiefly copper, but also tin, lead, and mundic.[3] Those that made the greatest visual impact from the major roads included the expanding Wheal Friendship near Mary Tavy, several small sites at Lydford, and a sprawling complex of mines at Vitifer. In 1834 china clay operations began at Lee Moor and at Brent Moor, which would result in mountains of white waste dominating the local skyline. Several acres at a remote spot near Postbridge were enclosed for a gunpowder factory, and in the early 1840s naphtha was produced in the Princetown area, first at Bachelor's Hall, then at the vacant prison. Peat, the raw material from which naphtha was produced, was dug from ties between Black Dunghill and Mis Tor and carried by horse-tramway to the processing plant. Naphtha oil would be extracted and used to produce a number of commodities including gas for lighting. Granite continued to be removed from a number of

63 *Ivy Bridge, Devon, engraving by H. Wallis after G.B. Campion, 1832.*

sites; some indication of the extensive impact a quarry might have, and not just on the immediate surroundings, may be gauged from the terms of a typical licence which gave the operators permission

> to quarry, get scabble, dress and make fit for sale and thence to carry away [...]. Erect and construct buildings, machinery and other works [...]. Form and repair roads and divert water.[4]

Diverting water meant that the moor was riven with leats, and the forming of paths entailed the clearing of surface stone for ease of passage, thus changing the face of acres of moorland. Permission 'to construct buildings' allowed temporary settlements to grow up close to the works. Ancillary development would be similar at other industrial locations.

On the south side of the moor the three-mile Zeal Tor tramway, from peat works at Redlake Mires to the treatment works at Shipley Bridge on the Avon, came into service in 1847. Employees tended to stay out on the moor during the week, the cairn on Western White Barrow reputedly fashioned into a home for some of the workers. At Petre's Pits traces of where horses were stabled are still to be seen – the remains are better known as Uncle Ab's house, a reference to the stableman who lived there. This venture, to produce saleable peat and charcoal, was – as you will have guessed – another short-lived enterprise.

Rowe was acutely aware of the scale of change, and no wonder! When he and his friends had begun their perambulation the fastest stagecoach from London took 16½ hours to reach Exeter; but by 1836 he was commenting in jocular fashion to Henry Woollcombe on 'railway surveyors looking with evil eyes' at the moor. 'It appears', he wrote, 'nothing is safe from them, they may find out and drain Cranmere Pool tho nobody else can.'[5] He was not quite right, but by the summer of 1844 the railway from the metropolis had reached Exeter, the journey taking just five and a quarter hours, and within a few years railway tracks would girdle the moorland region.

Now, it would seem that, with ancient monuments ravaged, enclosing of grazing grounds, and the swamping of the indigenous population with incomers, any local history and traditions would disappear. But this was not the case. Concurrent with the escalation of industry's delving into the moor, the mining of its literary potential intensifies, as part of a nation-wide fascination with the past. For example, the short-lived, wonderfully eclectic *South Devon Monthly Museum*, published between 1833 and 1836, included around forty articles, reports, or poems relating to Dartmoor. Poetry relating to the moor was unfailingly romantic, with Bair Down, Lydford, and the Plym valley described in terms of the picturesque, and much space devoted to Carrington's *Dartmoor*.[6]

64   *Viaduct at Slade, Devon, lithograph by J. Mason, c.1850.*

The principles expounded by the *Museum* were endorsed in a speech made by Henry Woollcombe, president of the Plymouth Institution. Addressing delegates representing literary and philosophical societies from across Devon and Cornwall at Plymouth, in 1835,[7] 'Progress', he believed, placed in jeopardy records 'of our history, our manners and our habits', but was inevitable:

> we may mourn over destruction [...] but it is absurd to arrest the progress of increased cultivation, and those facilities in travelling which the circumstances of the age requires.[8]

Progress, he continued, had to be tempered by acceptance of a duty to preserve wherever possible. Where destruction was unavoidable it was imperative to record for posterity what evidence of the past had once been present. This was exactly what Samuel Rowe intended in respect of Dartmoor.

Woollcombe drew attention to a variety of sources that should be interrogated in an effort to shed light on the past – in particular, archive material to which the public had formerly been denied access. The details recovered, he warned, 'may be rude, sometimes disgusting, and not commendable, but still they are facts'.[9] This speech sums up much of the ongoing work of local societies already responding to the democratisation of history, and places in cultural context a growing interest in Dartmoor's social construction, its dialect, and its customs.

In keeping with the tenor of Woollcombe's speech, Anna Bray (1790-1883), wife of Edward Bray, vicar of the stannary town of Tavistock, produced topographical works that would be republished over the next fifty years and nicely complement Rowe's work. Bray had begun producing the first historical novels with a Dartmoor setting, though she was not the first writer to find the moor a suitable location for fiction, for Richard Warner might be considered as pre-empting her. Some three decades before Bray, he had also travelled round on his pony collecting local anecdotes and fashioning stories from local trifles.

Warner describes the pleasures of exploring Britain around the close of the 18th century in epistolary form. Ostensibly his letters are written to a friend, thus allowing for personal reflections and a certain measure of informality. But Warner made it clear that he did not envisage his missives being enjoyed merely as a vicarious experience; they were 'intended for the direction of the Pedestrian', to encourage others to emulate him. Anecdotes centred on the Lydford area, some previously related by Laskey and Polwhele, are given a moral gloss in Warner's retelling, an early hint of the moulding that the few extant moorland stories would undergo to suit particular groups of readers. For Warner, moorland excursions are considered as forays into foreign territory, as he equates his trek 'travelling twelve miles over a desolate moor, wild as the African Syrtes, without a single human inhabitant or regular track', with those of explorers venturing into the interior of an unknown continent.[10]

Within the frame of his journal, Warner pauses to construct what might be regarded as the first Dartmoor fiction. Albeit slight and deriving from an actual event, it deals with local persons, and characters, exhibiting what would become familiar characteristics.

Breakfasting at Lydford, Warner notes that his landlord, 'while filling the teapot', recalls how, close to the part of the moor his guest plans to cross, the emaciated body of a sailor with the remains of a dog at his head had recently been discovered.[11] At this point our traveller indulges in a flight of the imagination, constructing a fictitious narrative, for, as he admits, 'fancy readily filled up the outline which I had heard, with the most affecting touches'. He postulates a tragic sequence of events, in which the young sailor returning from distant shores looks forward to a reunion with his 'faithful girl' and the 'raptures of his fond father'. A 'pityless' storm overtakes him and lost, cold, and hungry he dies of exposure, 'stretched upon the cold rock'.[12] In this short digression Warner encapsulates certain elements that will occur and reoccur at various times in Dartmoor fiction: of a wanderer, a storm, disorientation and tragedy. Like Warner, Anna Bray, as will become apparent, needs only the germ of an idea before plunging into print.

65 *The late Mrs Bray,* Illustrated London News, *1883.*

Anna Eliza Kempe, born in London, where her father was a bullion porter at the Royal Mint, grew up in a secure, loving home, sharing with her brother an aptitude for study, and an appetite for the works of Samuel Richardson and Sir Walter Scott, both of whose influence is apparent in her own novels. She married Charles Stothard, a gifted architectural draftsman, in 1818, and by the close of 1820 was pregnant and thoroughly enjoying her husband's encouragement of her plans to begin writing fiction. Her felicity was shattered in May 1821 when Charles suffered a fatal accident while working at Bere Ferrers parish church.[13] The child, born the following month, died in less than a year, by which time, as a means of assuaging her grief, Anna Stothard had already plunged into the composition of a memoir to her husband.

By 1825 she had settled in Tavistock, married the vicar, Edward Atkyns Bray, and embarked on her literary career. Two historical romances with exotic settings achieved considerable success before Mrs Bray turned her attention to Tavistock and the nearby moors as a suitable location. Mrs Bray determined to select details from 'real family history which, having already been made the theme of tradition, might be employed without impropriety'.[14] On this base, derived from her knowledge of the district and its history, which would 'give that stamp of originality and truth to the narrative', she intended to 'erect a superstructure of fiction'.[15]

66   *Kilworthy House, engraving by Rock and Co., c.1840.*

Within three months[16] she had completed *Fitz of Fitzford: A Legend of Devon*,[17] a novel set in the 16th century, which 'claims historical truth for representing the spirit of the age in which the action is carried on, rather than for any actual events'.[18] This work is the first to be published making extensive use of Dartmoor and the Tavistock area as a setting for fiction.

The tale revolves around the lives of members of the Fitz family and the Glanvilles, of Kilworthy near Tavistock. Sir John Fitz – Hugh Fitz in the novel – was known to be fearful of an astrological prediction that his son would meet a tragic end, a foreboding that was borne out by his son's eventual suicide after committing three murders.[19]

That little town, nestling amid picturesque scenery, seems to represent an ideal society. When the novel opens, there is, across the social spectrum, a sense of anticipation as the townsfolk prepare for the May Day celebrations. All classes are bound together through tradition, to form an orderly, harmonious community in which the Fitz family, and their friend, Lady Howard, whose pet is a giant hound, Redfang, are included.

Beyond the town is a landscape 'at once wild and desolate, but full of grandeur' (i, 37), inhabited by a motley collection of dubious characters living temporarily on the moor who

> have no law but that of the beasts which war together – the strongest overcome the weakest. And no conscience but that of passion. (i, 32)

The two Tavistock families lead lives entirely unconnected with the suspect gang upon the hills, until Betsey Grimbal, former servant to the Fitz family, now consigned to living among outlaws, and the renegade George Standwich intrude into the lives of the two extended families, when past errors, character flaws, and religious bigotry surface to destroy both families.

Betsey Grimbal and George Standwich emanate from the dark, secret places of the moor. They enable a reader to identify the moor as a region where base emotions fester until constraints accepted as the norm in a civilised community erode. It is an association that might be stretched towards a view of the sublime – that the landscape of the moor excites extreme passions. In respect of both landscape and persons the moor is presented as a heterotopia – as 'other', or opposed, to the comfort of town life in the ordered community of Tavistock. The lives of the indigenous moorlanders are subordinated to the point of extinction in Bray's novel, to be replaced by a 'desperate crew' (iii, p.4). As well as George Standwich, there are disaffected miners who exhibit anti-social characteristics, and persons who, visiting the moor in connection with their trade in illicit goods, have no commitment to any cause – save profit. Others, including some historically verifiable persons, whose presence on the moor would not impinge on or conflict with known records, are political and religious dissidents seeking refuge, whose ultimate objective is the restoration of Roman Catholicism as the national religion. Led to believe that, once the mission is successfully accomplished, their efforts will be rewarded by acceptance into mainstream society, the miners join the dissidents. Completing the factions is Levi, the Jew, despairing of religious toleration, surviving through exercising his skills as consultant and trusted broker of all sectional interests, but always remaining an outsider.

The activities of the malicious Lady Howard, and her attendant hound, are a fabrication. Tradition averred that the 17th-century Lady Howard was transformed nightly into a hound, but Bray 'determined to give her a real hound, a *blood-hound*, instead of turning her into one'.[20] Redfang Howard, protective of his owner and a menace to all others, a blood-hound, with limbs 'of a giant mould', whose 'countenance was fierce and stern' (iii, 129), is a forerunner of the hound who would become synonymous with the word 'Dartmoor'.

The novel was praised for 'accuracy of detail in its history' and for conjuring 'the romantic banks of torrent rivers, in the Arcadian recesses of verdant vales' and the 'sublimity' of the waste.[21] Of particular interest among the locations to which readers were attracted was the Virtuous Lady Mine on the banks of the river Walkham, as Mrs Bray explains:

> The mine is entered by the mouth of the great cavern, which is of a most Salvator-like description, and contains many small lateral caves. In my tale Betsey Grimbal and her companion in iniquity, George Stanwich, have for some time cause to conceal themselves in the cave of the Virtuous Lady. A year or two after the publication of *Fitz of Fitzford* this old mine was worked anew. My story was then popular among the natives, so that the miners employed, named the peculiarly–shaped mineral they found there Betsey Grimbal's slipper, and found out an apartment for her, showing a cell in the rock to visitors as her chamber.[22]

Thus a fictional incident is transformed into the real, and of the many abandoned mines in the district this is the one that will be known by name, even though it is slightly off the well-walked track along the Walkham. Three years after *Fitz of Fitzford*'s publication an article in *The South Devon Monthly Museum* recommended a visit to the mine, declaring that the mine is entered horizontally, and

> ladies who do not mind wet feet, and can be content without broad bonnets, or sleeves cut after the fashion of a Dutchman's breeches, may easily enter and see all the interior operations of a mine. It is, indeed, only when ladies are present that Captain John is known in all the cordiality and attentiveness of his character.[23]

Bray had worried over the presentation of local dialect, when planning *Fitzford*, but the problem was greater in *Warleigh*: the dialect of the Gubbins, even rehabilitated Gubbins, would be 'the drosse of the dregs of vulgar Devonian'.[24] Her solution was to re-invent Roger Rowle – from Browne's 'Lydford Journey' – as a disaffected former Royalist officer who had abandoned his career in order to join the Gubbins and become their leader. The scene in which he reveals the location of Pixies' Cave among the Sheeps Tor clitter is memorable for the intensity of its description, with the cosy little village below the tor presented as in counterpoise to rugged desolation on the hills above. The prospect of finding the cave would capture the imagination of many readers, and lead them to search for the elusive location.

Poet Laureate, Robert Southey, with whom Bray had initiated a corres-pondence, suggested, in the early 1830s, that she seemed to have precisely the talents required to embark on recording 'everything about a parish that can be made interesting; all of its history, traditions, and manners that can be saved from oblivion' including 'short and simple' annals of domestic life.[25] Armed with the promise of practical support from husband and brother, Anna Bray accepted the literary challenge, announcing that the most suitable and malleable form of presentation would be through a series of letters. Southey agreed to receive and comment on the epistles, with a view to their future publication, and between March 1832 and October 1835 Bray penned 42 letters, which, published in three volumes during 1836, met with considerable acclaim.[26] Much of the material is composed of extracts from early writers, but there is such a wealth of previously neglected information relating to Tavistock and its environs, that for half a century or so, most moorland topographies make recourse to her letters.

Mrs Bray proved eminently suited to the task of burrowing for the written history, admitting:

> I never yet could find any amusement in looking upon an old stone, or any other rude vestige, unless I could in some measure trace out its history (i, 144).

Although conscious that vestiges of ancient charms and customs were still extant, she realised there was marked reluctance among villagers to impart any such information to her. 'The lower orders', she explains, 'entertain an idea that if once these charms get, as they say, "into a printed book", all their potency will be for

67   *Crockern Chair at Dunnabridge, sketch by E.A Bray, c.1800.*

ever destroyed' (i, 332-33). Edward Bray had experienced a similar unwillingness to impart information, reporting how, on his enquiring as to the names of the tors around Princetown, the workers 'made no scruple to vary, and even completely change the names' of the tors (i, 290). Such passive resistance was, possibly, one of the few ways locals could show their resentment towards intruders who were, in effect, intending to commodify any material gleaned for their own gain and for the benefit of the homeland market. It is, in any case, apparent that neither Edward nor Anna Bray exhibits any sense of empathy with the moorlanders. His wife recounted with pride how, when travelling by horse, Bray once caught up with a man on foot who was leading several faggot-laden animals. Believing the pedestrian was deliberately lacking in deference, Bray purposely whipped the 'churl's' horses, so they shed their loads and bolted (i,.24). If this typified the fashion in which rustics were treated, it is understandable that they were inclined to be withdrawn and morose in the presence of the rector, and strangers in general.

Where inhabitants were forthcoming with stories, Anna Bray was frustrated in her attempts to comprehend their dialect: 'It is not English; it is not absolutely Devonshire, but a language compounded, I should fancy, from [...] any language that may have been spoken in these parts during the last 2000 years' (i, 26).

She also found it impossible to render the dialect either conventionally or orthographically:

> I would attempt to give you a few specimens, but I cannot possibly guess how I am to *spell* their words so as to convey to you any idea of them (i, 26).

Her three years' residency at Tavistock had not accustomed her to the rhythms and intonation, the blurring and slurring that characterised the dialect. Edward Bray also reported difficulties when speaking to the 'aborigines' (i, 286), finding that the reduplication of the final syllable of names of places created confusion, as did the interpolation of an extra sound between syllables (i, 121). – a strange remark from a man born and bred in the vicinity. It may be that his confessed inability to understand his compatriots was a pose adopted to emphasise, for the benefit of readers, the social gulf between him and the labourers. At times, though, his linguistic niceties act as a constraint to his historical researches, as when, in search of Crockern Tor's missing stone furniture not far from his boyhood home, he meets a man he 'considered one of the natives'. 'Perhaps', he says,

> I might have obtained the information I wanted long before, had I asked for what I was told to ask; namely for a stone that was placed over a *shoot*. But, absurdly, I confess, I have always had an objection to the word; because, in one sense at least, it must be admitted to be a vulgarism even by provincialists themselves. The lower classes in Devonshire, almost invariably, say *shoot* the door, instead of *shut* the door. And when it is used by them to express a water-pipe, or the mouth of any channel from which is precipitated a stream of water, I have hitherto connected it with that vulgarity which arises from the above *abuse* of the word. (i, 131-2)

Anna Bray eventually managed to complete her research through the cooperation of an unusual, aspirational servant woman, Mary Colling, who 'chatted to the village gossips, or listened to their long stories' (i, 80), and relayed the results back to Mrs Bray. It became apparent to both Colling and Bray that traditions were disappearing and, without positive effort, would probably be lost without trace by the end of the century as 'improvements' were helping 'to root out, in a great degree' the ancient superstitions of the peasantry (i, 337).

Dartmorians were not, in Bray's opinion, an attractive race. It would not, in the 1830s, be right and proper, she decided, to class them as 'little better than a set of savages', as had been the case 'at no very remote period', but they remained a 'very rude and primitive people' (i, 22). Such 'peasantry', she explained, are content to live in low huts built of loose stones, peat and mud, 'with a straw roof, or one not infrequently formed with green rushes, so that at a little distance it cannot be distinguished from the ground on which it stands' (i, 22). The sensibilities of these families seem to be blunted; they produced large families who were generally inadequately clothed, they lacked a sense of personal hygiene, 'though they are surrounded on all sides by mountain-streams'; and outside many huts, close to the door, might be found,

68   *Cottage at Buckland on [in] the Moor, Devon, lithograph by and after J. West, c.1830.*

as if they delighted in the odour it produced, a pool into which are thrown old cabbage-leaves and every sort of decaying vegetable matter (i, 24-25).

From the point of view of the comfortably-off outsider, such basic living standards would seem to justify efforts on the part of the dominant state to 'civilize' the natives.

Following less than a decade after the publication of Bray's topographical work, *Borders*, and visiting some of the same locations, Rachel Evans' *Home Scenes*[27] provides some useful cross-references, supporting Bray's general sentiments as to persons and place, although Evans makes a far more positive case for action to be taken to improve the morals of the locals and waken their aspirations.

Evans, like Bray, realises that old customs are dying. For example, the gathering of scattered communities at Whitchurch Down for horse racing and its attendant attractions including Punch and Judy and ballad singers is now only a memory. Suppression of rural pastimes and traditions was, in fact, part of a national trend, part of the process of disciplining and managing an increasingly wage-earning workforce, the excuse for banning events being the prevention of debauched behaviour and absenteeism.

Conscious of the need for industrial and agricultural progress and its promised benefits, Evans still feels regrets at the diminishing common land. On the northern outskirts of Tavistock, at Heathfield, she notes, the 'wand of industry' (local writers had latched onto this phrase) had passed over the scene:

> The gypsies, huntsmen and heath-flowers, [...] the furze-bush for the cunning hare were all gone. Enclosures on every side protected fields of springing corn [...]. Young plantations arose in the distance and cottages were appearing in various directions (66).

Her nostalgia is similar to that sense of loss expressed by Carrington in 'The Pixies of Devon'.

Rachel Evans's description of a visit with the British Association to the Wheal Betsey mining complex, near Mary Tavy, conveys her sense of pride, wonder, and excitement at the sight of the shafts and machinery surrounded by great heaps of halvans,[28] a sight duplicated in the several similar industrial clusters around the skirts of the moor. The mine utilised both steam and waterpower, the waterwheel used for raising ore being the largest in Britain. The wheel, '150 feet in circumference, 50 feet in diameter', was housed in a shed and beside it, in the gloom, Evans sees women and children employed as sifters and cleaners working in a 'perpetual shower' of water thrown out by the wheel (90). Water issuing from the mine to rejoin the main stream was yellow.

Majestic by day, the mine remains a landmark at night, for then 'long wreaths of smoke and flame' (91) could be seen pouring along the sides of the valley. Evans comments that a traveller at night might imagine 'some miniature pandemonium', while the miners, 'vulcans in their sooty gear, may well represent dark shadows traversing the regions of Hades' (91). For Evans, though, the mine represents not an intimation of Hell, but the triumph of science. Science could 'infuse a soul into the savage breast', clear the 'mists of superstition and ignorance', open the 'darkened mind', and destroy bigotry (93).

Rachel Evans feels strongly about 'darkened minds'. They belong, in her view, to the men and women who live on the remote farms and in the remote moorland villages, such as we see in 'On the Borders of Dartmoor', a pencil and water colour by Henry Bright (1810-73), showing a water-mill among trees near Lydford, with a weary looking woman and child walking by.[29]

The fresh population of miners who had settled on the moor, Evans observes, outstrips the indigenous labourers 'in quickness and intelligence' (29). In contrast Evans finds 'lamentable' ignorance among the 'slovenly' indigenous farm labourers: 'their shrewdness, which might be ripened into intelligence degenerates into cunning' (106), the women look 'sluttish', are lazy, content to 'drag-up' children in the 'same dark road' (108), their homes are dirty and miserable.

Evans's summation was that the labourers' instincts 'seem little raised above those of the brute creation'. Believing that 'vice and crime' were 'almost as rife in these remote parts as in the crowded and depraved haunts of a city', she is persuaded that the established church has failed and she suggests that the Methodists should step in to 'raise our petty agriculturists in the scale of humanity' (109).

There is little hint in Evans's work of the possibility of a happy, aspirational agricultural labourer's family; rather there is an implicit contrast between the incomers forming new, vigorous communities and the Dartmorians who retain a stubborn indifference to new ideas, new technologies, and Christianity. But, that the primitive existence Evans identifies is surely coming to an end is implicit in with the coming of the railway.

By the time *Home Scenes* was first published there was some basic educational provision in most villages, and sporadic communities were served by a system of 'cottage schools' set up as needed. That there had been indifference and resistance to educational opportunities is borne out by Dixon who finds that on the very edge of the moor

> the inhabitants of the parish, and others, subscribed a considerable sum, for the purpose of erecting a school-house and maintain the school afterwards; but, as the vicar, Dr Jago, had set his face against all such innovations, he contrived to retard the execution of this design during that space of time.[30]

There are reports of children bound apprentice at seven, and from scrutiny of school attendance records it is apparent that going to school was not a high priority. But another side to this picture, and to Bray's and Evans' remarks on the home life of moorlanders, emerges from the reminiscences of Elizabeth Bidder, a moorland child in the 1830s brought up in a cot at Ringmore, a remote settlement with Sheepstor the nearest village.[31]

Bidder's mother was one of the 'bettermore' sort, which implies there was, indeed, an indolent section of the labouring class, confirming Evans' and Bray's assertions.[32] The girls' parents took advantage of the educational opportunities available – Elizabeth's eldest brother obtained 'fine' free schooling at Walkhampton while the others were sent to Meavy, because the closer Sheepstor school was judged inadequate by the parents. Another mother reportedly was so anxious for her small daughter to enjoy the benefits of the school that she would carry her there.

Bidder's comments undercut some of the cavalier assumptions made by the middle-class Bray and Evans. The waste heap outside the front door, that so offended Mrs Bray, was a vital factor in the domestic economy. It 'went far to form the bacon, fowls, eggs etc. both for sale and home consumption'. The pile of turfs inside the front entrance that had appalled Rachel Evans was an example of foresight ensuring, together with supplies of barley meal, bacon, and potatoes, 'no fear if a blizzard came round'.[33]

Sound knowledge of labouring-class families is absent from both Bray's and Evans's works, their moorlanders generally exhibiting distinctly Gubbins tendencies.[34]

A perception of moorlanders decidedly different from that of either Bray or Evans is expressed in a short series of letters which purport to relate events at the *Three Crowns* inn at Chagford during the evening of 19 December 1811.[35]

The regulars are present, together with a scattering of visitors in Chagford on business. We are not offered a sentimental picture of a simple, happy bucolic gathering, for tempers momentarily flare, the host is churlish, the 'guzzlin' cobbler is known to abuse both wife and children, there is swearing and rough jesting.[36] The cobbler's irate wife, and a Moreton volunteer together with the French prisoner he is escorting and has accidentally shot, interrupt the quiet ebb and flow of the evening's pleasantries.

William, the writer of the 'letters', published in the *Exeter and Plymouth Gazette* describes the gathering to the supposed recipient, Bat, a childhood friend who has now left the area. William observes and records the unfolding of the evening's drama, pausing in his narrative only to comment on the reception of his correspondence by the recipient, Bat, and J**, the recipient's friend.

The publication of these slight missives is, in itself, a sign of the 'new' attitude to history. The working-class voice is heard and a defence of that voice, too. Casual bar-room conversation, presented orthographically, is accorded value. Through humour and by using Bat as a literary device to represent hostile attitudes, William pre-empts criticism from newspaper readers over his use of vulgar Devonian, and provides an opportunity for readers to question their own prejudices. Bat is annoyed at the 'vulgarity' of the writer in choosing to describe the dress and manners of the *Three Crowns*' host,[37] and at finding himself reminded of 'the inharmonious sounds of a barbarous dialect'.[38] William addresses those issues in the second letter, and his brief remarks serve as a sharp riposte.

It was in Chagford and among the villagers that the roots of his social relationships and social conscience had been formed, and the 'very words' by which William had been welcomed by parents and kindred are part of the associations of place, and should not be denied. He has no patience with the affectation of persons who attempt to conceal their rural origins and 'com to cal mux durt'.[39] It is not, he argues, that he does not appreciate 'pure English', but he believes that the value and significance of local dialect should not be constantly denigrated. Like John Laskey, William is ahead of his times.

The representation of Dartmoor in the first half of the 19th century is in response to a gradual national democratisation, of which a growing interest in Dartmoor's social construction, its dialect, and its customs is one small part.

9

'PARCERE SUBJECTIS' AGAIN

During the span of years covered in this chapter themes that will characterise Dartmoor writing and illustrations for well over the next half-century emerge. The notion of the lowering hills inducing dullness and lack of aspiration among a cabined and confined population will become an especially strong strand in fiction, while an alternative view of isolated Dartmorians as honest and artless commands attention. In respect of the landscape, both artists and writers strive to capture the rare beauties of those acres unsullied by human activity, and endeavour to convey the sense of freedom, and opportunity for spiritual renewal the place induces.

The concept of the moor as a place of confinement was given substance in 1850 when, after years of shilly-shallying over the use of the former war camp at Princetown, an item in *The Flying Post* in the autumn of 1850 announced that the dilapidated prison buildings were undergoing repair, '150 men being employed on them to get them ready shortly for the reception of convicts'. The report concluded by noting the benefit to 'small farmers and others in the neighbourhood, for the sale of their produce'.[1]

A major national ideological and political shift had occurred since the French and American war-captives had left the Depot at Dartmoor, years in which its grim buildings were either in 'mothballs' or leased out for short-lived commercial enterprises. Prison committals were rising in parallel with the growth in population, and, as the death penalty was less often invoked, so the number of long-term prisoners increased. Compounding the problem, the antipodean colonies, no longer prepared to concede to Britain's every dictate, refused to accept large numbers of criminals so, by mid-century, prison hulks were once again moored in the Thames at Woolwich and off Gosport. When the concept of a national prison system to supplement, not replace, local jails was finally accepted and inaugurated, the former Depot was among the earliest of the national prisons to be commissioned, thus helping to ensure the future of Princetown as a viable community.

On 2 November 1850 the first intake of convicts arrived. Five weeks later three escaped, the ensuing hue and cry stirring a popular interest that has never quite diminished. During the summer months, in particular, crowds, 'sometimes several hundred – would gather at the gate to watch the men marching to work – reclaiming land for pasture, cultivating land, cutting peat at a site over two miles distant'. Other visitors, eager to view the prison's interior, would have followed the advice proffered in Murray's *Guide to Devon and Cornwall* and obtained 'an order (readily procured) from the Home Office'.[2] Reporting for the *Devon Weekly Times*, Elias 'Tickler' Tozer waxed indignant at finding convicts

> seemed to have an easy time of it – they were in no hurry whatever; and the labour, being divided among so many, appeared to me to be more like gentle exercise, for appetising purposes, than anything else. [3]

Taken aback at the apparently easy life of men 'bad – very bad – in grain' (29), he points out that the

> honest and industrious labourer [...] works nine or ten hours a day, too often lives in a wretchedly uncomfortable cottage, fares on the commonest and coarsest kinds of food and supports himself, his wife and children, on about £25 a year (32).

The labourers, the journalist discovered, were living in such straitened circumstances that their children could be found foraging for morsels of food among the prison waste. There was concern in other quarters over the apparent stasis among the indigenous population and, casting around for solutions in the same year as the prison opened, The Western Literary and Scientific Union, with the support of private philanthropists, offered a prize for the best essay on 'The Cultivation of Dartmoor as a Source of Employment for the Unemployed of the District'.[4] Henry Tanner's winning essay indicated that some changes in agricultural practices were crucial if enough local produce could be grown to satisfy the expected increase in population, for he notes that

> there are practices now pursued, and implements used, which bear the impress of antiquity. Not only is the scene eminently calculated to carry the mind back into by-gone ages, but it requires no great abstraction of the mind for the spectator to imagine himself wafted to a region many centuries behind his native land.[5]

He concluded, as had others, that crop yields would not increase until farmers abandoned outmoded ideas and adopted modern methods and equipment. Tanner's report states, bluntly enough, that Dartmorians were behind the times and out of touch with the mainstream of life, a view Mrs Marsh (1791-1874) endorses in *Chronicles of Dartmoor*,[6] published in 1866, where she explores the entrenched beliefs and behaviour patterns dominating moorlanders' lives that have to be confronted, comprehended and sympathetically managed, before necessary cultural changes can take place. The novel, Marsh claimed, was inspired by Samuel Smiles' brief comments on Dartmoor in his *Lives of the Engineers*, in which he asserted that

> difficulties of road-engineering in that quarter, as well as the sterility of a larger proportion of the moor, had the effect of preventing its becoming opened up to modern traffic, and it is accordingly curious to find how much of its old manners, customs, traditions, and language has been preserved. It looks like a piece of England of the Middle Ages left behind on the march.[7]

Marsh's intention, as she explains in the introduction to her novel, would be to present life in a village 'which lies deeper in the moor than Chagford', before the railway penetrates, and the villagers 'suffer their own individuality to merge with that of the rest of mankind' (i, 5). She did not contemplate the prospect of change with any tinge of regret, considering that enforced isolation had been responsible for 'much ignorance' and the inhabitants of the moor 'remain stagnant, as it were, on their native moor, while the rest of England is advancing with rapid strides' (i. 4).

However, before examining Marsh's representation of moribund and abusive moorlanders, we will look at how the coming of the railway was anticipated by locals who lived deep in parts of the moor about to be served by a branch line from Newton Abbot. At the time she contemplated her work of fiction the London to Plymouth railway route around the southern skirts of the moor had been in operation for some years – since 1849 – bringing formerly remote villages within easy commuting distance of the large towns.[8] By the autumn of 1863 the Newton Abbot branch line to Moretonhampstead was under construction, utilising a section of the old Hay Tor granite tramway between Teigngrace and Bovey Tracey, before creeping up the Wray Brook valley, within the orbit of the population on the south-east of the moor.

There were, as might be expected, minor problems between some of the locals and the navvies constructing the line, as an aggrieved diarist reported:

> the villains stole all poor old * * *'s fowls. He had them under lock and key, but they broke in and took the whole, [...]. There is not a fowl or egg to be got hereabout.[9]

But, overall, there was eager anticipation at the prospect of the railway and, at Moreton, in June 1866, with the line near completion, a meeting was held,

> numerously attended from all parts of the district, [...] to take into consideration the best method for a public demonstration on the opening, [...] to make the day worthy the occasion.[10]

The following week the *Devon Weekly Times* commented on the benefits expected by Moretonhampstead:

> Hitherto it has been shut out from the advantages enjoyed by its neighbours. For commercial, as well as social reasons, this railway will, of course, be a great gain – not only to Moreton, but to Chagford, Drewsteignton and other places.[11]

On 26 June, two engines, the Lion and Lance, garlanded with flowers and evergreen, and drawing 13 crowded carriages, left Newton Abbot amid great excitement for the inaugural ceremony at Moreton. The Newton Rifle Band was present, playing 'inspirational airs' during the journey. The route officially opened to the public on 4 July 1866, with the local populace hoping for an influx of tourists and commodities. The impression from these and other news reports suggesting a local population generally only too pleased to be able to embrace

69 *Tavy Cleave, Dartmoor, water colour by C.E. Brittan, fl.1890-1930.*

innovation is quite at odds with Marsh's conviction, much the same as Tanner's, that moorlanders are moribund and hostile to new ideas.

Mrs Marsh never exactly defines the position of Lawsleigh-in-the-Moor, where the mighty tors stretch 'their huge forms in shadow' during twilight (i, 78), and it is best regarded as a fictional place, though there are certain parallels with Widecombe-in-the-Moor. From the Lawsleighans' point of view Exeter, Newton Abbot, and Ashburton mark the frontiers, beyond which just one inhabitant had travelled many years previously. Occasionally a few villagers venture to fairs in the borderlands between their elected frontiers and the village.

Through the experiences of newcomers to the village, the insobriety among the men, the physical abuse of women, the general level of illiteracy among the village young, and the entrenched superstitions among the adults become apparent. A new sewing machine,[12] called by the local women 'the critter', becomes the catalyst that rouses fear in the 'wise woman' Widow Simpson's mind, a fear that spreads among superstitious men and women in the village. Marsh explains, in one of her frequent interventions, 'that they should invest the sewing-machine with a species of diablerie is not to be wondered at' for their ignorance causes them 'to fear what they could not understand' (iii, 163).

Eventually a group break in to the incomer's home and carry off both 'the critter' and its owner. The machine is burned. Excited and in a rising tide of hysteria, the machine's owner is proclaimed a witch who should be 'swamped' on the moor.[13] After the riot is quelled, local landowners take an interest in the village. It is linked to Newton Abbot by a daily omnibus; a village reading room is built and daily papers provided; a telegraph station is installed. At the close of the novel there is a feeling of optimism that the villagers' outlook will be modified through gradual contact with 'civilisation'. Marsh has stressed that casual brutality, persecution, and ignorant superstition have become the norm in Lawsleigh because of its lack of participation with other social groups. The presence of the looming tors has acted as a mental barrier, arresting the development of questing minds, confining the inhabitants to a culturally and spiritually moribund existence. Lawsleigh is not a pleasant place, but it is entirely consistent with an opinion of moorlanders that had survived down the centuries, and, as we shall see, continued to persist.

Marsh's representation of moorlanders is bleak, yet her fiction is perhaps not without some truth, for it was not long since a vicar of North Bovey had described his parishioners as

> very turbulent people. The farmers, it is true – had recently given up the practice of fighting, in which they had formerly indulged – more especially on Saturday evenings; but the women were awful. The whole village was greatly demoralised, and much addicted to scandalous gossip of the worst description.[14]

The Dartmorians' uncouth ancestry had been recalled in *The Flying Post*, when a correspondent, drawing on the comments of early writers, finds his imagination stirred by the sight of Dartmoor:

> I had frequently marked the aerial pinnacles of the noble congestions of the moor, scarred with craggy rocks at a distance, and thought of strange old wives stories of British Giants and Druids, of wild men who wore raw hides or shaggy skins for clothes, whose drink was blood and with blood-gouts sometimes milk, whose dining-rooms were rocks, some hollow trunk their bed, with the 'brackin' curtains on the heath their bed, their children's lullaby the rattle of the javelin's head.[15]

Charles Kingsley's portrayal of 16th-century Dartmorians in *Westward Ho!* confirms descendants of the 'wild men' as retaining some of their ancestors' characteristics.[16] *Westward Ho!*, published in 1855, set in the late 16th century, 'a most ruthless bloodthirsty book, [...] just what the times want', was partly designed to rouse a sense of patriotism among its readers, the author being somewhat dismayed at the progress of the war then raging in the Crimea.[17] Ostensibly, the Dartmoor chapter simply provides a pause between two phases of the hero, Amyas Leigh's, overseas adventures, and encapsulates the manner in which true Englishmen act when passing through a 'foreign' land with a 'hostile' population. But, there is another theme: Kingsley's deep aversion to Roman Catholicism, re-established in England in 1850, will be detected in his presentation of the Catholic priest and, what is more pertinent, in his depiction of the Dartmorians. Readers are left in no doubt as to the character of the fringe moorlanders for, to introduce his chapter 'How Salvation Yeo Slew the King of the Gubbings', Kingsley includes the whole of Fuller's remarks.

Disembarking from the *Golden Hind* at Plymouth, in 1581, Amyas Leigh, together with a small group of compatriots, sets out for home, a journey that entails crossing the western edge of Dartmoor. These bold Englishmen, raised in the Protestant faith, ride towards Lydford and find themselves in a place that seems to be beyond England and its expected civilities.

Portents are ominous as Amyas, representative of all that England stands for, together with his compatriots, traverses the 'dreary' moor to approach Gubbins country in the 'wild glare of sunset' (268). Kingsley's vivid description of the conical Brent Tor, topped by its church, with threads of smoke issuing from its sides, suggests he intends it as a symbol. Just as volcanic activity may be simmering below the tor's surface, so the secretive Jesuits and their misguided devotees, the Gubbins, may be lurking there, planning to undermine the established church. The Gubbins represent both the uncivilised inhabitants of distant lands and the gullible poor of England among whom Roman Catholic missionaries are making converts.

Nearing Lydford Amyas and his friends feel uneasy – 'more than once they called a halt, to examine whether distant furze-bushes and ponies might not be the patrols of an advancing army'.[18] Just visible in the twilight they see a wayside inn, *Rogues' Harbour*, a name that could apply equally to the regular local clientele, or to the fact that its host harbours Catholic missionaries. The inn exuded an air of squalor, it was

> a villainous-looking lump of lichen-spotted granite, with windows paper-patched, and rotting thatch [...]; and at the back a rambling courtledge of barns and walls around which pigs and barefoot children grunted in loving communion of dirt (268).

The innkeeper's response on realising that Amyas and his party are approaching is to warn the visiting Catholic priest and his companion, also at the inn, to be on their guard, the implication being that, if not a Catholic, the innkeeper has Catholic sympathies.

Details in respect of the inn and the dress, appearance, and behaviour of its dwellers are all consistent with Fuller's remarks on the Gubbins. The description of the innkeeper is derogatory, redolent with animal associations: he 'claws' (269) at his feather-sprinkled hair, 'pricks up his ears' (269), 'grunts', 'howls', 'shambles' (269). His speech is barely intelligible; he is familiar with thieves' slang – 'Tell Patrico'.[19] He strikes his niece, and she returns the blow. Mary, the niece, is barely clothed, a reminder of the savages in distant countries whom the Jesuits were converting to their faith so successfully.

When the local Gubbins attempt to steal the horses a fight and a death ensues before they are routed. Amyas and his victorious group then leave the moor, which, together with its people, is firmly established as 'a Scythia within England'.

70 *New Bridge near Holne on the Dart, engraved by A. McClatchie after T.M. Baynes, 1830.*

Enough of these dour impressions of the moor and its people! Kingsley's private responses to the region reveal the extent to which he was promoting a particularly bigoted point of view in *Westward Ho!* Topographically precise, his correspondence expresses the joy he derived from roaming the hills. Kingsley (1819-75), born at Holne vicarage on the moorland border, soon removed to Nottinghamshire, where his family remained for some years until they returned to Devon, settling in the fishing village of Clovelly. When studying at Cambridge he would long for the county: 'Send down to Holne and make all requisite enquiries', he once urged his mother, 'for I wish for the "Far West" as soon as the leaves begin to show. It will be like a second childhood, a fresh spring in my life.'[20] After taking Holy Orders and serving as a curate in Eversley, he returned to Devon without his wife and family for a recuperative holiday during the late summer of 1849. His enthusiasm for the inner reaches of the region shines through letters to his wife:

> Got on the Teign about three miles up and tracked it into the Moor [...] Well, I got to Teign head – though a boggy glen [...] then, I climbed a vast anticlinal ridge, and seeing a great tor close by, I could not resist the temptation, and went up. O! what a scene! A sea of mountains all round, and in the far east wooded glens, fertile meadows, twenty miles off – far – far below; and here and there through the rich country some spur of granite hill peeped up, each with its tor, like a huge ruined

71   *Grey Wethers, etching by P.H. Rogers, 1826.*

castle, on the top. Then, in the midst of a bog, on the top of the hill, I came on two splendid Druid circles, 'the grey wethers,' as I afterwards found out, five and thirty yards in diameter – stones about five feet above the bog – perhaps more still below it –evidently a sun temple in the heart of a great oak forest, now gone. I traced the bog round for miles, and the place was just one to be holy, being, I suppose, one of the loftiest woods in the Moor. After that, all was down, down, over the lawn and through deep gorges, to the East Dart.[21]

He remains in his heightened emotional state on the following day when he decides to fish Cherry Brook, and sally on to Wistman's Wood where he picks an oak leaf, and gathers moss for his wife. Ramblers who had perused Bray's *Borders* might have been less venturesome than Kingsley, for they would have learned of the (supposed) abundance of adders in the wood. A number of visitors actually did claim they had heard serpents rustling about among the clitter there. Kingsley is quite enthralled as he climbs above the wood:

Oh! Such a place! I climbed to the top. I was alone with God and the hills – the Dart winding down a thousand feet below – I could only pray. And I felt impelled to kneel on the top of the rock – it seemed the only true state to be in any place so primeval – so awful – which made one feel so indescribably little and puny.[22]

In these passages, Kingsley's descriptions of the moor is consonant with that in Murray's *Handbook*, extolling the region as a subject for landscape artists who would appreciate how

the tints of the moor, although infinitely varied by the atmosphere, are derived from a few humble plants, viz. heather, a grass with white seeds, a pale green grass and rushes in the swamps. They are beautifully mingled with the grey of rocks and the blue of streams, and modified by the shadows which fleet over the expanse.[23]

According to William Crossing, James Northcote (1746-1831), Plymouth-born portraitist and biographer of Sir Joshua Reynolds, also noted for withering put-downs, had declared that 'Dartmoor was not worth painting'.[24] But artists had been giving the lie to such nonsense for many years and, from the mid-19th century onwards they would, increasingly, declare the merits of the region through their work. Mention has already been made of Samuel Cook's 'Sir Francis Drake bringing in the Plymouth Leat', a painting that owes much to his work for local theatrical productions. Born into a poor Camelford family, he was bound apprentice in the wool trade at an early age, to a kindly master who, recognising the youngster's artistic talents, set him to sign writing. Out of his time, Cook moved to Plymouth and, after working as a painter, glazier, and grainer, his proficiency in the latter skill earning the soubriquet of 'Limner Cook', and encouraged by some influential patrons, set up his own business. Among his supporters was Colonel Hamilton Smith, a local 'living encyclopaedia' who became the aspiring artist's mentor.[25] The knowledge of history and costume absorbed from his teacher was of immeasurable value when Cook was engaged in painting scenery for Aladdin, a travelling panorama of the war in Afghanistan, and for various peep-shows, tableaux vivants. But, he was also able to paint the most delicate and atmospheric watercolours, local historian R.N. Worth calling him 'the greatest water-colour artist of the West of England'.[26] That merit was recognised when, around the mid-century, Cook was elected a member of the New Water-colour Society. A sociable soul, he enjoyed an annual sketching tour with like-minded friends finding the scenery around Chagford congenial to his style.

Just overlapping with Cook, north Devon-born William Widgery (1826-93), two of whose works are included here, who would become one of Dartmoor's best known painters, had a similarly modest childhood and early training as a craftsman, before setting up his own studio and concentrating on landscape painting. By 1853 he was attracting local praise:

> his handling is bold and firm, but free and fluent where needful [...] the artist has ample merit to entitle him to the patronage of those who have the means and inclination to foster or encourage talent in humble life.[27]

Working in oil and water-colour Widgery produced over 3,000 works in a style 'quite peculiar to himself, a style in which he catches effects, portrays rural scenes and wild landscapes boldly, and with very little finish'.[28] That his pieces were popular is evident from the fact that his paintings were routinely bought before completion, and he was able, by 1880, to move to a substantial house in Lydford. According to William Crossing (1847-1928) – discussed in a later chapter – Widgery's interpretation of a scene could be imaginative rather than realistic.

> One day, when he was busy painting, a passer-by who had a slight acquaintance with him stopped to look over his shoulder at his work. He could not recognise the view before him as that which the artist was painting. In the foreground instead of a marsh there appeared a rocky stream. 'Mr Widgery', said the visitor mildly, 'there is no river at the foot of that hill.' 'Isn't there?' returned the artist, without looking up; 'well, there ought to be'.[29]

Bra Tor, above Lydford, which Widgery topped with a fine cross about 13 feet high in 1887, to commemorate Queen Victoria's jubilee, is commonly known as Widgery Cross, an appropriate tribute to an artist who exemplified the Victorian doctrine of upward mobility.[30]

The literary equivalent of Widgery's bold brush approach is found in the kind of effusive writing that would have seemed beyond the realms of possibility at the beginning of the 19th century:

> Let others boast of mountain ranges high,
> Whose cloud-capp'd summits graze the azure sky,
> The pride of Devonshire shall ever be,
> The Dartmoor hills, so wild, so proudly free.[31]

72 *Evening on the River Teign, Prince and Sharipton Rocks Above Fingle Bridge, Dartmoor. Water colour by J. Barrett. fl. 1875-1900.*

Such a vision of the moor is capped in the early chapters of Jules Poulain's novel *Les Deux Soeurs*, published in France in 1852.[32] Sometime during the 1840s the narrator, a young Frenchman, and his compatriot plan to set out on holiday from Plymouth for the Dartmoor hills above South Brent: an 'uninhabited land [...] far from the roads traced by the hand of man' (1). The narrator's imagination soars, he promises 'caverns which resemble fairy palaces, [...] rocks pierced by torrents, and forming natural suspension-bridges, which tremble at the tread' (2). The Drewsteignton cromlech is transformed into a 'monolith sixty feet in height, a shapeless obelisk, which vibrates, giving forth a dull murmuring sound whenever the base is touched' (3). There were mountains upon whose 'sides man has never left the print of his feet' (6), and places where witches, fairies, pixies, and deformed dwarfs who carry off children were still to be found.

Edward William Lewis Davies (1812-90) in his narrative poem *Dartmoor Days*[33] recalls the pleasures of a house party at Brimpts, near Dartmeet. The

73 *Tors 'Where Solitude and Silence Reign', c.1860.*

opening, in which the author declares that from youth he has been addicted to all forms of hunting, is followed by a descriptive and historical overview of the moorland scene. Tribute is paid to current geological theory: the tors were not ruins occasioned by a comparatively recent flood, but aeons older; they 'mocked the deluge as it rose' (1. iii. 22). Davies imagines the notion of Britishness deriving from the ancient rocks, 'rough cradle for the infant tree' (1. iv. 5), encapsulated in the aged Wistman oak that

> laughs at hurricane and storm,
> And braves securely every shock,
> A British oak from stem to stock.
> 'Dartmoor Days', 1. iv. 8–10

Tufts of moss depending from the oaks 'recall funereal plumes' (1. iv, 14), a reminder that nationhood was achieved through blood spilt in the effort to achieve freedom from feudalism. As the poet's eye alights on the ancient tenement of Brimpts[34] his mood changes and he refers to a mythical British past of which

> no living hand is left to trace
> That dim and parenthetic space.
> 'Dartmoor Days', 1. vi. 17

The mythic British past dissolves to be replaced by the more familiar frame of classical allusion. From the poem's outset enough references to classical mythology are interposed to indicate some quite deliberate connection, finally clarified when mutability is revealed as the poem's underlying theme, with

> Ah! Postumé, it makes me sigh
> To ponder on the years gone by.
> 'Dartmoor Days', 1. xii. 1

Here the author/narrator is borrowing the mantle of Horace,[35] to create a Dartmoor-in-Thessaly where, twenty years ago, sporting gentlemen 'more or less connected with the County of Devon' (n.p.) would gather at Brimpts, near Dartmeet, for a few days twice each year to exist in an Elysian vacuum, unconcerned with the domestic infrastructure that supported them – animals were cared for, food, fires, clothes appeared as if by magic at this house from which stretched the moor, 'illimitable, wild and free' (1. vii. 8). Following the introductory paean to the moor and the establishing of the reader in the role of friend and confidant, the activities of the 'happy band' are described. Their early morning ablutions, adventures in the field, and the hours spent in good fellowship around the fire are recalled with pleasure mingled with nostalgia:

> Ay, time itself can scarce efface
> The golden light that gilds the place.
> 1. ix. 23

There are brief glimpses of the Dartmoor workers: the turf cutter pauses in his labours to enjoy the sight of the huntsmen streaming past, and the 'stout yeoman' voices his respect for a fox just killed. Davies recalls the day when, close to the spot 'where Yealm and Erme have kindred source' (2. ix. 10), and the will o' the wisp 'flickers wildly oe'r the mire' (2. xi. 9), a horseman appears, his flowing hair and loose garments indicate a contempt for prevailing fashion. The Brimpts' group receive him respectfully, learning of his care for wild animals, particularly the endangered females. He is in reality a forester, but his appearance works on a symbolic level; he is the representative of an idealised image of pastoral life, the good shepherd, the green man, the philosopher, one who lives in harmony with his environment, a counter to the lawless band who exist at odds with nature.

Finally, the poet recalls the overwhelming sensation he had experienced on returning to Brimpts after the final day's hunting, that the perfection of the present time was 'an earnest of the home above' (2. xxxvii. 20). By setting the poem within a loose mythic frame Davies was free to ignore the reality of mid-19th-century Dartmoor, and conjure instead a terrain unsullied by agriculture or industry, lonely and quiet, in which he and his happy friends, 'far from the crowded city's strife' (2. xxxvii. 2), like gods, pursue the chase they love so well.

From the descriptive extremes encountered so far, this chapter will close on quieter notes, touching briefly on a farmer's enjoyment in his work and 'Tickler' Tozer's observations on Dartmorians he encountered in his rambles. With the publication of George Hamlyn's (1819–1905?) verses the unmediated voice of a Dartmorian is at last heard. *Rustic Poems*, published in 1869, embraces his reactions to local events, his working life, and his appreciation of the natural world.[36] Born at Bickleigh, in the Plym valley, and receiving little formal education, Hamlyn first served an apprenticeship to a local wheelwright, followed by a period of work in London and a spell back at home working with his parents. After trying his luck in Australia he returned to Jump, near his birthplace, to farm and bask in his peers' approbation as the 'Dartmoor Bloomfield'.[37]

His particular facility lay in composing verses very quickly and immediately relaying the results to his companions. His reply to a query on the state of his swedes elicits verses in which that vegetable's whole cultivation cycle is recalled, the poet drawing his companions, sometimes by name, into the piece, with 'you will remember', 'you may all understand'. He shares thoughts on everyday practices with which his listeners would be familiar:

> It was very good guana,
> Brought over from Peru,
> Which answered very well indeed,
> I may observe to you.
> 'On a Field of Swede Turnips', line 25

'The Ploughing Match', composed and recited during the festivities following a competition, is in praise of the pleasure in participating

> For honour, mirth, and fame
> And not for winning money.
> 'The Ploughing Match', line 23

Poetically the pieces may be dismissed as little more than doggerel, yet, on the other hand a solid respectability, sense of patriotism, and commitment to a labouring life define his work, presenting an alternative to the notion of Dartmorians fostered by Mrs Marsh.

To 'Tickler' Tozer it seems that he steps back in time on his excursions, but, unlike Henry Tanner, he appreciates the experience and, respecting the locals' deep knowledge of their land and their determined individuality, he communicates his empathy in his series of articles. Tickler and his friends would leave Exeter by horseback, pony and trap, foot, or train for a starting point, where they might meet a guide, sometimes a local farmer or the indefatigable James Perrott, the noted guide.[38] Invariably, during the ramble there would be an encounter – more often than not at an inn – with a local who would impart some wisdom, a story, or a song, that Tickler would transcribe phonetically for his readers. In this manner his apparently casual reports of 'unconsidered trifles' represent a collection of local material rescued from almost certain oblivion. He finds locals who believe that 'animals are often bewitched', and who draw 'charmed circles' into which pigs, sheep, and bullocks are 'backed' (74). He describes characters in a few deft touches: at Sourton there is the 'Moorman, with his hat fastened to his head by

74   *Corbel Stones by the Dartmoor Tramway, intended for London Bridge.*

"whisks" of hay, [...] feeding with great gusto' (46). Near Belstone there is the middle-aged man 'whose dress was pre-eminently primitive. The stem of a short black pipe was sticking out of his waistcoat, and his hair seemed to have remained uncombed since his birth' (75). But, as if to obviate any possible hint that he might ever be trying to create some humour from the locals' disregard of fashion, Tickler explains that they

> as a rule eat to live, and dress to please themselves and the weather. There is no strain of fuss here – no artificial veneering and lacquering (76).

In sympathetic strain, he tells of meeting a widower in the Chagford churchyard 'in attitude of devotion', having 'completed another day's pilgrimage to the tomb of his departed wife' (87). Joining Tickler's group at the inn, the grieving widower sings the lament he had composed in memory of his wife. This touching little scene, redolent with Wordsworthian overtones, seems to complement Tozer's observation, that 'the silent, solemn hills criticise not, but admonish those who live near them to be simple, and real, and substantial as they' (76).

Artists, poets and all manner of writers tended to ignore the signs of industry. Sweeping landscapes could look untouched by man, but a close encounter would reveal a different picture. Davies, in *Dartmoor Days*, realises this and while for the most part he recalls how he and his happy friends, 'far from the crowded city's strife' (2. xxxvii. 2), range over an unexploited, quiet and devoid of human activity, it is clear, towards the close of his work, that he is aware of current pressures to exploit the region. Unlike the poets of a previous generation he deplores such a prospect:

> Far removed be the day ere Fashion deface
> The feature and charms of this primitive place!
> May her schemes prove abortive, by ruin dispersed,
> And force the pet-bubble of Science to burst!
> The Freehold of Nature, though rugged it be
> Long, long may it flourish unsullied and free!
>
> 2. xxviii. 112

But the day of defacement had emphatically arrived and granite was being exported to city sites. Even as Davies was composing his poem the streets of London were being paved with Dartmoor's stone, and the piles of discarded material were actually altering the outline of the 'primitive place'. Kingsley's untrammelled acres were not as untrammelled as he makes out considering the gunpowder works were not far away. Samuel Rowe's *Perambulation* seemed to have failed in its purpose, for in the midst of promoting the region as a mecca for artists, sportsmen, naturalists, poets and antiquarians, the *Handbook to Devon and Cornwall* notes how

> the venerable tors [...] are successively reduced to heaps of rubbish by that spirit of wanton destruction which posterity will fruitlessly deplore. [...] The moor resounds with the din of iron clashing against granite.[39]

10

Military Manoeuvres

Even while 'the hammer and the axe' appeared to be in the ascendant on Dartmoor, and outwardly the prognosis for its future as a public open space looked bleak, there was a quickening of interest in the waste as a subject for painting, and for a variety of writings.

A speech made during the 1871 annual gathering of the Devonshire Association may be regarded as marking the start of the campaign to preserve what remained of the moor as open space. 'To civilised men', observed W.F. Collier, who lived on the moor, contemplation of nature was a 'delight, a relief and a rest; a pure unalloyed enjoyment, drawing their thoughts away from the toil of civilized life, putting the sense of beauty into the mind of the jaded worker'.[1] Protests, argued Collier, should be mounted against enclosure, quarrying, pollution of moorland watercourses, and the proposal for a steam railway to Princetown. An inquiry should be instigated with the aim of establishing access for the public to the 'wild uncultivated tracts of land to which they have for ages resorted'.[2]

This impassioned plea was made within a very different milieu from that of his predecessors – Laskey, Bray, Dixon and Rowe – who had been solitary voices crying in the wilderness, for now a national chorus was making itself heard. Efforts to retain commons as open spaces seem to have stemmed from the self-interest of the middleclasses who had settled within easy commuting distance of large cities, in areas that were still green, clean, and rural in appearance. While they wanted to retain their various localities in that condition, they were fearful that continuing high demand for housing developments would result in the diminution of the very aspects of out-of-town living they were enjoying. They were not amused by such a prospect, and, by 1865, had formed the Commons Preservation Society.[3] Within a year the society became embroiled in what would prove to be a protracted test case against the enclosure of part of Epping Forest.[4] Affirmation of the Forest commoners' rights was achieved in 1875, followed by the Commons Act of 1876 forbidding enclosure of mountains and moors.

It was perhaps as a consequence of this Act and the precedent set by a number of other local preservation groups around the country that members of local associations were galvanised into action to unearth 'fragments of history from the deluge of time' in support of their case to preserve Dartmoor. The map illustrated on page 6 is an example of material they brought into the public domain, and after considering how the efforts of the Association could be

best directed to the practical object of preserving the peculiarities and the beauties
of the Moor, together with the relics of former times, so much valued by antiquaries
and archaeologists.[5]

Enthusiasts embarked on a programme to discover and restore many of the
moor's long-neglected ancient monuments. The wonder is that they were able to
maintain their commitment in the face of the reality on the ground.

Above the village of Sourton, at one point the ground rises in a series of turf
covered steps. Terrace farming? No, the remains of an ill-conceived and short-lived
moorland enterprise: an ice works, established in 1875. The terraces mark the
remains of ponds into which water from a nearby spring was diverted. During the
winter ice was removed from the ponds, stored in on-site underground icehouses
until taken by train to Plymouth for the fish trade. That was the theory. In practice
the ice tended to melt en route, and within a decade the business ceased. Also
passing close to Sourton, a five-mile rail link from near the head of the Rattle
Brook stream was constructed, to join the main line at Bridestowe. Completed in
the autumn of 1878, the line was intended to facilitate removal of peat from the
high moor.

Although peat-cutting on a commercial scale would appear to be a violation
of commoners' rights, the Duchy had granted a lease to the West of England
Compressed Peat Company for cutting one square mile, and so began a production
cycle that limped on intermittently until the track was lifted in the 1930s. The
route of the line, rising around 1,000 feet, is now a clearly defined track leading
to mouldering remains of the work's machinery in stark contrast to wide vistas of
scenic splendour.

The 1870s saw mining of tin and copper production in decline due to cheap
imports, but the demand for granite – needed for buildings and roads in the
rapidly expanding towns – was on the increase, as was the production of china
clay.

Once clay extraction seemed to be established at Lee Moor, families joined
the quarry workers, bringing a fresh population to form a new settlement, wholly
dependent on the success of one product. The mountains of discarded soil, mica,
and quartz, visible from afar, might be regarded as symbols of success in creating
economic wealth, or as symbolic of the ravages human beings inflict on their
environment.

On the northern moorland fringes, Okehampton's civic leaders, aware, by
the early 1870s of the possible economic advantage to its needy little town,
proposed that the adjacent moorland would be a suitable location for military
training. Such a proposal was not entirely without precedent, for during the
French Wars exercises were held at Hemerdon, and at Roborough Down, where
John Andrews described the 'Tents round, with a Stake in the Middle; the Men
lying in the Position of Radii'.[6] When the British were fighting in the Crimea, there
had been volunteer camps again at Roborough and at Hay Tor. Those temporary
incursions were as naught compared with military activities once the War Office
decided to realise the moor's potential as a training ground. There must have been

75   *Military Manoeuvres*, Illustrated London News, *1853.*

a sense of chagrin amongst the Okehampton townsfolk when their suggestion of a venue close to the town was dismissed by the powers-that-be, in favour of an area to the south, where, during August 1873, some 12,000 men and 2,100 horses engaged in the first Autumn Manoeuvres commanded from headquarters on Roborough Down.

Never had so many strangers suddenly been introduced to Dartmoor. Not only the thousands of military personnel, but readers of national, local and weekly papers were provided with the details of every aspect of life under canvas. The locals were delighted. Princetown could hardly believe its luck when one of the camps was pitched nearby, for hotels and inns of the place were crowded and so great was the demand that there was 'little doubt that many a kitchen hearth, hay-stack, and waggon was turned into a bed'.[7]

Initially, press reports indulged in fancying the moor as a strange, outlandish region, of 'gnomes and the ghouls, and the fairies of the glens and the caves'.[8] *The Illustrated London News* describes how 'huge pinnacles of grey rock [...] seem to have burst out of the scanty turf'. Unfamiliar place names conjure

> an extinct race of British people, whose gloomy superstition, like that of the Gael in
> mountainous Scotland, invested Dartmoor with the terrors of a wild mythology in
> keeping with the scenery of this strange western region.[9]

As the military settled in, the moor's annexation is symbolised by the ground around the camps being 'crossed and re-crossed with the electric threads

THE AUTUMN MANŒUVRES.

What can surpass in grandeur and magnificence a military display, especially when the evolutions are gone through by English troops and graced by the presence of Royalty ? The soldiers in battle array, amid the clashing of arms, and the terrible roar of musketry and cannon ? Such a scene is shortly to be witnessed on Dartmoor. Doubtless, many thousands of strangers and visitors will pass through Exeter on their way to the scene of action ; but there are many who do not know the establishment of J. H. NEWMAN, the eminent Grocer, 48, High-street (nearly opposite Goldsmith - street, Exeter), where they can obtain first-class Teas, Coffees, and all the various kinds of Groceries of the best quality, at a saving to themselves of the extraordinary sum of from *two* to *four* shillings in the Sovereign ! !

76 *Making the most of the manoeuvres, advert from 1873.*

of the field telegraph', by 'mysterious looking lanes' rendered 'topographically intelligent by little white boards stuck upon rough hewn posts'.[10]

For colour, verve and imbuing the field exercises with a sense of excitement the press excelled, a number of reporters elected to be assigned to various companies to share the soldiers' experiences – some consorting with 'the enemy', others with the 'British' contingent. They then entered into the spirit of the manoeuvres, setting aside any attempt at objectivity, allying themselves with their chosen side and offering a partisan account of each day's exercises.

A series of engraved sketches enhanced dramatic descriptions in *The Illustrated London News*, and distant views of moorland scenery were followed by close ups of the minutiae of camp life. The supporting paraphernalia of war is pictured: the portable printing office, harness shop, the Welsh Fusiliers' mascot – a pet goat, ambulance wagons (much in demand) and the guns. Details of mimic battles conveyed 'an air of rude reality'.[11]

On the army's rest day thousands of persons visited the camp at Yennadon and a special train ran from Plymouth in aid of the Royal Albert Hospital conveying more than 2,000 passengers to the moor. The excursionists were 'highly delighted with their visit, and during the afternoon were entertained by the band of the 93rd Highlanders'.

On weekdays, too, spectators flocked to the moor, as a report sent by telegraph noted:

> During the morning a great many holiday folks arrived here, some in the stylish fours-in-hand, others in harvest carts, and altogether Princetown was never so busy [...] Most of the spectators are on their way to Bellever Tor, which is accounted the best place for witnessing the fight.[12]

A number of the proposed campaigns was curtailed on account of bad weather:

> In mimic war they meet, but there they've found
> The elements an unrelenting foe
> Pouring its torrents till the swampy ground
> Has made their captains their white feathers show.
> 'Dartmoor'[13]

Inclement weather may have frustrated the authorities, but not the spectators – maybe the men, but apparently not the women, for

77   *Military camp on Dartmoor,* Illustrated London News, *1873.*

when the showers came down as they only can come down on the moor, young
ladies, and old ladies for the matter of that, showed themselves quite willing to
accept the shelter of the soldiers' tents, and to fraternize with the occupants thereof.
This friendly invasion of the tents was, of course, out of all order, but discipline had
to give way to the exigencies of the weather.[14]

Fortunately, on the final Thursday the weather cleared and, in brilliant weather,
local excitement reached fever pitch as a crowd, estimated between 40-50,000,
made for Buckland Down, near Horrabridge. There were such crushes at the
stations that timetables were abandoned and trains ran a shuttle service and all
approach roads were packed.

One result of the three weeks of the
manoeuvres was that Dartmoor had entered
the public consciousness as never before.
Whether the place would remain open for
the public to enjoy seemed problematical
once the War Office laid its claim. By 1877
the army was negotiating the lease of 3,000
acres of moorland for their annual training,
having concluded that, as the burghers of
Okehampton had originally suggested, the
northern area would prove a better location
for future war-games. A permanent camp
was established on Okehampton Common
and six weeks' annual training became the

78   *Jotting at the Autumn Manoeuvres, 1873, by Mackenzie.*

norm, until 1895 when, over 15 square miles of the northern quarter, firing was permitted on any day between May and September. Commoners' reservations over the limitations placed on access to grazing during the army occupation were tempered by the possibility of financial compensation. There was opposition from groups and the general public, deprived of their 'freedom to roam',[15] but, however vociferous the protests, the military had arrived and intended to stay.

The military grip on the moor might be tightening, the tors quarried, mounds of clay waste growing, but once the excitement of the army's presence had vanished from the pages of the newspapers, artists and writers turned to different aspects of Dartmoor's landscape and life. Novels, poems and tourist compilations would seem to confirm the artists' images of an industry-free Dartmoor. Generally, there is a literary delving into the past as if to preserve knowledge of moorland life and customs.

Richard John King adds to a fund of stories transforming the moor into the site of legend with 'The Forest of the Dartmoors',[16] a 'vision of the dim old days' (87–88). On the moor at twilight the poet is conscious of ages past, when

> The mountain wolf led forth her cubs
> Beneath the dark pine tree; [...]
> The giant deer with branching horns
> Passed upward to the hills
> 'The Forest of the Dartmoors', lines 67-68; 71-2

Those were times, he thinks, when Tristram and Percival may have traversed the moors, then, as if heralded by 'fairy horns' (23), the presence of King Arthur, leading his knights 'homewards to Carlyoun' (28), is conjured in some detail. This vision is succeeded by that of a solitary knight who looks ever towards Cornwall and his 'ladye'. The poet's fancy then shifts to an image of a bright day, when Guenever, the ladye, visits the moor in a magnificent procession, and the ringing of the horses' bridal reins 'fills all the forest glade' (48). As night falls the scene changes and Morgana is heard telling of her life and the death of Merlin. The poet senses that the 'dark strength' (83) of knights who perished on the moor still lingers in the lush foliage of the glens.

In more prosaic fashion, Frederic Adye, former rector at Lydford, realised that knowledge of the time when the establishment held foreign captives seemed to be forgotten determined, through his novel *Queen of the Moor*,[17] 'to say something about the old prison on the moor'.

Following descriptions of the inner buildings, daily routine, and general intercourse between town and prison during the autumn of 1814 and following spring, the escalating strains as hopes for early release as hostilities draw to a close are thwarted, reach fever pitch and spill over into riot, are graphically revealed through the persona of one sensitive French inmate, Captain Arnaud de Valence.

Queen of the Moor is a small landmark in Dartmoor popular literature, for it is Adye who introduces incidents that will define moorland novels: the gaol, a prison breakout, a local's aiding an escapee, a stumble into a bog, a night spent in the open, an encounter with an angry animal, a hunt. A few years later these motifs may be considered to reach their zenith in *The Hound of the Baskervilles* but, well before then, we find such dramatic occurrences in *Donovan*[18] and *Christowell*.[19]

Edna Lyall (1857-1903), the pseudonym of Ada Ellen Bayley, a prolific writer of moral romances and champion of women's rights, published *Donovan* in 1882. Dartmoor, for Lyall, is a suitable terrain to use as a metaphor for her hero, Donovan Farrant, to undergo a life-changing experience.

On a physical plane Donovan's journey across the moor is a metaphor for his life as a young adult, his present moorland wanderings mirroring his recent aimless attitude and lack of clear objectives. Falling into a reverie, and unaware of the mist descending, he wanders hopelessly, stumbling into a bog. With an effort he heaves his dog to safety. In the dark, in the mist and slowly sinking in the mire, Donovan reaches his spiritual nadir. The hours he endures this dreadful plight are, symbolically, the years he has spent trapped in the ugly mire of his own moral weaknesses. He muses with sadness and accepts responsibility for his failures. He has quite literally fallen into a 'slough of despond' and like Bunyan's Christian becomes aware that he is both physically and spiritually lost.

Writers and poets had for years suggested that an experience of the sublime might be induced by exposure to the extreme conditions of the moor, and there seems to be such an echo in Donovan's position. While 'stogged' in the mire, he mentally moves beyond a state of terror into a heightened awareness of existence, and makes a 'final resolution to keep the silence that would inevitably lead to death' (236). Resigned to his fate Donovan hears his dog return, leading a team of rescuers, and he is dragged out of the mire, dazed and 'in a half dreamy state' (237). At the nearby farm he is stripped of his clothes, a bath is prepared and, clean again, he is given a set of fustian clothes to wear – as the mud was washed away so was his dubious past, his bathing was a baptism and his borrowed clothes – those of the rustic – suggest a new commitment to the Christian values so evident in the lives of his rescuers.

From the use of Dartmoor as a place for self-discovery, we turn to Richard Dodderidge Blackmore's portrayal of village life in *Christowell*, a village on the cusp of change, when symbols of the restless, thrusting world are drawing ever closer to the moor, when

> steam coaches are beginning to run madly all about. Next year they are to come to Bristol. [...] The whole world is in a hurry. [...] The *Quicksilver* average is fourteen miles an hour; and the horses must be changed, in thirty seconds, to show they can beat steam coaches (99).

According to the novel, somewhere between Moretonhampstead and Lustleigh the village of Christowell has grown up around the shallows of the Christow brook, 'lintelled by planks for dear gossip'. It possesses no 'ceremonial line of street or road or even lane' (18). As even a perfunctory glance at a large-scale map will reveal, it is a fictional place, no village conforming precisely to all Blackmore's specifications. While details of the layout of the village are vague enough to apply to several places, the novel's climactic incident closely resembles the terrifying experience at Widecombe in 1638. Although Widecombe's confined location does not match Christowell's open position on the scarp, Miss Gibbons of Sidmouth is convinced that Christowell was Widecombe, as she describes in 'We Donkeys' on Dartmoor:

> We soon descended, and then ascended, some hills into Widdecombe, and could easily recognise Pugsley the carrier's journey [...]. We are afraid we thought more of Captain Lark's well-defended cot than of North Hall, the dwelling surrounded by a moat well-stocked with fish, and crossed by a drawbridge which once stood here, and from which Blackmore took the idea in his delightful book *Christowell*. [...] Truly you must read *Christowell* to appreciate Dartmoor in general and Widdecombe in particular. And you must visit Widdecombe to appreciate *Christowell*.[20]

The 1893 'Devon' edition of the novel was illustrated with views of various moorland locations: the 'real' *Saracen's Head* transformed into the *Raven*, the inn kept by Gruff Howell in the novel, and the inclusion of the church at Widecombe tending to further the impression that this is the location of Blackmore's village of Christowell, whereas Blackmore evidently intended his village to be regarded as a fictional zone when he wrote:

> Christow is not my Christowell; though I took the name partly from it. My Christowell is a compound of several places. Christow is down from the moor, and among less rugged scenery.[21]

His village encapsulates a view of rural life, an intensely conservative model that ranges across the local social spectrum. The villagers live reasonably contentedly, respecting their neighbours, and having a nodding acquaintance with the world beyond the village. Some are illiterate but competent in the necessary life-skills needed to survive above the poverty line, some are avaricious, some jealous, but all know and accept their place in the status structure within their own class. A degree of balance is maintained by consensus, for the rustics who occasionally 'manage to fall out very cordially' (17) accepted that every man 'grew wiser by seniority', thus ensuring that 'youth was kept in its place' (93) while the opinions of their seniors prevailed.

But change is imminent and the innovation, which provides impetus to the plot, is the linking of the village on 1 May 1840 to the newly created, centrally administered postal network. Villagers regard the prospect of change with some cynicism: 'Let un coom; her taime won't be long. 'Tis a get up to sell gate-postesses; and nubbody buyeth they in these here parts' (112). In the villagers' opinion the penny post rather diminished the importance of any communication:

> Whoso got a letter for a penny, [...] was it fair to expect him to pay twopence, every time he got it read to him? [...] The post had no right to deliver letters for a penny, without providing somebody to come and read them *gratis* (111).

Immediately upsetting the delicate village social structure, a youth is promoted above his years to the position of postman.

Far from the hurry of town life, the villagers respond to the rhythms of their pastoral environment, keeping 'no account of time, too partiklar', for as John Sage, the village Solomon, had pronounced, 'the Lord hath ordained for us martals not to do so, with our eyes looking forward to the kingdom' (227). Moretonhampstead is the nearest 'big' village, famed in tourist literature for its 'dancing tree', and, with quiet humour, we learn of the slow pace of life there. Unlike Christowell, Moreton lacks a stream and bridge by which to linger but, 'if any bridge were needed, no one could ever find the energy to build it' (100). Before the passage of many years, as the author knew, the happy somnolence of the place would be shattered, 'when the railway rushed into its bottom' (101).[22]

Blackmore illuminates how the seemingly quaint custom of dancing among the tree branches still serves the same practical purpose as of old. For the girls a platform hoisted up into the branches of the elm is reached by means of a tallat ladder, while the lads are required to shin up 'a half-inch rope hanging down from a bough and anointed well with mutton suet' (107). The effort involved in gaining the platform allows the sexes to appraise each other's dexterity thus serving as part of the pre-mating selection and discriminating process, for certainly, in the past, physical strength would have been a necessary attribute for life on the moor. The dancers needed to maintain their wits and suppleness for 'fear of an 'orkward clout' from the pendant branches (108).

Another sign of change is the scattering of newcomers who settle near the village, precursors of those who would, in reality, come to exercise considerable influence on the way village life developed in future years. These folk are among the local middle classes who meet for a day out at Fingle Bridge, 'where folded, and unfolded, the long hazy windings of the Fingle vale' (167), a spot often described in eulogistic terms by the compilers of tourist guides as a venue for picnics.

The waste above Fingle and beyond Christowell, where the novel's villains meet is, unless driven by work or necessity, a place Christowellians tended to shun. John Sage, noted for his sagacity, would not spend nights there alone for fear of the devil, Jack o' Lantern or pixies. But, attitudes were changing and, through Sage's young relative, Blackmore voices the concern of many regional writers that old traditions are fast dying out. Young Joe explains why this is so: '"Grandfather be aveared of pixies, [...] but I been to scule, [...] I ain't got no faith, in none on 'em"' (231).

Christowell's 'stogging' incident happens when, attempting to wade through the swampy margin of a pool to collect five duck, an innkeeper tumbles into the quagmire. Stuck fast and sinking, 'the harder he fought, the worse he fared; [...] everything turned black above him, and his breath went into gurgles'. He is rescued, 'just as he was disappearing softly, with only his grey hair left behind' (309).[23]

Reinforcing the guidebook warnings, Blackmore explains that, even though the moor is dry, the terrain in the vicinity of Cranmere remains formidable, for

> deep black channels, interlacing one another, and lapped with heath, required great outlay of long leaps, or much light downing, and heavy upping, of boots encrusted with the cake of mire. As wearisome a plod, as a light foot can go through with, or a heavy one stick fast in, with much aching of the knee-caps (377).

Widecombe's 1638 storm, so often mentioned in tourist literature, is the basis for the climax of Christowell, Blackmore's description having much in common with the well-documented events as recounted on a tablet in the church when

> the tower was cleft, the church was rent, the people cast like blasted straws. [...] Pitchy night, and stifling vapour, shrouded all who were unconsumed (387).

As a metaphor the storm presages intense intrusion from the world beyond Exeter. The prognostications, while gloomy, are not without hope, for just as the damaged church will bear repair, Blackmore indicates the villagers will pull through unsettling times and survive.

Once again, although novelists like Blackmore might be looking back to Dartmoor's past with regret, the late 19th-century moorlanders seemed to relish the future – as is apparent when the steam railway line to Princetown opened on 11 August 1883. At Princetown three triumphal arches were erected. School children assembled outside the new recreation hall – erected by convicts – were provided with banners and, preceded by a band, marched to the station to greet the first train. Proceedings lasted all day with more marching, a sports programme and a free tea for the children and more than 400 adults, prepared by the prison's master baker. Fireworks concluded the festivities. Villagers at Dousland, Sheepstor, Walkhampton, and Meavy clubbed together to celebrate with banners, a public tea and races including one for the navvies who had worked on the line.

New buildings, commercial and industrial enterprises and shell-holes, were not the stuff of paintings. Artists were busy on Dartmoor during the 1870s and 1880s; William Widgery was working hard; several artists were attracted to Chagford, all conspiring in the construction of a beautiful misty dreamworld, far from the 'sick hurry and divided aims' of contemporary urban existence.

11

Moves towards Preservation

With hindsight, the 1880s would prove to be a turning point in respect of keeping the moor as a public open space, and preserving venville rights. The effects of the 'human hand rapacious' were never greater. Think of it – in this small area, roughly 20 by 17 miles, mines were operating intermittently; granite was still being removed; the china clay industry was booming. Taking advantage of a granulite deposit near Meldon, a glassworks was set up on site, the War Office was making overtures to extend its ranges, and London County Council was eyeing the region as a possible source of water for the capital. Paintings and photographs of wide vistas, uncluttered by machinery and spoil heaps, might soon, at this rate, be of historical interest only.

Preservationists might be down, but certainly not out, for the 1880s heralded a period of intense concrescence between various local individuals and groups in their urgent efforts to save what remained of the ravaged region, to protect the rights of those living there and those who hoped to visit. In this chapter we will range over some of the ways in which public interest in the moor was maintained.

On behalf of a small band of supporters, in August 1882 E. Fearnley Tanner announced in the local press that an autonomous pressure group had decided to campaign on issues relating specifically to the moor.[1] He stated that the Duchy's stealthy action, which had 'failed to rouse any practical or combined opposition', threatened to alienate all rights from venville tenants and other parties with rights.[2] He urged those with an interest in Moor-rights to 'aid in abating the ill effects' of enclosures and encroachments, by all permissible means. In order to test the difference of opinion between the Duchy and the moorlanders, a case needed to be presented at law, and to that end it was proposed to form 'The Dartmoor Preservation Association'.

Attempts were made to enthuse the general public, keen enough to enjoy the moor when it suited them, but generally indifferent when told:

> It is entirely to your interests that the exercise of these rights should be protected, nay, encouraged. It is through these rights that you acquire the unquestioned liberty over these wild regions which you enjoy, and therefore to you the Commoner is a man of importance and a true friend.[3]

The various groups' attempts to rouse Devon County Council who were habitually 'silent as the grave' on the subject of Dartmoor rights resulted, after years of

79 *William Crossing, pen and ink sketch, c.1895.*

lobbying, in a vague acknowledgement that measures should be taken to protect the area, under the 1894 Local Government Act which granted local councils the power to protect commons and open spaces. The council might be desultory in its approach but not so the DPA who decided to take legal proceedings against any further attempts at enclosing.

While the working-class populations in towns and cities within reach of the moor did not flock to join the DPA, public interest was maintained through journals, novels, the local press, and the ongoing 'battle of the sites', fought over three decades and culminating in the construction of a dam across the river Meavy to supply water to Plymouth.

During the last two decades of the 19th century, William Crossing (1847-1928) and Sabine Baring-Gould (1834-1924), Devonians both, were able to transform papers and reports presented to their associations into popular works, thus creating an awareness of Dartmoor's past and present that no solemn exhortation from a platform could achieve.

Born in Plymouth, William Crossing grew up on the moorland fringe, with the family's business located at South Brent and their private retreat at Jump. After a period abroad and a fruitless attempt at running a repertory theatre, he eschewed the idea of business life in favour of exploring and writing about Dartmoor.

From his home at South Brent, Crossing had been quartering the moor by foot or horseback, compiling records of all aspects of the terrain and the moorland dwellers' lives. His compatibility with the locals made him privy to stories that had survived purely in oral form. He found that tales of the 'little people' were only told him as 'what "old people used to say"', that currently moorlanders were inclined to be sceptics, disinclined to ascribe any untoward events to the agency of pixies.[4] Nevertheless, as he discovered,

> Their curious pranks still form a theme for conversation when, the labours of the day being over, and darkness covers the moor, the cottagers gather round to spend the evening hour by the comfortable peat fires.[5]

Pixies' favoured abodes, it was said, were Sheepstor and close to Dartmeet, although they wandered far afield visiting tors, farms, and occasionally indulging in mischief-making. A few years previously Richard John King had concluded that moorland superstitions and traditions derived from a common stock of European tales but, apart from the purists, no one really cared. Visitors were coming to Dartmoor expecting to be regaled with stories of pixies and not only pixies, for collectors of traditional tales had discovered that a surprising number of spirits made themselves manifest in the region – particularly on dark and stormy nights.

During his moorland rambles, Crossing had found around 27 granite crosses, many prone, some mutilated, others serving divers purposes on farms. After much thought, and with the support of the DPA, a process of restoration was planned. The problem, Crossing recognised, was that in respect of Dartmoor there was jostling between 'preservation' and 'restoration' and the terrain would bear witness to the manner in which he and his colleagues interpreted those key words. Moorland stones fashioned by humans would over time fall down,

80 *Recumbent cross in the wall near Laughter Tor.*

81 *Bennett's Cross near the* Warren House Inn *has defied the vicissitudes of time. Drawn by W. Crossing, c.1880.*

prey to time and weather, and also, over millennia, it was beyond the realms of probability that succeeding civilisations had respected the symbols of their predecessors. The annexing of stones from old monuments for some new practical use was a manifestation of cultural change, and the present position of the stones signified the current phase of Dartmoor's social history. As part of the current cultural sanctification of the past, judgments had to be made as to which should be sensitively re-erected and which left in situ, bearing in mind that the moor was primarily a workplace, not a museum.

On 8 August 1885 William Crossing's dream of a time when crosses would once again stand proud above the moorland herbage was made real. With the assistance of a member of the DPA and some labourers, holes were drilled, cement poured, solder melted, clamps fitted to brace stones – four crosses were re-erected, either in their original position, or nearby. Since then the process of preservation has continued, and the crosses still stand proud against the sky.

In the hope of uncovering sound evidence as to the nature of early moorland culture, a number of barrows – earth mounds – had been investigated in 1872. There was great excitement when, among fragments of ash, bone, and pottery the tumuli at Two Barrows on Hameldon yielded a gold and amber pommel and, from the earth carted away from the site for further investigation, a bronze dagger blade emerged. Twenty years later, aware that what was really known of the region prior to the conquest was 'a little trembling light, more like a shade'[6] the newly formed Dartmoor Exploration Committee decided to approach antiquarian studies in a systematic and dispassionate manner. They would begin by concentrating on clusters of hut circles, with those at Grimspound the first to submit to pick and shovel. There were other similar enclosures but Grimspound was well known, having been identified by Polwhele as of particular importance. Having set aside at least ten theories relating to the site, it was hoped their excavations would provide some new information relics as they set to work

Around these roofless huts, these feeble walls,
Thus solitary, thus decay'd, amid
The silent flight of ages. In these, once,
The fierce Danmonii dwelt ...
These silent vales have swarm'd with human life –
These hills have echoed to the hunter's voice –
Here rang the chase, – the battle burn'd, – the notes
Of sylvan joy at high festivities
Awoke the soul to gladness! Dear to him
His native hill, – in simple garb attired,
The mountaineer here roved.[7]

'Dartmoor', verse 30

No startling discoveries were made, but the material evidence accumulated and documented between the founding of the committee and their last report, in 1905, has proved of value to future archaeologists as their techniques have developed.

As speculation gave way to facts antiquarians agreed, some reluctantly, that rock basins, granite 'gods', and tolmens were formed by weathering; that no culture had been based on the veneration of those natural features, and any relation 'borne by the cairns and kistvaens, and stone rows, to the hut clusters'

82 *Drizzlecombe Antiquities.*

83   *Tolman, North Teign, near Chagford, lithograph by P. Cauci after C.F. Williams, 1848.*

could not be established.[8] While, intellectually, former theories were discarded, Crossing feels there is a sense of emotional loss, for

> the tors of Dartmoor as the older antiquaries knew them were invested with an interest they can never possess for us. The light of the torch held up by the geologist and the archaeologist enables us to read, if not the whole truth, at least very much of it, but this may not be all gain. The romance that once clung to these hoary rock-masses has been ruthlessly torn away, and we can no longer associate them with bards and venerable seers. It is now known that the raindrop, and the frost, and the wind, have scooped out the basins on the tors, and not the hand of man. The Druids have vanished before research like the morning mist that the rising sun dispels, and Nature has taken their place.[9]

Sabine Baring-Gould, ardent member of the Dartmoor Exploration Committee, agreed – in principle – that the 'lucubrations'[10] of earlier antiquarians should be dismissed as 'rubbish' and 'tall twaddle'.[11] But 'rubbish' and 'tall twaddle', part of Baring-Gould's stock-in-trade, were much enjoyed by the public as he moulded conjecture with the results of his fieldwork into the stuff of popular romantic novels.

84 *Watern Tor, on the north moor.*

Exeter-born, Sabine Baring-Gould grew up with a passionate love of the moor, recalling that, in his youth, he

> rode over it, round it, put up at little inns, talked with the moormen, listened to their tales and songs in the evenings, and during the day sketched and planned the relics that I then fondly supposed were Druidical.[12]

After a period as a schoolmaster he took Holy Orders, holding curacies at Horbury, Dalton, and Mersea until inheriting the Lewtrenchard estate in 1872, where he settled, as squarson – parson and squire – when the incumbency fell vacant in 1881.[13] A curate was engaged to care for the souls of the 250 or so inhabitants, leaving Baring-Gould free to undertake civic duties, pursue antiquarian interests, travel on the continent, oversee extensive renovations of his estate and church, and write. It was through his prodigious output as collector of folk songs and author of over 100 books, covering a breadth of subjects from the abstruse to the vulgar, that church and estate were restored and his large family able to live in style.

John Herring[14] is the first of his cluster of Dartmoor stories, the location of the tale and names of places are accurate, and the Battishill family were, in the 1830s, living at West Wyke near South Zeal, a small village lying below the north slopes of the moor, as is evidenced in church records.

Through the Battishills, the Tramplara father and son who are corrupt lawyers, and the Cobbledick members of the Gubbins tribe, different aspects of life at West Wyke and on the adjacent moor are revealed.

Histories of Dartmoor had generally remained silent on the social and working lives of the yeoman farmers and squires with modest holdings who lived around its borders, such as the Battishills, the last survivors of 'seven families of gentle blood', who had maintained a paternal influence over their small domains. They are remnants of those classes living around the Dartmoor fringes who had been in slow decline since the days of the Commonwealth, Baring-Gould maintaining that

> hard drinking, gambling, an extravagant style of living, have destroyed these little
> gentry, and the same causes have effected the extermination of the yeomanry (33).

Having obtained a lease on part of the Battishill land the Tramplaras set up a bogus gold-mining venture. Possibly as a comment on the large number of short-lived speculative mining operations initiated on Dartmoor in the mid-19th century, the author pokes fun at the way in which the wishes of the credulous and avaricious can be manipulated for profit by the unscrupulous – 'when fools are hungering to be deceived they are not particular about the meat that feeds their folly' (85).

On dedication day at the Ophir mine, potential investors carry lumps of ore to the crusher, watch the washing and pick the gold grains from the pan, each carrying home one guinea's worth of the precious metal, with the result that 'applications for shares poured in by every post' (138). They are so intent on watching the progress of their lumps of ore that they fail to notice Grizzly Cobbledick 'salting' the crushed and washed material.[15] This is the scam revealed by John Herring.

A strong narrative strand centres on the Cobbledicks, Joyce and her father, Grizzly, who live in a cromlech poised on a spur of Cosdon Beacon, above West Wyke, where Grizzly and his wife, both members of the Gubbins family, had enclosed a little land under squatter's rights.[16] Except for stealing turnips and potatoes the father and daughter, her mother now dead, respect the property of near neighbours, existing in isolation as 'half-naked savages' (2), 'autochthones' (3), by their own rules. The Cobbledicks represent primitive societies with ideologies alien to those of late 19th-century Britain. As Joyce and Grizzly move from their high moorland isolation, the moral qualities of their 'civilized' contacts prove crucial to their own social and moral development. Baring-Gould illustrates that some 'savages' will 'seize the moment and mount', while 'others are cast into deeper degradation than they knew before' (345). Joyce, influenced by the honest Battishills and John Herring, will represent those who 'mount', while Grizzly will be utterly ruined as his propensity for dishonesty is encouraged by the morally bankrupt Tramplaras.

Besides *John Herring*, Baring-Gould addresses the relationship between Dartmoor and its dwellers in *Urith*, 1891,[17] and *Guavas the Tinner*, 1896.[18] Both

C.F. Williams, del.ᵗ   P. Gauci, lith.

85   *Longstone Rock-Pillar, Gidleigh Common, lithograph by P. Gauci after C.F. Williams, 1848.*

works deriving from the author's field-studies reveal how 'the careful and critical examination of the remains of the dead can be woven into an account of the living'.[19]

Urith opens dramatically with the reader's attention drawn to 'a rude granite monolith' below Devil Tor, said to bear 'resemblance to the Great Enemy of Man'. The connection with Hell is heightened as towards the monolith a fire 'ate its way along, [...] the whole atmosphere was impregnated with smoke, the smoke red and throbbing with the reflection of the fires over which it rolled' (i. 9). At the foot of the standing stone crouched a girl staring 'with a vacant unconcern at the mingled darkness and flame' (i. 10) and who, under closer scrutiny, appears to be wounded. Striding through the barrier of flames a young man, Anthony Cleverdon, reaches the young woman. The inference of a timely rescue from some horrid pagan rite involving human sacrifice proves to be unfounded, for

Urith Malvine confesses she had left home in a bad temper and inadvertently wandered into the path of a swaling operation. Before carrying Urith to safety, her saviour stops to explain that, while the immediate danger may be over when the flames are extinguished, yet the peat might 'smoulder down into its depths for weeks, for months, mayhap' (i. 14). Here is a link between the environment in which Urith, Anthony, and their peers live, and an aspect of their several personalities that will be revealed in the novel when simmering grievances, harboured over years, burst into the open. The description of swaling, the first of several didactic passages, also serves to inform readers about what was deemed to be a necessary part of moorland management, but to an urbanite might seem quite frightening.

Anthony Cleverdon and Urith fall in love, much to the chagrin of family and peers and after much trauma, compounded by the slow-burning jealousy of their marital partners, they find some consolation together.

Ever ready to turn his interests to financial gain, from 'the dry bones of antiquarian research into the past of tin-streamers' he conjured *Guavas the Tinner*, set around Yealm Steps, Crockern Tor, and the Swincombe Valley.

By intertwining details of stannary laws and recent discoveries relating to early methods of obtaining and smelting tin ore with a strong romantic fictional plot, the author, once again, makes arcane information accessible and palatable for the popular market. Moorland tinners' living conditions, working practices, beliefs, and customs are described at length, and the novel allows the harsh, intransigent Stannary Laws to be understood in a 16th-century perspective, as an attempt to curb men who, driven by greed, are utterly ruthless in their determination to succeed. It demonstrates the need for those appointed to uphold the law to live lives beyond reproach, if the society they represent is to be considered just.

The work opens in melodramatic fashion:

> Fastened to a stout oak beam, that was planted deep in the soil and wedged with stones, was a young man without jerkin, in his coarse linen shirt, the sleeve of the left arm rolled back to the shoulder, and the left hand attached above his head to the post by a knife, driven through his palm.[20] His right hand was bound behind his back. About his feet leapt a huge wolf (2).

The young man is Eldad Guavas, who is being punished for allegedly transgressing the tinners' code of conduct. Released from his agony by Isolt Rhodda, the bargemaster's daughter, Guavas accedes to her demands for a pledge of loyalty in return for her action.[21] In a long analeptic sequence it becomes clear that, as Isolt remarks, 'all things are fair in love – and mining' (20).

Once freed, Guavas, protected by his wolf, Loup, and anxious to have his wounded hand tended, walks to a cottage at Swancombe,[22] where the widow Ford and her daughter, Lemonday, live. Through the Fords the author presents an imaginative reconstruction of subsistence living on the high moor. Left relatively comfortably off, they have 'a cow and a pig and half a score o' ewes' (59), and a lad to help out. Details of their domestic activities, of the superstitions, social

I   *The Source of the Tavy by J.B. King (1864-1939).*

II   *Christmas Morn, Lydford, Devon, by William Widgery (1826-93).*

III *Drake Bringing Water from the Moor, by S. Cook (1806-59).*

IV *Evening sunlight, Dartmoor – The Road from Pew Tor to Vixen Tor, by J. Barrett fl. 1875-95.*

V *Bren Torr by William Payne, c.1800.*

VI *Subterrane on the Dock Leat, by John Swete, 1797.*

VII   *Sheepstor, Dartmoor, W. Widgery (1822-93).*

VIII   *Cranmere Pool, Dartmoor, F.J. Widgery (1861-1942).*

IX *Lustleigh Cleave by Francis Stevens (1781-1821/2).*

X *[On the Cowsic], Untitled, by T. H. Williams, c.1804.*

XI   *Taw Marsh, Dartmoor, Exeter, G.H. Jenkins Jnr (1886-1937).*

XII   *Steperton Tor, Dartmoor, F.J. Widgery.*

XIII *Amicombe Hill, Dartmoor, by F.J. Widgery.*

XIV *On the Tavy at Gur Tor, Dartmoor by E.A. Tozer, c.1892.*

XV   *Vitifer Mine by E. Neatby, 1929.*

XVI   *Towards Hey Tor by R. Balkwill, 2006.*

activities, and religious practices that shape their lives are conveyed, restoring a kind of life to the decaying ruins of former Dartmoor homes that many late 19th-century visitors would have seen.

Guavas wheedles from Lemonday details of an old 'keenly lode' her father had re-discovered. Before he can work the mine Guavas faces a final confrontation with his enemies. Since his semi-crucifixion, whenever Guavas has been threatened, Loup, the sole surviving wolf in the country, has leapt to his defence. The wolf becomes legendary: 'that bain't a nat'ral beast neither. I've heard o' such things as devils runnin' about in animal shapes' (138). The above descriptions and those following, of Loup's appearances, will prove to be curiously similar to those of the animal in *The Hound of the Baskervilles*, discussed in the next chapter.

Scheming against Guavas near to Swancombe, his enemies hear a mournful baying, then the

> landscape was illumined by a flash of lightning, and in the blaze they saw the wolf run by – black against the flame – but with eyes turned on them and fangs that gleamed in the evanescent flash (218).

A day later they are aware of their proximity to Fox Tor Mire,

> over which at night danced the will-o'-the-wisp, and into which, when a horse plunged, if he came out again, it would be with phosphorescent gleams flickering along his wet hide (265).

Then they become aware of the wolf's presence as a bullock rushes into the morass and, after a brief moment, vanishes from sight; 'a tossing of the surface alone indicated where it had gone down' (270). A remarkably similar incident will be found in *The Hound of the Baskervilles*.

A motif running through *Guavas the Tinner* is a preoccupation with light sources. At critical moments in the narrative, the location's background becomes subfusc while a single light source illuminates the foreground action. The ghostly light of the moon, prior to its effulgence, reveals the tortured Guavas; there are glowing embers; a turf fire; rushlights; a candle-lit corpse; the light of a taper; flaming gorse; burning peat; fragments of shining cloam; phosphorescent gleams; and the will o' the wisp.[23] As will become apparent, Conan Doyle employs the same device to emphasise dramatic moments.

In *Urith*, the *Hare and Hounds*, a place where 'all classes met, and gossiped, and smoked, and boozed together' (i, 108), provides an opportunity for the author to preserve memories of old, strange tales, such as the eerie tale of the 'walking arms' (i, 126–31), and of the ballad-singer, who rendered 'The Lady's Coach' to a 'weird air in an ancient mode', that by the mid-17th century was 'already beginning to sound strange and incomplete to the ear' (i, 120).[24] These were tiny examples of Baring-Gould's collection of music resources, which, with words suitably censored and rewritten, would filter into many classrooms over the next fifty years.

86 *Going to Widecombe Fair, postcard, by C.E. Brittan.*

While William Crossing was accumulating his store of moorland tales for posterity, Sabine Baring-Gould was embarking on a similar crusade in respect of folk song. He relates on more than one occasion how, in 1888, he left a dinner party near Tavistock with 'his mind in a ferment', feeling he was 'on the outset of a great and important work'.[25] This proved to be the gathering of folk songs and music. He first sought his information among the farming classes, but finding it would be 'necessary to drop to a lower level if we were to tap the spring of traditional folk music',[26] he decided that 'if I want the melodies and ballads and songs of our peasantry, I must get them from the peasantry themselves',[27] from the illiterate aged.[28] In his travels around the western counties he found the old village song man 'rapidly becoming as extinct as the dodo and the great auk'.[29]

In spite of some reluctance on the part of the older generation he was able to garner a substantial amount of material. Lyrics accompanying songs included in his collection are not entirely as originally taken down, many being too sexually explicit for publication so, as Baring-Gould cheerfully admits, he composed anodyne versions to spare public sensibilities.[30] 'Widecombe Fair',[31] with its simple, pathetic story tinged with cruelty, and its robust chorus, attracted tourists to the village, while other words and tunes were assimilated into the school curriculum or folk song repertoire. The old tunes and old words would maintain their new life within folk song societies, divorced from their localities. Baring-Gould believed that on Dartmoor 'customs, modes of thought, of speech, quaint sayings, and weird superstitions' were all on the verge of extinction.[32] The root cause he identified as the 'rubbish [...] that at great cost is given to our children'. He deprecated attempts to widen young persons' horizons away from their locality and their class.[33] Such protestations were generally unheeded, for life in the towns seemed considerably more attractive than the prospect of a moorland existence.

While books were one means through which an awareness of the moor could be stimulated, a familiar problem kept the moor in the news at Plymouth. The town's population had risen as a consequence of the drift from the country and – here we go again – there was a problem in providing an adequate water supply. During the exceptionally cold winter of 1881 snow accumulating in the leat had necessitated water carts touring the streets and the hurried re-opening of local wells. When, a decade later, the Great Blizzard caused similar disruption the municipal authorities ceased their 30-years-long Battle of the Sites – the long-standing argument as to where a dam should be built – and settled on a plan to impound the river Meavy at Burrator to provide a holding reservoir. On 21 September 1898 over 6,000 Plymothians took advantage of a special holiday, travelling by trains, in wagonnettes, char a bancs, by bicycle or on foot, to witness the moment when the water from the Plymouth leat would be diverted into the Meavy valley. Just as had Drake's Leat, the opening of Burrator Lake would generate its own folklore and, in its way, introduce the spectacular tree-fringed waters on the Dartmoor border to future generations, who would learn of the drowned village beneath its waters. Not exactly true – the 'village' was a couple of farmhouses and bridge – but the tale still persists.

While arguments raged over the various uses of the waste, writers began to produce socially realistic novels of moorland life, and artists worked on serenely, visiting locations their predecessors had identified as painterly, and besides reaching further into the moor.

By the 1880s Widgery's son, Frederick John (1861-1942), who studied art at Exeter, London and Belgium, returned to Exeter to follow in his father's footsteps. With a house at Lydford giving easy access to the moors, and his father's former studio at Exeter, FJ, as he is usually known, concentrated on landscape painting and, in the 1890s, received a commission to illustrate a new, revised edition of Rowe's *Perambulation*. Reproduced in monochrome for the 1896 *Perambulation*, the 22 original water-colours are now held at Exeter's Royal Albert Memorial Museum and Art Gallery. 'At their best', as Brian Le Messurier comments, in his recent book on Dartmoor artists, 'F. J.'s paintings have an Elgarian *nobilmente* about them'.[34] The great broad sweep of tors in 'Tavy Cleave' confirm Rowe's comment as to the magnificence of that 'range of castellated tor with which nature appears to have fortified this fine peninsular hill',[35] while his image of the then recently re-erected Sacred Circle on Langstone Moor exactly matches the author's feeling that 'the appearance of this Antient monument as the day is closing – is weird and solemn in the extreme'.[36] Following his father's footsteps, Frederick John Widgery also painted Cranmere Pool, a site that had not generally attracted artists' attention, perhaps on account of its being such a desolate, often mist-bound spot. By emphasising the gap in the peat bank at the northern side of the pool Widgery is suggesting that the old stories might contain a modicum of truth: that during a drought the bank had been deliberately breached and never restored, leaving only a boggy rain-filled hollow. FJ's moor is at times magnificent and at times solemn, but never frightening. But, it was a frightening representation of the region that would thrill and terrify an appreciative public four years after the publication of *A Perambulation* when, after the first instalment of *The Hound of the Baskervilles* in August 1901, the word 'Dartmoor' would become synonymous with horror lurking on a dark waste.

12

The Hound of the Baskervilles

'The hound of the Baskervilles!' This is likely to be the response if you mention 'Dartmoor' when you are next in a convivial group or if you are out walking and hear a strange noise. The phrase has become part of the national cultural baggage, and understandably so, considering there are around 30 film versions of the novel, besides numerous stage, radio and television adaptations. Seduced by hints of the supernatural, and suspense, readers ignore the fact that, had Dr Watson applied a modicum of common sense to the situation, the mystery could have been quickly resolved. Instead, a choice is made to suspend disbelief, and enter into a fictional realm where an insubstantial animal roams on an unstable wasteland. *The Hound of the Baskervilles*,[1] Dartmoor's gothic novel, overshadows every other writer's representation of the moor, and imbues the region with a particular kind of shivery notoriety. Conan Doyle invents a version of the moor to suit a specific literary purpose – to resurrect Holmes who had been dispatched to his death at the Reichenbach Falls. Events in *The Hound*, supposedly happening a decade or so prior to Holmes's 'death', reintroduced the detective to an expectant public. As it had been eight years since his 'final' appearance, Holmes' and Watson's characters needed to be unequivocally re-established, and a construct called 'Dartmoor' proved to be the perfect environment.

When Arthur Conan Doyle (1859-1930) spent a few days in the spring of 1901 at the *Duchy Hotel* in Princetown it was not his first visit to the West Country. After completing medical studies at Edinburgh and following a short stint as surgeon on a steamer bound for West Africa, he had travelled to Plymouth in the spring of 1882 at the behest of a companion from his student days, George Budd, who needed a practice partner. Doyle lodged with Budd at Elliott Terrace, from where the western slope of the moor is visible, but within weeks there were such tensions between the two doctors that Doyle left, moving to Southsea to set up his own medical practice. According to his article in *The British Journal of Photography*, he returned to Plymouth in August that same year with two friends, en route for a short moorland photographic expedition.[2] While 'nothing remarkable' in the way of pictures was produced, the article reveals, in embryo – through its exaggerations, phrases and fragments of description – a perception of the moor that would later surface in *The Hound of the Baskervilles*.

As Doyle's party, burdened with equipment, advances on foot toward Roborough (formerly Jump), he notes how the character of the scenery begins to change. 'Rugged "tors" and tangled masses of half-withered vegetation' close in on the party. They experience a sense of being observed, as sheep 'eye' the party curiously, as if 'speculating' on the motives of the travellers.[3] 'Charming little nooks', the subject of photographs, do not deflect attention from a profusion of signs telling 'a grim story of the bygone dangers of the Moor – where men had wandered in circles until they dropped dead of hunger and fatigue'.[4] After a night's rest they reach Tavistock where the short expedition is aborted on account of inclement weather, and they hurriedly return to the town in 'a hermetically sealed four-wheeler'.[5]

A year later, Roborough House, close to the road Doyle and his friends had passed while trudging towards Tavistock, became the setting for *The Winning Shot*.[6] On a night stroll the narrator and her partner are unaccountably assailed by feelings of depression and fear that have no basis in reason, before being startled by a figure, 'ghastly and silent':

> the moon was just topping the ridge behind and the gaunt, angular outlines of the stranger stood out hard and clear against its silvery radiance.[7]

Such a sudden powerful emotional response to place, together with the image of the silhouetted figure, would later be reproduced in *The Hound of the Baskervilles*, when Dr Watson recalls:

> outlined as black as an ebony statue on that shining background I saw the figure of a man upon the tor. [...] He stood with his legs a little separated, his arms folded, his head bowed, as if he were brooding over that enormous wilderness of peat and granite [...]. He might have been the very spirit of that terrible place.[8]

For *Silver Blaze*[9] the action moves to the Tavistock district, which is inaccurately described as lying 'like the boss of a shield, in the middle of the huge circle of Dartmoor',[10] a foretaste of the cavalier attitude to Dartmoor's topography so apparent in *The Hound of the Baskervilles*.

Then, in 1896, Brigadier Gerard's account of his escape from Dartmoor prison during the Napoleonic Wars is related in 'How the King Held the Brigadier'.[11] Gerard realises that in order to evade capture the best policy is to obtain a change of garb and defy the pursuers' expectations by lurking on the moor until the hue and cry dies down, which is exactly the action followed by Selden, the escaped convict, in *The Hound of the Baskervilles*.

The novel stemmed from discussions between Conan Doyle and Bertram Fraser Robinson, an ebullient sometime war correspondent from Ipplepen, near Newton Abbot, the pair having struck up a friendship during their voyage to England, in 1900, following duties in the Boer War. In the early spring of 1901 when they met at Cromer, Robinson regaled Doyle with tales of Dartmoor from which was born the plan 'to do a small book together *The Hound of the Baskervilles* a real creeper'.[12] Doyle followed up his interest a month later by visiting the moor with Robinson. Writing again to his mother, from *The Duchy Hotel*, Princetown, Doyle refers to the progress he has made on a novel that would show Holmes 'at his very best'. 'A highly dramatic idea', he enthused, 'which I owe to Robinson.'[13] At some stage during the moorland visit Doyle must have met Robinson's coachman, Henry Baskerville, but the Cromer correspondence indicates that the name 'Baskerville' had already been selected for the story. Whether the choice of name for the family at the centre of his latest work was a coincidence or an early suggestion from Robinson is open to dispute, although there is the coachman's own testimony that, as thanks for the use of his name, he, Henry Baskerville, had been presented with a proof copy of the novel.[14]

There was no doubt as to the excitement *The Hound of the Baskervilles* generated when the first instalment reintroduced the character of Sherlock Holmes after a lapse of eight years,[15] boosting the circulation figures of *The Strand Magazine* to unprecedented levels. Interest was maintained over the nine monthly episodes and, as Marshall recalls, 'was nowhere more popular than at the high tables of Oxford and Cambridge'.[16] He relates how, having obtained a copy of the story in book form, it being published just prior to the final instalment in *The Strand*, both the Dean of King's College, Cambridge, and

87   *Harry Baskerville, Bertram Fraser Robinson's family coachman.*

the Registrary of the University left 'an important University function' in order to enjoy the novel's denouement.[17]

Locally, the earliest publications in which any singular Dartmoor hound corresponds to Doyle's animal seems to be Mrs Bray's invention in the 1830s of the non-spectral massive Redfang Howard, in *Fitz of Fitzford*, a hound 'of giant mould', with a 'fierce and stern countenance' and extraordinary skill in tracking its quarry down.[18] More recently a dog with 'bristling hair, bloody eye, and foaming mouth' had made a brief appearance in the translation of *Les Deux Soeurs*,[19] another animal that, with Doyle's hound, shares physical qualities with Mrs Bray's creations.[20] Closer to the vicinity of Robinson's home a legend commonly found in guide books tells of the black hound doomed to empty the Dean Burn near Buckfastleigh,[21] and there was another local story that must have been well-known in the area, even if only through the memorial in the churchyard at Buckfastleigh, of the infamous Richard Cabell of Brooke, and how 'fiends and black dogs breathing fire' raced over Dartmoor on the occasion of his death.[22]

There are strong resemblances between Doyle's hound and Sabine Baring-Gould's creation, Loup. The wolf plunges into view, 'fangs gleaming in the firelight and his eyes glowing like carbuncles'.[23] Later Loup is sighted at the edge of Fox Tor Mire, amid 'smokelike vapour',[24] just as Doyle's hound would spring 'from the shadow of the fog' (149) for his final appearance.

Although there was 'a large kennel of spectral hounds'[25] as proto-types from which Doyle and Robinson may have culled ideas, and it is possible to recognise similarities between local animals and Doyle's creation, the fact remains that the author needed no prompting from outside his own imagination, for he had

88 *The Hound, daubed with luminous paint, magazine illustration, by S. Paget, 1901.*

featured fierce dogs in previous tales. Almost a decade earlier, he had, in *Micah Clarke*, introduced his own hound: 'A great brute, with flaring eyes and yawning mouth [...] white fangs glistening in the moonlight', who is gunned down by the hero.[26] But, the inspired difference between all other fearsome dogs and the Baskerville hound is the daubing of the hound with a luminous mixture, to make it appear diabolical:

> Fire burst from its open mouth, its eyes glowed with a smouldering glare, its muzzle and hackles and dewlap were outlined in flickering flame (149).

A late 19th-century invention, the use of luminous paint had been the subject of an experiment at the prison in 1881, when, in the interest of economy, it was hoped 'that artificial light could be dispensed with in a cell so painted.'[27] The glowing hound's final attack is among the novel's climactic moments dramatically illustrated by Sydney Paget (1860-1908), in the *Strand*'s serialisation. For readers unfamiliar with the moor's terrain Paget conveys the impression of the granite outcrops, provides an imaginative reconstruction of an ancient dwelling place and, above all, creates a darkly forbidding region.

The action of *The Hound of the Baskervilles* consists of two separate but overlapping series of events that occur during the autumn of 1888.[28] The central strand revolves around the strange demise of Sir Charles, the late occupant of the Baskerville estate in the heart of Dartmoor, the 'footprints of a gigantic hound' the only clue to his fate. The secondary plot strand concerns Selden, a convicted murderer who, having escaped from the Princetown jail, is lying low until arrangements can be made for his passage abroad. The escapee's sister and brother-in-law, both employees at Baskerville Hall, are reluctantly providing food and clothes and making the necessary plans for him to get to a port. Dressed in Henry Baskerville's cast-off garments, the convict dies as the result of a fall while fleeing from a pursuing hound, thus providing the detective with the indisputable evidence of a plot involving a hound trained to follow Henry Baskerville's scent.

The villain of the central story, Jack Stapleton, distantly related to the Baskervilles, is outwardly conformist. A former schoolmaster turned lepidopterist, he is one whose appearance and apparent behaviour mask a life of criminal activity. Coveting the estate he moves to Dartmoor, and with the compliance of a servant keeps a large dog concealed on the waste. As part of his master plan he deliberately fosters the hound legend to produce an atmosphere of terror among the locals, and manipulates Laura Lyons, an impoverished gentlewoman, to act as an innocent decoy.

Doyle constructs both Beryl Stapleton and Laura Lyons as representative of women trapped in unsatisfactory relationships: Beryl exists wholly on her bullying husband's terms and Laura as the victim of a brutal marriage. The sadistic control exercised by men over women is a theme that winds through the novel.

In previous accounts of Holmes's work the detective's methods had been particularised, locations sketched in with economy, and Watson's part largely reduced to that of admiring amanuensis, but for this novel, in order to highlight Holmes's singular talents, Doyle alters the pattern. Watson, the epitome of Englishness, sent to Dartmoor to guard Sir Henry Baskerville, becomes increasingly disconcerted by the unfamiliar environment and hopelessly embroiled in an apparently supernatural situation. Watson is revealed as a man whose judgement is impaired by his emotional response to his environment in contrast to Holmes who approaches problems with scientific detachment.

By having Holmes obtain an ordnance map of the moor, over which 'his spirit has hovered' (28) all day, Doyle fosters the impression that the Dartmoor which will be the location of the story is topographically accurate. Holmes explains that within a 'radius of five miles' of Baskerville Hall there are 'only a very few scattered dwellings' on the 'desolate, lifeless moor', with Grimpen, the nearest village, and Princetown, the great convict establishment, 14 miles distant from Baskerville Hall. The moor is, Holmes observes, a worthy setting 'if the devil did desire to have a hand in the affairs of men' (29).

The author exaggerates features of Dartmoor in order to rouse fear and terror in his readers, and is not overly concerned as to topographical accuracy. In order to achieve his purpose names are one means to an end, and to that end

89 *Holmes Shoots the Hound, magazine illustration, by S. Paget, 1901.*

he uses the fragments of names suggestive of places, familiar elements of fog, the mire, an escaped convict, and a sparsely populated area.

There is no argument as to the extent of mist and fog on the moor, and there had been a number of escapes from the prison. But, as we have learned, the area was hardly desolate: while the area was, indeed, sparsely populated in comparison with the teeming towns, there were more than 2,000 persons in the parish of Lydford and nearly that number in Moretonhampstead. Doyle's Dartmoor is an imaginative spatial construct, a fantasy, a country of the mind conforming neither in size nor in social composition to the actual place, but it contains enough vague generalisations to seem to refer to the existing area. In this invented locality places slip and slide in kaleidoscopic fashion, never remaining in a consistent relation to each other. Generating a sense of dislocation seems to be a deliberate strategy intended to enhance a sense of unease, for as Doyle explains:

> In short stories it has always seemed to me that so long as you produce your dramatic effect, accuracy of detail matters little. I have never striven for it and have made some bad mistakes in consequence. What matter if I can hold my readers? I claim that I may make my own conditions, and I do so.[29]

Prior to Watson's accompanying Sir Henry Baskerville to Baskerville Hall, as his protector, Doyle has provided enough information for the supernatural element to be discounted. Sir Henry's missing shoe implies the existence of a material hound, as do the footprints. Holmes knows this but such facts hardly register with Watson, who becomes increasingly unsettled by the moorland environment.

Watson now becomes a representative of 'everyman' discovering the moor for the first time. His objectivity diminishes as he leaves familiar sights of fertile and well-hedged country. He sees 'a grey melancholy hill, with a strange jagged summit, dim and vague in the distance, like some fantastic landscape in a dream' (55). A momentary feeling of foreboding is dispelled at the small wayside station, the embodiment of rural England, where station staff cluster around helpfully. Yet there is an indication that the 'sweet country spot' (56) is at the edge of something unfamiliar, for Watson sees 'two soldierly men in dark uniforms who leaned upon their short rifles' (56). As he leaves the known world behind the atmosphere of stability and order indicated by clearly defined boundaries, and the charm of the picturesque houses, dissipates as the wagonette swings ever upwards, through 'drifts of rotting vegetation' (56).

Presaging the terrors to come, Watson sees 'dark against the evening sky, the long, gloomy curve of the moor, broken by the jagged and sinister hills' (56). Already the waste seems to be a place suggestive of confinement and possible violence and sadness. The sombre atmosphere prevails for the remainder of the day, for, after leaving the 'shadow and gloom' (60) of the dining-room at Baskerville Hall, Watson is conscious, from his bedroom, of the sound of trees that 'moaned and swung in the rising wind' and the sight of the 'long low curve of the melancholy moor', this sombre atmosphere enhanced as the 'sob of a woman' heard during the night contrasts with the chiming clock and the otherwise deathly silence (61).

It is Stapleton who cleverly instils in Watson a fear and horror of his new surroundings. In a key meeting, developed in a series of oppositions, Watson's initial impressions are undermined. His pleasure in the distant view across Grimpen Mire, of the 'undulating downs, long green rollers, with crests of jagged granite foaming up into fantastic surges' is countered by Stapleton's assertion of the moor as 'so vast, and so barren, and so mysterious' (67). The great plain, 'a rare place for a gallop', in Watson's opinion, is not as it seems, for 'a false step yonder means death to man or beast' (67).[30] As if to emphasise Stapleton's claim, a pony is heard and seen in its final moments of struggle before disappearing. Immediately following the shock of the pony's fate, as 'its dreadful cry echoed over the moor' (68), another chilling sound is heard as 'a long, low moan, indescribably sad, swept over the moor' (68). Unnerved to the point when he cannot accept he has heard the howl of a confined dog, Watson allows himself to be persuaded that the noise is 'the cry of the last of the bitterns' (69).

Spatial unfamiliarity to the point where even the solid ground proves to be a morass becomes a metaphor for Dr Watson's state of mind as reality and reasoning power seem on the point of deserting him. Watson reveals his feelings in the intimacy of a letter to Holmes. The moor, for Watson, is

> this most God-forsaken corner of the world. The longer one stays here the more does the spirit of the moor sink into one's soul, its vastness, and also its grim charm. When you are once out upon its bosom you have left all traces of modern England behind you (75).

Perhaps Watson's impressions should not carry us away for Holmes and his young assistant, both of whom, temperamentally controlled and unencumbered by superstitious beliefs, are able to exist in the wilds without any trouble.

Beneath its evocation of the moor, and its study of the extent to which suggestion and psychological pressures influence attitudes, there are, in *The Hound of the Baskervilles*, darker strands, concerning cruelty and the subjugation of women.

The whole work is suffused with conventions redolent of the popular gothic novel: the shifting narrative mode, the old manuscript, credulous rustics, mysterious letters, a spectre, significant portraits, and fog. A gothic connection is implied through the description of Baskerville Hall, with its massive ivy-draped frontage, 'twin towers, ancient, crenellated, and pierced with many loopholes' (58). There is emphasis on the gloom, shadows, and blackness beyond Watson's immediate vicinity only fitfully broken. The 'muffled, strangled gasps of one who is torn by an uncontrollable sorrow' (61) are attributed to abuse from a 'domestic tyrant' (80).

It is in Stapleton's house, in a room fitted out as a museum for butterflies and moths, that evidence of physical mistreatment is made plain. Previously described as having 'something tropical and exotic' about her (76), words often used in connection with the butterfly, Beryl Stapleton is treated in her captivity with a horrid irony suggestive of the macabre. The explicit detail of the manner of her confinement is a clear indication of sexual sadism, for she is discovered tied to an upright beam, 'swathed and muffled in sheets [...]. One towel passed around the throat, and was secured at the back of the pillar. Another covered the lower part of the face' (151–152). There was 'the clear, red weal of a whip-lash' across the victim's neck, and her arms were mottled with bruises (152). There is an undertone of the masochistic in the victim's assertion that she could endure the brutal physical ill-usage and the torture of her mind and soul provided the outcome was knowledge of her husband's love.

The moor around Grimpen becomes the equivalent of the graveyard in the gothic novel. Here are elements of the macabre: the descriptions of the two ponies struggling and drowning in Grimpen Mire; the signs that Stapleton suffered the same fate; the death of the doctor's little dog, savaged by the hound; and the manner in which Selden's body is discovered.

Happening in muted light, either at night or in misty conditions, climactic events are the stuff of nightmares: the woman sobbing, chasing a figure over the moor, catching sight of Holmes, the convict's death, the appearance of the hound, and the culminating scenes when Sir Henry Baskerville is pounced on and Stapleton falls into the Mire.

Possibly it is the components essential in a gothic novel, those of sadism and cruelty and a damsel in distress, which prove to be compelling factors in the novel's enduring popularity. The work is set in a time when women were beginning to clamour for their 'rights', and a degree of independence, but in *The Hound of the Baskervilles* women are utterly dependent on men, the very stuff of male fantasy, but hidden in a novel suitable for reading and discussion in public.

There is the implicit acknowledgment that newcomers to a region may bring both good and ill. The locals long for the Baskerville family to return to the Hall and instigate 'schemes of reconstruction and improvement' that will bring them material benefits. Watson's letters and diaries convey grim prophecies of the collapse of the region's prosperity once the peasants are deprived of the valued leadership emanating from Baskerville Hall. The late 19th-century moorlander appears to have stepped back in time.

Dartmorians, according to Stapleton, are a primitive race of 'credulous' peasants (65). Similarly, Watson feels that a natural human presence on Dartmoor would be that of 'a skin-clad, hairy man [...] fitting a flint-tipped arrow on to the spring of his bow'.[31] He regards the current indigenous population as only slightly further up the evolutionary ladder than those ancestors, primitive in outlook and, without supervision, incapable of modern land management. The peasants, observes Watson, lack restraint and are unable to make balanced judgments.[32] Apart from these scanty references to their ignorance and incredulity Doyle allows the natives to vanish – to sink, as it were, into the mire, their only sightings suggest an unbridgeable cultural gap between the local population and the metropolitan dweller.

There are many editions of *The Hound of the Baskervilles* in print, but should you find a first edition complete with dust jacket in your attic, you will have in your possession a small fortune for, in 2006, a copy sold at auction for £81,000.[33]

13

'STARK STARING REALISM'

Whereas Doyle's moorland novel has proved enduringly popular, John Trevena's descriptions of the region and its people, the subject of this chapter, soon spiralled into obscurity. His depiction of the population dwelling between the Teign and Tavy, sometimes unkind, raw and uncomfortable, also reveals his increasing sensitivity to social deprivation.

During the late 19th and early 20th centuries there was, just as in rural districts all over the country, a drift from the moor to the towns. Aaron Rowe, respected farmer and proprietor of the *Duchy Hotel* at Princetown, doubted the wisdom of labourers leaving the district workers in the expectation of a less arduous, more prosperous existence. Familiar with the squalid conditions in which the urban poor existed, he told Henry Rider Haggard, who was researching into agricultural and social conditions, that

> the man who earned 15s a week and had his cottage, garden, pigs, and fowls upon the Moor, was infinitely better off than his fellow who had migrated to the slums of that city.[1]

But, maintained Rowe, there was no stopping moorlanders, seduced by natives who returned on holiday 'wearing rings and an Albert chain'.[2] Perhaps because fluctuating village populations were part of the moorland demographic pattern, the drift did not disrupt the general tenor of existence. At any rate, according to William Crossing in his *A Hundred Years on Dartmoor*, local life continued quietly, its various customary gatherings, markets, fairs, and sports fixtures facilitating social interchange.[3] Village schools were well established, though attendance tended to be casual; many parish churches had been renovated, non-conformists had been busy establishing chapels, and there was a scattering of new villas, their occupants attracted to the area on account of its efficacious climate. Several packs of hounds and harriers were kennelled around the moor and fishing streams still provided abundant baskets, although game birds had been hunted to extinction. The prison continued to be an asset to the local economy.

The relative exclusivity of the region had steadily eroded since railways completely encircled the moor. Now Dartmoor was advertised as an exciting destination for the masses, and a day excursion from London was possible; a typical combined rail and road excursion ticket included a four-hour journey

90 *Dartmoor in four hours from London, advert, 1905.*

from Paddington, lunch at Newton Abbot and a trip to the moor.[4] There was also the new craze for bicycling. Tavistock was advertised as the local headquarters of the Cyclists' Touring Association, the moor being touted as most suitable for an activity, in which

> the saving of time and fatigue is immense in getting from place to place [...]. The rider who cares more for pleasure than pace will find his cycle a real convenience.[5]

School parties were welcome at Sticklepath and 'camping out' was promoted as one of the 'most delightful experiences possible'.[6] The Okehampton Royal Artillery Camp had been established on Okehampton common, with bungalows for officers, dormitory accommodation for the men, cookhouses, and stabling for the horses.

Increasingly appreciated as a facility meeting health, leisure, and spiritual needs, the commodification of the moor worked to the advantage of the locals in providing additional income. Besides accommodation in villages circumjacent to the moor there were now hotels in what only a generation previously had been quite remote places: Hay Tor, Postbridge, and Dartmeet, where telephones, electric lighting, hot baths and 'sanitation perfect'[7] were the norm. Several stables kept from twenty to seventy or eighty horses for moorland coaching expeditions, and steam coaches ran in conjunction with the Great Western or the London and South-Western Railways. Chagford was among the villages developing as a popular holiday destination, with many visitors, seeking advice on how to make the most of their stay, consulting the Perrott family who had been well known guides for many years.

It was James Perrott, who way back in 1854 had set up a little cairn at Cranmere into which he placed a receptacle for visitors' cards. The popularity of this 'small bit of black bog ... a delusion and a snare for tourists',[8] had not diminished – and it had become customary to place a stamped card or letter in a

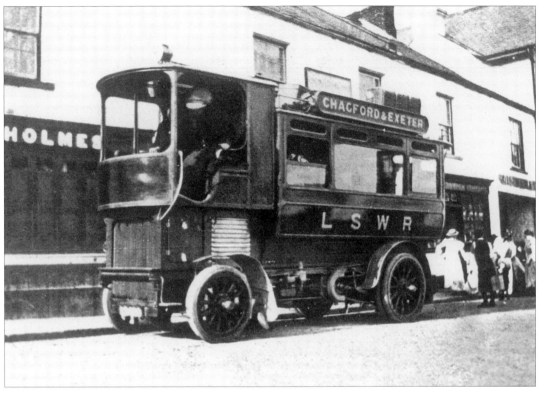

91 *Steam coach at Chagford, early 20th century.*

receptacle, for the next visitor to retrieve and post. A visitors' book placed in the cairn inside a watertight – very necessary – zinc box during April 1905 had, by December, collected 609 signatures. The many books filled since then are held in the local studies library, Plymouth.[9]

Hoping that the much-vaunted bracing moorland air would prove beneficial, the ailing writer, Ernest George Henham (1870-1948), better known as John Trevena, settled on the moor. Born near London, after living in Canada where he studied law and began to write poetry for local publication, he returned to England in 1903. Diagnosed with tuberculosis, and advised to forsake the capital for the country, he moved to Belstone on the northern slopes of Dartmoor, where he rented a cottage at Birchy Lake on the village outskirts.[10]

Belstone at that time had a population of 230, the rector was partial lord of the manor, and there was a Wesleyan chapel and a village post-office. Children attended school in the nearby village of Sticklepath. In addition to traditional farming and granite quarrying as sources of employment, several guesthouses offered a range of accommodation and Tawcroft, a small sanatorium, cared for about half a dozen patients.[11] After protracted negotiations, Trevena purchased a piece of land in South Zeal, a village that could boast of two chapels, a school,

92 *John Trevena, Journal, 1908.*

a reading room, a hotel, and three public houses, where farming, granite quarrying and copper mining provided work.

The villages and persons he describes in his Dartmoor novels, while accurate in terms of demography and social composition, posit an alternative vision to that so heavily promoted by the tourist industry, and implied in the newly available range of picture postcards of village life. Until 1902 only an address had been permitted on the reverse side of a postcard but once a message, besides the address, could be written on the reverse, the picture postcard industry took off.[12] In contrast to the numerous popular and enriching images of Dartmoor life received through such images, the novels discussed in this chapter reveal the 'skull beneath the skin', of local conditions, seen through the gaze of a newcomer to the region.

Arriving at Belstone after living in a new, thrusting country such as Canada, and latterly in London, the move to Dartmoor was evidently a culture shock for Trevena, who suddenly found himself in a unique enclave, separate and different from the rest of the country, a place that

> had neither been conquered nor legally annexed. [...] As an independent and unconquered state it passed into the jurisdiction of the Duchy of Cornwall, although the Duchy obtained no legal title to it. Legally Dartmoor was not in Devonshire; politically it was not in England.[13]

The sense of loneliness experienced by an educated, middle-class young man constrained by the circumstance of indifferent health to live a quiet, solitary, open-air life in a strange land amongst strangers, in an almost feudal society, surfaces in a number of his stories. He feels his life has been 'decapitated',[14] is 'abominably unpleasant', an existence of 'clods and dirt, of gritty food and black-rimmed finger nails'; and he longed to exchange all the 'grey tors, every cloud-scape, for a nice little row of jerry built stucco villas on the edge of the gorge'.[15]

In *Pixy in Petticoats* and *The Dartmoor House That Jack Built*[16] his jaundiced opinions of local dwellers is made clear, but, by the close of his trilogy, *Furze the Cruel*,[17] *Heather*,[18] and *Granite*,[19] he is able to convey sympathy and voice concern over the moorland community's present difficulties. Reviewers' initial pleasure in Trevena's work turned sour, for his novels, as will become evident, went against

93   *South Zeal and Ramsley Mine, postcard, early 20th century.*

the grain of the national perception of rural life, and undercut the comfortable existences of Chase's and Phillpottts' characters.

Published anonymously, the first edition of *A Pixy in Petticoats* received favourable reviews; but it created an unpleasant furore in Belstone. Locals, identifying themselves, were not amused. No matter that the chosen signifiers were, as the Belstonians agreed, strictly accurate, they felt they had been vilified and made ridiculous.

Old Wannell is famed for never having taken a bath, Kentisbeer is unable to write, Muzzelwhite is illiterate, Veale is the village toper, and Dufty is cross-eyed.

One local cannot stand straight, another is unable to walk straight, and the vicar is senile, vaguely lecherous and physically abused by his drunken housekeeper. Gossip, drinking, and lounging about are favoured activities.

Ann Cobbledick is a besotted mother, who habitually milks her cow in the centre of the road, while 'her geese waddled and cackled around her, and her son Willum leaned against the wall of the linhay' watching.[20] The young man is a loafer, for as Ann proudly explains:

> Willum walks around the village all day, [...]. He takes it easy and that be good for 'en. And he smokes a lot. Smoking does Willum good. And he drinks a lot of beer. Beer be fattening, William says, and he knows 'cause he be a scholar.[21]

Willum, obviously not as lazy as the author suggests, helps with the family guesthouse business, is postman and a leading figure in village life.

Local anger was expressed through a campaign of harassment and someone took a pot shot at the author but, ironically, the real Belstonians' expressions of spleen and threats of legal action provided Trevena with substantial material for *The Dartmoor House that Jack Built*.

The building of Trevena's new home, described in *The Dartmoor House that Jack Built*, is not the sole sign of change bubbling up. During a local parish council meeting the chairman announces that a complaint has been received in respect of a milking-stool blocking the centre of the road, impeding the safe passage of a motor-car, 'still something of a monstrosity in that district' (118):

> "Tis mother's!' exclaimed Willum at once.
> 'Couldn't you get her to remove it to the side of the road,' suggested the vicar.
> 'Mother wouldn't move 'en vor any one, [...]. There be always room to pass outside if 'em goes slow and careful wi' one wheel in the ditch.'
> 'But I am afraid her action is illegal,' said the chairman.
> 'It bain't here,' said Willum (119).

Even the milking stool could not indefinitely impede progress, and this exchange foreshadows an intrusion that will profoundly affect the village. Towards the close of the novel, the motor-car is driven late at night through the village, with the result that the stool is destroyed, and:

> Every principle of liberty, and every part of the stool, had been violated by that abominable machine (404).

To the villagers the crushed stool has 'fallen victim to civilisation and science', neither of which they wished to encourage (410). While the incident is related with humour it also portends, with authorial insight, the effect that this new mode of transport will eventually have on village life.

Already the village is changing, for its inhabitants are defenceless against the strategies of middle-class business practices. A wily lawyer from Exeter had exerted unrelenting psychological pressure on Old Wannell who eventually agrees to sell a portion of his land for the building of the house. 'The Man', for whom the lawyer had been acting, is representative of a class who have no ancestral connection with the area but who, for health concerns or aesthetic reasons, not with a need or desire to develop some connection with the land, would settle in the district. Change may happen insidiously: Ann Cobbledick, opening her house to patronising paying guests, is representative of independent villagers who, electing to become part of the service industry, will unwittingly enter into a kind of servitude, dependent on gratifying the needs of strangers. Lacking exposure to social change, most moorlanders, Trevena implies, are in an evolutionary backwater, actively hostile to any attempts that might encourage them to look beyond their immediate locality.

The Moorland communities' lives seem to be teetering on the edge of extinction:

> The last dregs of the folk, still ignorant and primitive, who are being killed like the Red Indians by the civilisation which has for a long time surrounded them, driving out the old, bringing in the new.[22]

But, Trevena presents, in *Furze the Cruel, Heather* and *Granite,* a race who, affected by the demands of their environment, have absorbed qualities that will ensure some kind of survival. A brief author's note introduces this dominant theme:

> Almost everywhere on Dartmoor are Furze, Heather, and Granite. The Furze seems to suggest Cruelty, the Heather Endurance, and the Granite Strength. The Furze is destroyed by fire, but grows again; the Heather is torn by winds, but blossoms again; the Granite is worn away imperceptibly by the rain.[23]

Through the human mind, Trevena maintains, humans are linked to the origins of life, and the species might have inherited memories, 'passed on unconsciously', of 'that terrible fight for existence'.[24] Although not to the exclusion of the others, in each novel one of these inherent characteristics – cruelty, endurance, or strength – is shown to be crucial in determining one or more character's behaviour patterns. The works are infused with bleakness and brutality, so it is as well to remember that the author deliberately panders to the perceived demands of his readers and attempts to slake their appetite for vicarious excitement:

> Folk are not to be thrilled with a tale, unless it be highly coloured, or has a certain amount of wild and bloody complications. Just because their lives are colourless they crave for a bit of romance and they prefer it red; it stimulates them that way, and the horror never touches them because they are not called to face it.[25]

The deeper the author delves into the condition of life in Wapsworthy, the setting for *Furze*, the more divisive and disturbing he finds it: a place of 'strange lives dragged out in lonely places',[26] where cruelty often passes unnoticed and endurance and strength, which might serve some positive moral good, are often debased.

Trevena's 'dark, staring realism'[27] contests the norms and values assiduously promoted in tourist writings, as associated with moorland life. The light of civilisation has barely penetrated into his Dartmoor. This mood in *Furze* is made clear:

> Nothing in the entire system of creation can be more inexplicable than the persistent cruelty of nature. [...] Animals not only kill but torture those which are inferior to them. [...] It is the same all along the scale up to and including man.[28]

The characters' names suggest their position at the lower end of the evolutionary scale. There is Weevil, Maggot, Pentfoggat, who sniffs the woman he lusts for; there is Brightly, routinely compared with a seal, Thomasine with a cow, while Mary Tavy, when provoked, acts like 'a wild beast'. Siblings Mary and Peter Tavy are 'savages', descendants of a pair of Gubbins; their unusual appearance – Peter is like a gnome, 'not much taller than four feet in height, with a beard like a furze-bush', and his sister Mary has a 'man's face and a man's feet' – implies that interbreeding has produced stock verging on the degenerate (17). This suggestion of poor breeding also surfaces in respect of Brightly. He is an example of how Nature 'jerry-builds' (67). With him, the author observes, 'nature seemed rather to have overreached herself. [...] What was the use of such a defenceless creature, this sort of human rabbit whom any one could attack?'(207).

Farmer Pendoggat is the embodiment of a thoroughly cruel individual, resembling furze in 'its fierceness, its spitefulness, its tenacity of life' (38–39). Outwardly Christian, Pendoggat is covertly a sadistic sexual predator. This vicious man takes pleasure in inflicting pain, his large physical presence and bullying mien preventing others from challenging him. He plans to raise money through a fraudulent mining proposal and decamp once the required 'capital' is obtained. In the meantime he seduces an ignorant local servant who, conditioned to be obedient and never encouraged to think, joins Pendoggat at a linhay at Tavy Cleave. Their couplings in the shed reeking of cattle are brutal. He mauls his victim roughly, is stirred by biting 'like a dog playing with a rabbit' (177). The novel reaches a climax when Pendoggat is trapped in a burning gorse brake. His cries mingle with the scream-like noises of the burning furze, and like that plant that survives moorland swaling, so Pendoggat, dreadfully scarred, maimed and blind, lives on.

Examples of communal unthinking cruelty are obvious when, during a shoot, the locals revel in prolonging the suffering of animals, and as the 'ghastly pile of dead pigeons and rabbits grew' (241)

> the men were happy; not only happy but drunk with the passion, and half mad with the lust, of their bloody game (240).

In *Furze*, acts of cruelty, a dominant fact of subsistence survival, are casually regarded as an acceptable behaviour pattern. The wanton shedding of blood is an example of regressive behaviour, an 'echo' (236) from barbarous times. Had Hogarth seen a Dartmoor rabbit shoot, comments the narrator, 'there might have been a fifth plate added to his Four Stages of Cruelty' (242).

Cruelty is not always obvious; it can be manifest in a community's general lack of compassion to the weak and vulnerable. This is shown in the thoughtless attitude towards the partially sighted purveyor of rabbit skins. Timid and defenceless, he is bullied by farmers and deliberately targeted for harassment by the local police until, desperate for relief, he is driven to suicide.

Heather is located in the fictional north Dartmoor village of Downacot.[29] The central woman character, Winnie Shazell, a patient in the small sanatorium, is suffering from tuberculosis. Brought up on the moor, her illness had developed only after she moved to Plymouth. Having made a good recovery she leaves Downacot for urban life, only to find herself trapped in an abusive relationship. Somehow, like heather, she endures, clinging on to life with fierce tenacity. Gradually she realises she is existing in an alien environment and, abandoning town life, returns to the moor. It is only there, she reluctantly accepts, that she can flourish physically and spiritually.

The quality of endurance, Trevena points out in *Heather*, does not preclude change. Through the persona of Gregory Breakback the author explores how a closed mind leads to stultification and unhappiness. Gregory deliberately and unnecessarily endures poverty because he will not compromise his freedom by being yoked to a an employer. At 62 he longs to marry, but when the woman of his choice answers him truthfully that she is not a virgin he abruptly dismisses her as failing to meet his standards of integrity. Strength and endurance are qualities in him that have been unconsciously absorbed from contact with the moor he loved. Its wind warmed him, 'his blood and bones fed on it, and when it increased he became stronger, too'.[30] But, unlike heather, Gregory lacks one characteristic of the plant – in exposed places it can bend with the wind to survive. But, with his entrenched attitudes, Gregory passes up the chance to breed and by Darwinian standards is a failure.

Judged by one critic as displaying 'insight' and 'true knowledge of nature',[31] *Granite* was castigated by another as 'unutterably morbid and depressing', a novel in which certain characters 'are used to illuminate strange, unwholesome depths of depravity and waywardness in the life of a remote moorland community'.[32]

The strength inherent in granite is revealed as the major characteristic in two members of the Yeo family. Will Yeo is a dry-stone wall builder, content with his life – just the type of character burlesqued in *Pixy in Petticoats* – but now treated with understanding and sympathy. With great dignity Will had devoted his whole life to fighting granite:

> There was the intoxicating fascination of a gigantic work in which strength alone could serve, with just a little cunning added. There was the wild music made by the iron and stone to be listened to through life; chief of all the privilege of being out alone every day subduing a force, while looking over what appeared to be the whole world stretched below, with the keen winds tossing the clouds along, and strange voices coming out of the nooks and corners – that was to live and not know weakness.[33]

Injured while blasting, Will is restless in hospital: 'his soul yearned for the rocks'.[34] His intuitive sensitivity to forms of beauty is revealed when, listening for the first time to the Exeter Cathedral organ, he is emotionally moved:

> 'I ha' heard mun avore,' he muttered.
> 'Where?'
> 'Dimsy. Out o' the rocks.'[35]

Sadly, he cannot articulate his experience, and his incoherence, his inability to communicate, may mean that some wonderful creative gift has been lost to the human race.[36] Now in his mid-seventies and looking as if the granite had been 'stirred into life and had taken the form of a man', Will, restored to health, joyfully returns to work:

> He was so massive and dark with scars, and his old clothes clung to him like moss and lichen; the dust of granite had become engrained in his skin; his beard was full of it, and flakes of mica glittered upon his arms, and his teeth were like quartz-splinters, his face was red with iron-ore, and his boots were green with copper.[37]

Will's son Mark's granite-like strength is also apparent. He studies for the ministry, returning home to campaign against the drunkenness endemic among the men of his north moorland villages. His mental strength is apparent in that, aware of the extent to which the villagers resent his mission against drink, he resists their efforts to thwart him. His iron will is evident when, arraigned on suspicion of murder, he refuses to reveal the name of the real killer and is hanged.

Mark Yeo shared with his father the feeling that some inexplicable bond exists between him and the granite, but whereas for Will Yeo the deep sense of communion is an uplifting experience, for Mark it was disturbing. He was often conscious of a shadowy figure sitting on a granite boulder, too distant to be recognized. He dimly apprehended that the rocks were, mystically, offering a warning sign that, when tested by life's vicissitudes, he must display the great strength characteristic of certain types of granite rather than crumble into growan.

When the final novel of Trevena's trilogy, *Granite*, was published in 1909, *The Bookman* reviewer judged that when those works were compared with the records of the Rev. S. Baring-Gould, the reader would reject Trevena's novels, turn quite impatiently aside and class them heatedly as 'the product of a perfect nightmare of mental disorder and physical indigestion'.[38] On the other hand, it might be considered that, brimming with ideas not pursued, with plots unresolved, veering abruptly from one literary tone to another, the works are intentionally constructed so that the form corresponds with the essential unpredictability of the moorland environment, where 'one day is sometimes composed of a dozen different specimens of weather'.[39]

The inconsistencies characteristic of the region in the variability of its weather and the ever-changing ground underfoot are mirrored in the persona of Beatrice Pentreath, a summer visitor, the 'the glorious lady of the moor',[40] the unattainable, the ideal, 'the spirit of health', 'a pixy queen or the white witch of Cranmere'.[41] She seems the embodiment of the terrain and the elements: she leaps across the tussocks that characterise the north moor, making headway without effort. There is an intimation of the wraith in her rainwashed appearance with hair streaming and the wind stretching her 'scanty clothing tightly upon her' revealing 'every line from waist to ankle'.[42] She teases and disorientates a group of excursionists when, like the will o' the wisp she leads the walkers off their planned route and on to treacherous ground, vanishing before they appeal for help.

Long days alone, wandering on the heights and along the margins of the rivers that spring from the north moor, developed Trevena's sensitivity to the terrain. Particularly in *Pixy in Petticoats*, he is aware of the moor's changing moods and its deceptive appearance viewed from afar when, for example,

> Lower down upon the moor, around the cottage by the gorge there was probably nothing more than a slight wind and a flurry of snowflakes. Still lower it would be calm and cold. The terrific wind, the freezing missiles of snow, heavy mist, liquid mud, and interminable bog, were the normal conditions of Cranmere in winter.[43]

In this episode the author strips away any notion that the experience of foul moorland weather is 'romantic', the suggestion proffered by guidebook writers. Readers are made aware of furious disorientating noise, of an 'interminable maze of crevasses filled with slime, choked with mud and gurgling horribly with wind and water'[44] and the ravages caused by great shell holes. Above Steeperton Cleave the ground is

> torn into pits and jagged fissures by projectiles. It was impossible to walk more than a few paces without seeing one of the ugly iron cylinders. A spectral figure stood near in the pose of a scarecrow. It was a dummy man. A well-aimed shell had pierced its wooden chest.[45]

In contrast, the author is conscious of a 'dream-like air of mystery' about the area, and the possibility of 'the sound of gnomes'.[46] He notices how, on a moonlit night, phosphorescence emanates from 'straight stiff stems tipped with ruby of the curious lichens known as pixies' matches', and wonders at the glimmering 'place of twisted oak, intersected by mysterious old walls, some in ruins, like old temples, overtopped with beds of moss'.[47]

Despite the material poverty of the region and the ambivalent attitude of some moorland dwellers, Trevena believes that there are persons who find themselves 'called' there, impelled to return to the region,

> Tramping the day away in the solitudes, searching for what they can never find, looking for what they can never see.[48]

Not so Trevena, who, restored to health, abruptly left South Zeal in 1915, without a word to any neighbour and under an assumed name settled in mid-Devon before moving to Dorset. He was never 'called' back to the moor.

14

The Epic of Dartmoor

The coincidence of a clutch of overlapping artists and writers making Dartmoor a subject for their work during the early 20th century is felicitous, for it puts into sharp focus how varying ideological, and personal predilections, and commercial pressures shape interpretations of the region. Yet, we will find, beneath apparent diversity, similarities in attitude to place and people prevailing, even between Eden Phillpotts (1862-1960), whose moorland series is considered in this chapter, and his contemporaries.

In his own way, Phillpotts demystifies the region. He presents, in his novels, what seems to be a knowable, working environment whose population confront the same basic problems and aspirations as their urban counterparts. But, underlying apparently straightforward romantic tales, the 'epic of Dartmoor'[1] is infused with the author's non-Christian ideology. For Phillpotts, Dartmoor is a theatre on whose stage characters are manipulated to act out his conviction that all life is part of a great cosmic struggle in which those most fit to master the prevailing conditions will survive.

In the foreword to *Widecombe Fair*, published in 1913, Phillpotts announced that the 'modest comedy of Dartmoor, planned more than twenty years ago is now finished', inviting his readers to 'judge his work as a whole, and from no fragment'.[2] Until making this announcement Phillpotts does not seem to have mentioned that certain novels among his prodigious output were intended as a series, and it is not until they are read as a whole that they are seen to be set apart from the rest of the author's regional work. Then the sense of closure in *Widecombe Fair* becomes apparent. I am convinced that with its publication the author had said all he had to say about the moor and its dwellers living there between the mid-19th century and the early years of the 20th century. Although Phillpotts published a variety of other works set on the moor, it is through the series that we will discover another interpretation of the region.

It is hardly surprising that critics failed to recognise that certain works were connected by an underlying ideological structure whilst others stood alone for, as was observed of Phillpotts, 'his pen is never idle, and his works come from the press in such rapid succession that we can hardly assimilate one before another claims our attention'.[3] Yet, when the 14 novels of the series – which he later extended – is separated from the mass of his writings and read as a whole, a melding of theme and form becomes apparent. The trajectory of each narrative is the same: Dartmoor becomes a theatre on whose stage the Dartmorians act out the cosmic

[172]

play. Amid the austere surroundings of the moor, divested of the accretions of urban existence, the passions that drive all species are revealed. The author often pauses in his narrative to remind us that the contested and complicated human relationships he is describing are part of the perpetual Darwinian battle.

Eden Phillpotts was a particularly private person. Scraps of information relating to his private activities can be gleaned from his memoirs, his friend and sometime collaborator Arnold Bennett's journals,[4] and from a small collection of tributes published in 1953.[5] With the publication of Phillpotts's daughter Adelaide's autobiography, *Reverie*,[6] in 1981, followed by James Dayananda's *Selected Letters* in 1984, some further insight into the relationship between the author and his attitude to life and work was made possible.[7]

He was born in India, at Rajputana, living there until his father died and his mother returned to England with her three young sons, Eden being the eldest. Leaving Mannamead College, Plymouth when he was 17, he worked in a London insurance office, gravitating to a literary circle that included Arthur Conan Doyle, Jerome K. Jerome and Arnold Bennett. In 1900 he was appointed assistant editor at *Black and White*, resigning within two years, emboldened by the success of his first novel with a Dartmoor setting, to leave London for Torquay in south Devon, determined to support his family by writing.[8]

During his school days, Dartmoor had been the author's 'playground', a time, he recalled, when 'its history dawned upon me, its secrets yielded to my exploration and I read all the wise had to say about it'. As an adult, the place would become his 'workshop'.[9]

Early in his career Phillpotts summed up his attitude to his professional life: 'Wife and bairns must live, so I publish magazine work, though do not, of course, take as serious anything I set down that is not inspired by the West'.[10] In fact, much of his prolific and varied output across several genres he dismissed as 'potboilers', 'twaddle', 'trash' or 'nothing', written for the sake of his family,[11] and to maintain an increasingly comfortable mode of life.

As an agnostic and a humanitarian he placed his trust in 'science and a profound belief in that principle of mind and matter we are content to call evolution'.[12] His attitude to evolution he referred to as 'optimistic', based as it was on a presumption that ultimately change would be for the better:

> The superman of Nietszche must come as surely as the upward sun must rise; [...].
> The Unborn will exceed us as we exceed the Neolithic or as they exceed nature's
> earlier manifestations from which conscious intelligence rose.[13]

Phillpotts sums up his own ideology, in correspondence and in his Dartmoor novels, as saying '"yea" to life'. 'Life', he declares, is 'the message of the day – life abundant – superabundant – fulfilling itself, pouring itself out [...] multiplying, running like a fire', a sentiment that informs the Dartmoor series. In pursuing this theme through his series of novels, he challenges

> the assumption of many critics that only within the metropolitan cab radius can
> a comprehensive system of philosophy be constructed, and that only through the

plate-glass window of two or three clubs is it possible to see life steadily and see it whole.[14]

The compulsion to survive and procreate, he believes, is the force that dominates all forms of organisms. Fulfilment of the biological drive for sexual congress, he postulates, has become entwined and confused with a concept of 'happiness'. But happiness, as Phillpotts argues in his Dartmoor series, is not a concomitant of the human condition: 'My tragedies are triumphant', he maintains, 'and point to a better future order of things'.[15] The drive to procreate, unconscious in Nature, is self-conscious in humans who endeavour to temper their instincts through a set of learned moral laws. But, when the sexual drive is particularly strong humans will challenge and defy the accepted order. This aspect of human nature is revealed in the Dartmoor series, as we meet men and women, who are prepared to flout or subvert the prevailing moral or social pattern. In small ways, these are often the human beings who help move society forwards.

By some critics, scenes in which Phillpotts reiterates his authorial aims were regarded as mere impediments to action. A review in *The Bookman* is typical:

> At the beginning of most of the chapters there are chunks of eloquent dissertation on the moor, or some part of it, not as the people of the story would feel it, or could describe it, but as the author sees it, [...]. One wonders, on beginning each chapter, how soon the author is going to stop talking about Dartmoor, and let the story begin again.[16]

But, the characteristic 'dissertation' is not simply scene-painting, it serves a didactic purpose. It is the conduit through which Phillpotts presents his core belief in the utter indifference of Nature, his conviction that humans are part of the ceaseless natural struggle. They are subject to the same drives as all other organisms, and influenced, consciously or unconsciously, by the environment in which they exist. This personal philosophy shapes the author's representation of Dartmoor.

Each of the 14 works of the 'Dartmoor epic' is concerned with the same central theme, a romantic tangle ranging from two women interested in the same man to two men pursing the same woman, with sundry suitors complicating the basic situation. The most ruthless and guileful, or the most sexually attractive, succeed in winning the mate of choice. By taking a closer look at *The Whirlwind* we should be able to understand how persons and place are constructed to support the author's ideological infrastructure.[17]

The first two novels of the series, *Children of the Mist*,[18] and *Sons of the Morning*,[19] are set in and around Chagford during the 1880s. *Children of the Mist* was well received, while there were reservations over *Sons of the Morning*, on account of its indeterminate ending and because of its heroine, 'a type happily abnormal', being 'violently in love with two men at the same time', a point that will be considered later in this chapter.[20]

Characters were not invented in the comfort of his home; the composition of each novel was concurrent with extended visits to the moor. 'Desperately cold up here but I am tramping the theatre of the new long story and spending a good

94 *Location of Eden Phillpotts' Dartmoor series, map.*

deal of time with my warrener', Phillpotts reported[21] during his preparations for
The River. This novel, located around Wistman's Wood and Two Bridges on the
West Dart, illustrates the importance he attached to environment:

> Dart runs through the lives of many humble folk and unconsciously influences them
> – sometimes by its life which is nature and sometimes by its death which seems to
> me to be in the strange man-made superstitions that haunt it.[22]

By April 1903 another 'serious' work was maturing, 'a very dreadful story' set in and around Belstone, that would tax the author 'to the uttermost to tell it properly'.[23] The following month Phillpotts reports that this tragedy, *The Secret Woman*, is proceeding apace as he works 'on the northern slope of Dartmoor to the sound of the cannon's roar'.[24]

The events of *The Portreeve*, 1906,[25] are played out in Bridestowe and Okehampton, with the action of *The Whirlwind*, 1907[26] occurring in nearby Lydford, a novel of which a critic commented:

> Here is a story which I shall not read again – which I would not have followed to the end except under compulsion. It belongs to the great modern French school of antitheism and suicide, increasing the world's melancholy, breeding darkness. [...] The story is false – false in motive and in grain. [...] Apart from its landscape, the book is to me, I frankly own it, horrible.[27]

The Mother followed in 1908, a 'simple' story, set around Merrivale and Vixen Tor, in which maternal influence 'dominates the hero at the critical stages in his career'.[28] Years later Phillpotts dismissed the work as 'saccharine [...] written for my dear mother who said, "I want a book in your series, and I do not want a tragedy"'.[29]

Published in 1908, *The Virgin in Judgment*[30] is the story of love within a family, the obsessive and ultimately destructive love of a sister for her brother. The novel, according to *The Bookman*, was 'marred [...] by the somewhat frequent descriptions of scenery',[31] some of that scenery, in the valley of the Meavy, near Sheeps Tor, lost beneath the Burrator reservoir after 1898. Further downstream, above the confluence of the Plym and Meavy, the village of Shaugh Prior is the central location for *The Three Brothers*, 1909, a study of three elderly siblings.[32] In preparation for the novel Phillpotts stayed at what is now the *Burrator Hotel*, Dousland, although for some years he had been refused a room there: '"I don't wasn't en yur"', the landlady told her daughter, '"I knows the toad. 'E's mind to hearken to me, and put me in a book."'[33] (Actually he did – in *The Three Brothers*).

In 1910 the high open moor around Postbridge and the East Dart was the locale for *The Thief of Virtue*, 'a tragedy of false fatherhood' with a chorus of 'bar loungers and parish gossips'.[34]

Then, in 1911, Phillpotts wrote to a friend, saying,

> My Dartmoor story is nearly told. Three more volumes will finish it [...]. Then the task I set myself twenty years ago is done and I shall seek fresh ground.[35]

This remark is significant, confirming what he had not publicly stated: that of the many works set on Dartmoor certain publications were part of a planned whole.

With *Demeter's Daughter*,[36] 1911, the tale of the Cleave family is unfolded around the south-eastern slopes of the moor at Holne, then still in the same year there was a move to South Zeal and Cosdon Beacon on the northern side of the moor for *The Beacon*, 'the psychologic story of a woman trying to lift a weak man,

95   *Teignhead Farm, below Sittaford Tor.*

and when she despairs and deserts him the miracle is performed and he rises above himself for her sake – too late'.[37] Yarner Wood and the village of Ilsington were the chief locations of *The Forest on the Hill*, 1912,[38] a novel including, according to one reviewer, 'four pictures of a Dartmoor scene at chosen seasons of the year. The four pictures make four chapters written without direct reference to the story'.[39] The nearby village of Widecombe is the setting for *Widecombe Fair*, 1913, the final novel in the series, the action almost wholly confined within the village environs. The novel was praised for its topographical detail, judged as forming a component part of the works, 'not merely the frame', and for the fact that while

Dartmorian lives were shown in relation to the environment, the author achieved much more by showing Dartmorians in 'relation to life itself'.[40]

Set towards the close of the 19th century, it differs in tone from its predecessors, completing the series with a final flourish, with few oracular intrusions; the work is anarchic and carnivalesque as, in a whirl of gossipy stories, the 'series of life' is concluded. The novel's title was an inspired choice – a fair customarily being arranged in a rough circle, the outer ring of caravans enclosing the space of the fair, just as the hills enfolded and encircled Widecombe. The fairground manager is Phillpotts, offering his readers, through Tryphena Harvey, the opportunity to share a whole range of experiences and sensations offered by the ranges, booths and rides that correspond to the various homes and sites around the village.

The foreword to *Widecombe Fair* not only enjoins readers to judge the work, 'planned more than twenty years ago', but asks that it should be considered as a

> frieze, [...] whereon victors, vanquished, and spectators of the ceaseless struggle play their parts in the great hypaethral theatre of the Western Moors.[41]

The word 'hypaethral' (roofless) reinforces the classical image. The phrase 'ceaseless struggle' is reminiscent of Darwin's: 'Never to forget that every single organic being around us may be said to be striving to the utmost to increase in numbers, that each lives by a struggle at some period of its life'.[42]

The Portreeve encompasses a cosmic view of evolution:

> Matter is eternal, but no form of it; and there is nothing absolute – neither at the foundations of the round world, nor in the domain of conscious intelligence. Morals and matter alike know no constant form [...]. As man swarms upon the face of this his home, exists and passes endlessly until the end; so the golden galaxies of innumerable suns and the wonder and glory of the systems that they sustain [...] are darkened, perish, and depart.[43]

And in *The Beacon* he reaffirms that 'matter alone is eternal but no form of it'.[44] Such sentiments are elaborated in *The River* where, on the slopes above the West Dart, in Wistman's Wood, 'crystalline giants of quartz, feldspar, and mica that seem to defy time' are 'playthings for winter and the latter rain'. But change is inevitable as 'the years nibble and gnaw each monstrous boulder, the frost stabs them; the ages wait their attrition with patience'.[45]

For organic beings life is invariably equated with struggle and restlessness; as in the forest at Yarner where

> life manifested itself everywhere, and the diurnal creatures on wings and paws minded their business above and below. [...] They followed the never-ceasing, necessary business of preserving life by hard work of beak and tooth and claw. [...] They lived in lusty rivalry [...] and wist not whence or why or whither. But war was the recognised state; all were fighting; none knew that it was so.[46]

Both the impact of human activity and the ravages of climate apparent on the landscape are part of the evolutionary process: 'the furrowed face' of Hambledon 'might be read like an open book, for its heather-clad and snow-clad bosom was a palimpsest, written and re-written, erased and corrected by Time and his children'.[47]

Even when all sign of herbage seems to have been destroyed, as on Amicombe Hill, where peat had been cut on a commercial scale, the drive for life is reasserted

> like a sea the waste billowed round [...]. Raw mountains of peat slowly grew green again under heath and grass [...]. Liverworts and tumid fungus ate the woodwork [...]; beds of emerald sphagnum swallowed the old peat-knives and spades.[48]

Nature's fecundity is apparent on the high moor at Metherill, above Chagford, where

> fields snatched from the moor in time long past, now showed a desire to return to their wild mother again. The bars of civilisation were broken [...] at every point the Moor thrust forward hands laden with briar and heather. They surmounted the low stone walls and fed and flourished upon the clods and peat that crowned them. [...] These heathen things and a thousand others, in all the early vigour of spring, rose triumphant above the meek cultivation.[49]

A sure sign of the human 'will to life' is evident at Bridgetstow (Bridestowe), in *The Portreeve*, where

> ripe matrons were suckling the race to come, and many a young wife budded to motherhood. [...] Men were shining at the forge; men were panting by the river. There fleeces fell and shorn sheep bleated and galloped snow-white on the shorn meadows. Men built with brick and stone, where unlovely dwellings rose raw about the confines of the hamlet. [...] The daily battle waxed under the sun's fire.[50]

In a cosmic context, each Dartmorian life, every sign of organic life and inorganic process must, according to the author, be perceived as fleeting incidents in a perpetual repetition stretching from 'the awful revolt of matter' that brought the moor into being, to the 'chain of human evidences extending from prehistoric ages to the ruined shepherd's cot of yesterday'.[51]

Dartmoor, as represented in the series, is a 'theatre of elemental force',[52] a place 'austere, primeval, unsubdued'.[53] Beyond the centres of civilisation, it is a place where the natural impulses are less masked by the requirements of polite society; therefore it becomes a suitable arena in which to illustrate the similarities between flora, fauna, and human behaviour patterns, and to consider whether the local environment is responsible for any distinctive adaptive traits in its human inhabitants:

> To what extent and in what direction had their dwelling-place impressed itself upon these transient dwellers. Had they directly though unconsciously won from Dartmoor the needful patience and fortitude of character to face and conquer the tough challenge of circumstances.[54]

96 *Kistaven near Hound Tor, lithograph by P. Gauci after C.F. Williams, 1848.*

But, as Phillpotts shows, his characters' actions are not wholly determined by biological drives, for when 'natural' instincts are held in check humans have the power to make reasoned choices – that they are not the playthings of a capricious god is essential to Phillpotts's philosophy. However, characters' actions are largely circumscribed within social and economic limits. Progress towards some notion of 'good' or 'evil' is achieved when a puppet manages to transcend what had appeared to be the encompassing boundaries.

An epic quality is evident in *The Whirlwind* when Daniel Brendon, en route to take up a new post at a farm near Lydford, in a manner typical of the series, emerges, or evolves, from the moorland. In this sequence Brendon's action in climbing on to a grave 'of heroes' links him with the past, and he seems to imbibe the hopes and aspirations held dear by his ancestors. Brendon, who has 'the physical beauty of a Greek statue of youth', is a devout Christian, sustained by the teachings of the Old Testament.[55] His God is 'one who commanded whole nations to be slaughtered, [...] who prescribed rules for slavery; who destroyed the first born of all Egypt, [...] who loved the smear of blood upon his altars'.[56] As he surveys the scene from his vantage point

a high wind raged along the sky and roared over the grave-crowned bosom of White Hill on Northern Dartmoor. Before it, like an autumn leaf, one solitary soul appeared to be blown. [...] Grey cairns of the stone heroes of old lie together on the crest of White Hill, and the man now climbed one of these heaps of granite, and stood there, and gazed upon an immense vision [...]. Like a map rolled out before his eyes, lay the man's new home [...]. Upon this great stage he would move henceforth, pursue hope, fulfil destiny, and perchance win the things that he desired to win.[57]

Here is Phillpotts's familiar image of a stage with all its connotations. Similarly, the extended descriptive opening of *The Thief of Virtue* lingers on in the 'amphitheatre', wherein 'twinkled the eastern arm of the Dart' – where Kingsley had roamed – the focus gradually moving to the central character, Philip Ouldsbroom, 'lying supine in the heath on Hartland Tor' debating over his possible choice of wife.[58] In *The River* the classical connection surfaces as the troubled hero walks the moor alone:

No cothurnus magnified his stature, no garment swelled his shape, no graven mask concealed his ruddy countenance. [...] As he played his part to the sun, the moon, the stars, for chorus came the cry of the river.[59]

The typical Phillpotts device of first describing a panoramic landscape and then gradually moving closer until a particular character comes under his scrutiny works on two levels: it is reminiscent of the moment of a play when, on an apparently empty stage, a character, previously unnoticed, is gradually illuminated; and it reinforces the frame around which the Dartmoor novels are constructed – that the author is observing and noting, in the manner of an anthropologist, the behaviour of humans under particular circumstances. Just as a scientist adjusts a microscope to focus on the behaviour of minute organisms he has chosen to study, so Phillpotts the author selects a few human animals for each of his novels, focusing on their responses to minutely differing sets of circumstances, amassing evidence to show that the pattern of human behaviour conforms at a basic level to that of other life forms.

To return to *The Whirlwind*, Daniel experiences an instant rapport between himself and Sarah Jane Friend who, pagan-like and primeval, embodies her high moorland environment. When Daniel declares his love – 'feel me – fire – fire – burning like the bush in the wilderness [...]. Bless God for his goodness'[60] – Sarah Jane, who has not learned to dissemble, and is unbound by social conventions, responds to her lover's advances with passion:

'Leave God till after,' she said. 'Go on burning now. Love me, hug me. There'll be black and blue bruises on my arms tomorrow. [...] Don't drag God in now.'[61]

Compelled by the evolutionary drive, without questioning her social or moral compatibility with Daniel, Sarah Jane unceremoniously dismisses the man to whom she is unofficially tokened and marries Daniel.

Sarah Jane, she with generous breasts and stately hips, and apron bearing the words Amicombe Peat Works, understands the physical needs of her employer, the repressed and ailing Hilary Woodrow, and responds instinctively. In the course of her duties as milkmaid, this beautiful, natural woman persuades Woodrow to drink milk fresh from his cows. The giving and receiving of milk becomes a bond between the pair, and sustained by her joy in sexual fulfilment she becomes convinced that Hilary would be restored to health if 'he should have a female after him'. This response is instinctive, assimilated from years growing up on the high moor insulated from learned conventions. Driven by her conviction, Sarah Jane becomes Woodrow's mistress, until he 'finds' religion when the adulterous relationship ends.[62]

After three or four years Jarrett Weekes, her previously rejected suitor, whose jealousy and desire for revenge have never abated, belatedly discovers the affair and organises an event once customary, but long fallen into history, a mock burial in which effigies of the adulterous pair are paraded and buried after a 'funeral' service. Thus, knowledge of a liaison that had already run its course burst upon Daniel Brendon:

> To find what he had believed a Creator's sustained and benignant attention proved instead one cruel, long-drawn trick and jest, shook the man to the roots of his faith. [...] He believed in predestination, and through that hypothesis he came back humbly to the footstool of his idol. [...] The fruit of his spirit was about to ripen in murder. [...] He meant to kill Woodrow with his naked hands.[63]

As the restraints of religion temporarily desert Daniel he regresses into savagery, assuming the characteristics of a wild animal; ploughing through a crowd with the 'sudden charge of some great beast', his eyes burning 'redder than the flames of the torch-fires round him'.[64] He lurks for a night and a day among the silent woods above Dawlish, in south Devon, where Woodrow is staying, mentally pondering over the scriptures for some revelation as to his next action. Convincing himself 'that the World-maker had chosen him to drive the knife into these evil hearts',[65] he determines to destroy both his wife and her lover. Finding Woodrow already dead from consumption, and thus foiled from taking revenge, Daniel howls 'horribly' as he attacks the body.[66] This late-Victorian worry over regressive behaviour also surfaces in *The River* and *The Secret Woman*.

Sarah-Jane, realising the depth of her husband's wrath, returns to her roots at the remote Amicombe Peat Works and commits suicide, a sacrifice to Brendon's unforgiving God. Life has proved not to be fair. Heir to the farm as a result of his wife's affair with Hilary, Daniel sells the place, burns the money and joins the Salvation Army. His fatal flaw has been his hasty temper compounded by his intransigent belief in the jealous and vengeful God of the Old Testament. Faith enables him to accept the terrible events as part of God's purpose in testing him – this conclusion to the novel quite at odds with the author's own beliefs.

In his novels, Phillpotts avoids attributing any specific meaning to any topographical or climatic detail, rather, the same place or object will be invested with meaning according to the individual through whom it is perceived. The open moor is a place of fear for some, while to others 'it is a manifestation precious as the presence of a friend'.[67] When young persons are courting, or a young woman has a rare moment of leisure, the moor may be a place for relaxation and enjoyment.

As an employer of farm labour, Myles Stapleton in *Sons of the Morning*, comfortably off, with time to wander the moor at will and indulge in the luxury of philosophising, takes a romantic view of his home region:

> The great, candid, undissembling home of sweet air, sweet water, sweet space. [...] It is an animate God to me [...]. I too am all of this – spun of it, born of it, bred on it, a brother of the granite and the mist and the lonely flower.[68]

In contrast, for Honor Endicott, his companion, the place is 'death and destruction in winter, and hidden skeletons under the quaking bogs'.[69]

Striving to wrestle a living from the high moor, farmers find their aspirations, 'speedily cowed by ill-requited toil and eternal hardship, quickly dwarf and shrink until even the most sanguine seldom extend hope much beyond necessity'.[70] Such is the case of Will Blanchard in *Children of the Mist*, for his efforts to make Newtake Farm productive whittle away his previous delight in the place to a dour battle for survival.[71] As pressures mount the past becomes meaningless, only the immediate present fills his mind, and his frustration boils over at the suggestion that a Christian cross buried head downward in the distant past 'to make a gate-post' on his farm, should be removed for restoration.[72]

> I'm weary of all this bunkum 'bout auld stones an' circles an' the rest; I'm sick an' tired o' leavin' my work a hundred times in summer months to shaw gaping fules from Lunnon an' Lard knows wheer, them roundy-poundies 'pon my land. 'T is all rot as every moorman knaws; yet you an' such as you screams if us dares to put a finger to the stone nowadays. [...] What's a cross to me? 'T is doin' more gude wheer 't is than ever it done afore.[73]

97   *The Nine Maidens near Okehampton, sketch c.1850.*

On the other hand in the same novel, part-time farmer Martin Grimbal, supported by wealth acquired in the colonies, has the leisure to indulge in the pleasure of antiquarianism:

> These cryptic stones are my life. What are these lonely rings? Where are we standing now? In a place of worship, where men prayed to the thunder and the sun and the stars? Or a council chamber? Or a court of justice?[74]

There are, among the series' cast of women, those who are obviously successful in what is predominately a man's world: Hannah Weekes, of *The Portreeve*, as a huckster with a stall in Plymouth market, Betty Bradbridge, in *Children of the Mist*, as innkeeper at the *Ring o' Bells*, and Barbara Hext, of *The Thief of Virtue*, who rules the shop and post office at Postbridge.

But although a few women are known to be capable beyond the domestic sphere, their struggle for parity is quietly blocked in some quarters. Celebrations to mark completion of the Lydford water-leat would exclude women, the general male opinion being that women were 'not fitted in their intellects to stand the strain of a public procession without getting too overbearing. They'm better kept under'.[75] The best solution for a self-opinioned girl, the older men agree, is to see her married. Marriage, the Dartmoor men believe, marks the end of a woman's interest in developing skills beyond domesticity: a proper married woman's work being to 'get boys – plenty of 'em'. After the business of child-bearing was over, farm worker Joe Tapson reckoned, women 'ban't so much use as cows'.[76]

At a time when popular literature generally upheld Christian principles and tended to be morally uplifting, Phillpotts seems to be condoning and perhaps encouraging attitudes that did not conform to the notion of lower-class respectability.[77] Discussion at Postbridge over the scandal of the hedge-cutter's wife who had eloped with a carpenter closed on what must have seemed a liberal note, condoning adultery and casting doubt on the pleasure of everlasting life. Farmer Ouldsbroom asserts that, if his wife wished to live with her lover, he'd say

> Go to him. You can live your life but once, and there's none of the glory of being men and women in heaven, by all accounts.[78]

Most of the numerous characters in the novels are 'people of the soil',[79] those who 'never had more than a board school education', and who depend on agricultural work or local industry to survive. They are not credulous peasants but labouring-class men and women, searching, knowingly or not, for some kind of meaning to their existence.

At some stage in each novel the 'great amphitheatre of the moor' becomes an economic landscape. Information relating to wages, working conditions, and pensions is revealed. The relationship between tenants and Duchy is examined, the tenants expressing ambivalent attitudes towards the Duchy as landowner. For a few persons the leasing of land to the military provides work and income; for others,

> The Duchy's a law-breaker. The very place we be walking on now is sold over our
> heads to the military, for them to bang their blasted cannon an' rob us of our grazing
> rights for miles an' miles.[80]

Moorland life is dominated by work, most of the characters dependent in some way on agriculture for income, as small holders or agricultural labourers, with just a few employed on road maintenance and the railways. Apart from granite quarrying around Meldon and South Tawton, and Henroost Mine near Hexworthy, the extractive industries or manufacturing complexes towards the centre of the moor are in decline. Vitifer mine, once a region of former activity is now, in the 1890s, a 'dreary, broken region of rotting mounds, dry watercourses, and deserted machinery'.[81]

Work may be a kind of communication with nature. Without romanticising, attention is focused on the ease and fluidity with which 'menial' tasks are performed: from the making of a rabbit snare, the splitting of a piece of granite, to the rounding up of stock from the reaches of the moor, thus demolishing the notion of the moorlander as an unskilled and ignorant 'peasant' or 'rustic'. Avoiding the danger that the Dartmoor workers may be regarded as operating in some kind of pastoral time warp, they are shown coping with the demands of late 19th-century technology, but still preserving a fierce attachment with place, as instanced by Abner Barkell, who had worked with such commitment on the construction of the railway line near his home that now some 'fragment of the world's energy represented by his working days' is 'embalmed' amid the numberless rivets of Meldon Viaduct.[82]

Conforming to the national pattern, Sundays are reserved for worship and relaxing, there is time for extended visiting, gossip, and 'outings', but social interaction is not confined to that day. Farms where employees live on site form a lively social nexus; there are weekday church, chapel, and village meetings, much 'dropping in' on neighbours, particularly among the women, or downing tools for mealtime chatting. Through all these social channels, but chiefly through the local inns, where the doings of the villagers are dissected and the tone of local life is set, Phillpotts conveys the thoughts and opinions of the moorlanders.

Over the series as a whole, Phillpotts has space to reveal the extent of community activities that punctuate the moorland year: the Drift, agricultural shows, the circus at Tavistock, wrestling and boxing matches, play acting, shopping trips to Exeter, training with the local militia, the pony fair at Princetown when the town throngs with visitors: [83]

> Aged and middle aged, youthful and young, grey and white, black and brown,
> bearded and shorn [...]. Perhaps few could have explained what drew them thither
> or kept them for many hours wandering up and down, now drinking, now watching
> the events of the fair.[84]

Those who are content to live on the moor are not presented as atrophied by isolation in the station to which they believed God had ordained them. Rudimentary schooling, visitors, and newspapers have extended their horizons.

98   *Scorhill Circle, etching by A. Dawson after J.Ll W. Page, 1889.*

The series abounds with references to relatives who have rejected rural life, a local manifestation of the general drift of the working classes from the country. Some have left the area in search of adventure, employment or marriage 'off the moor', while among the young persons remaining Phillpotts suggests a number find the whole ambience of the place 'a weariness', are unprepared to be part of an austere existence and evince no interest in their roots.[85] Girls plan to 'marry upwards', abandon being 'in service' to live in London determined never to return to the moor. Jill Bolt of *The Mother* confesses she can no longer face living all her life 'among these old crook-backed men and women and in such a home as mine! I wish to God I was dead and out of it'.[86]

Where Phillpotts's villagers instinctively recognised the honouring of old customs as a social mechanism that strengthens their community, they make efforts to pass on traditions to the younger, sceptical generation. Little Silver labourers, in *Sons of the Morning*, make a pilgrimage to Scor Hill on Easter Day to 'see the gert sun a-dancin for sheer joy', because their forebears did so, and because the act of going there would instil in the youngest members of the party 'a proper understanding' of the customs at which many of the younger generation chose to scoff.[87] After sunrise the young learn of 'omens and callings, and messages from the dead voices heard at nights', and how to interpret 'cryptic mysteries hidden in hares and toads', traditional beliefs that form part of the community's sustaining fabric.[88] In *Children of the Mist* Billy Blee, of Monks Barton Farm near Chagford, assembles some 25 persons to enact an ancient rite, of 'wassailing' – christening – the fruit trees:

For the boys this midnight fun with lantern and fowling-piece was good Christmas sport [...]. To the old men their ceremonial possessed solid virtue, and from the musty storehouse of his memory every venerable soul amongst them could cite instances of the sovereign virtue hid in such a procedure.[89]

But, even handed, Phillpotts shows by the 'mock burial' at Lydford, in *The Whirlwind*, that old customs might have a darker, cruel side and were best left to lapse into obscurity. Although there were folk who still believed in pixies, the witch hare, and the heath hounds, and some for whom 'the evil eye still shone malignant', for most 'the time of these mysteries' had passed by, and the latest generation saw 'only an unlikeness to truth that stamps the faces of these far-off things'.[90] Bearing in mind Phillpotts's consciousness of the younger generation's scepticism and the drift to the towns from villages, his pressing the novel into service as a means of preserving knowledge of old traditions 'moribund at the date of which we are concerned, and probably dead tomorrow'[91] exactly mirrors the work of Sabine Baring-Gould.

Based on the superstition that there is an annual drowning in the River Dart, *The River* illustrates both how superstitions obstruct 'mental breathing', and how an obsession may have a psychological foundation. Sorrow Scobhull's life is dominated by his fixation with the Dart, for on the night he was born his father had drowned in the river and he fully expects to meet the same fate: 'I look down by the hour into that awful, crawling, sleek water, an' I see the eyes underneath it [...] allus waiting for the next'.[92]

Watching his employer fall into the river, unable to swim, Scobhull makes no attempt to raise the alarm until he believes the Dart has claimed a heart 'at last'.[93] His fixation dominates and masters the normal human response of proffering aid to someone in dire need. Scobhull's peers reject his explanation that the river needed to be propitiated, and shun him. The locals' action suggests that, among the moorlanders, reason is replacing belief in old superstitions. Men and women are beginning to think for themselves, appreciating they must master their personal obsessions in order to function in the modern world.

Bringing the Dartmoor series to a close in the final scene of *Widecombe*

99 *On the River Dart, aquatint/etching, by and after F.C. Lewis, c.1840.*

Fair, Phillpotts juxtaposes two contrasting attitudes towards moorland life, that of the 'foreigner' and that of the temporary 'insider'. The 'foreigner', a lawyer from Newton Abbot, represents those persons who remain ignorant of the rich variety of human activities that comprise moorland life, while Tryphena Harvey becomes all those readers whose new insights into Dartmorian life might illuminate and enrich their own perspectives on society in general. Looking down on Widecombe, the lawyer muses aloud:

> Such a sparse population is most depressing [...]. The gregarious instinct of humanity rebels at such a sight [...]. By slow degrees the mind becomes brutalised and accustomed to this dreadful primitive silence and loneliness in the lap of Nature. [...] It is most unhealthy and reactionary. It should be no longer possible, in my opinion.[94]

Tryphena, whom the 'foreigner' is escorting for the first stage of her journey to Australia, makes no comment. She knows that, far from Dartmorians 'living lives the slow continuity of which would drive a "band-box" townsman mad',[95] her stay has been a round of colourful and dramatic events. Local scandals have concerned land, money, unsuitable and highly suspect proposed pairings. There is the pathetic situation of the dominated son hoping marriage might release him from parental bondage, and the robust humour derived from a Christian stalwart convincing himself that it would be perfectly proper to take a young relative as his concubine.

Tryphena, and those readers who have followed her experiences, have found all the stuff of human life on Dartmoor.

15

SENSIBILITY AND SENSE

By the early years of the 20th century a great deal of writing relating to the moor is available. Much of that work, continuing initiatives set up by the several associations, consists of accounts of explorations, surveys, social and economic history; and reports on military activities and any commercial or industrial ventures. Of the factual material published during those early years, William Crossing's *Guide to Dartmoor*, which closes the chapter, will be discussed as representing the major work through which generations of walkers would discover the region. The selection of illustrations – paintings and postcards, the novel, and the play we touch on in this chapter will, when appreciated within the context of their time, be seen to consolidate by now familiar images of the region. The reasons why artists' work, and Beatrice Chase's books were popular, while Eden Phillpotts' play was considered subversive, will be considered. First, though, an overview of the context in which those works were created.

From the late 19th century there had been increasing concern that the poor quality of life among the urban masses would lead to national degeneracy – particularly physical degeneracy. This was because the country was perceived as the breeding ground for healthy workers, sound in body and mind. If the healthy, aspirational rural young were leaving for the towns, the result would be a depletion of that national gene pool. The poor conditions in which the urban newcomers frequently existed were not conducive to the production of healthy children, with the result that, over time, the quality of the whole population would decline. Such thinking brought about a politically and socially driven 'back to the land' ideology, in which rural living was promoted as an ideal. The promotion of rural arts and crafts, the teaching of folk dance, the fashion for mock-Tudor and cottage style homes, and the content of the first edition of *The Oxford Book of English Verse*, are among the many manifestations of this developing culture. The emergent notion of 'country' from such activities and art forms was of managed land, nucleated villages, gently rolling hills, inhabited by a hard working biddable people, is the stuff of Beatrice Chase's books.

Just before immersion in Chase's idealised moor, the reality of recent moorland developments reveals a recently opened china clay quarry at remote Red Lake, the clay carried in suspension to works on the southern slopes, while machinery, supplies, and men were transported to and from the site by the 7½-mile Redlake Mineral Railway, opened in 1911. At times as many as one hundred workers might stay out at Red Lake for days at a time, living in barracks close

100 *Castle Drogo, above the river Teign, postcard, early 20th century.*

to the quarry. The burys (warrens) around Red Lake suggests that the men supplemented their meat rations with rabbits, thus following an established moorland practice. Quarrying was abandoned in 1932 – since then the line of the old track, which crosses some boggy terrain, has proved a safe route for moorland walkers.

By 1911, down-river from Chagford and high above the Teign, an edifice unlike anything on the moor was under construction. Convinced that some drops of Drogo de Teign's Norman blood ran through his veins, businessman Julius Drewe, founder of the Home and Colonial chain of grocery stores, bought the Drogo estate, Drewsteignton in 1910 and employed Edwin Lutyens to build a castle. Completed in 1930 and visible for miles around, the great granite pile – not as large as had been envisaged – is spectacular. Whether living inside a granite shell was altogether comfortable is debatable. An inherent design fault, and the use of unreliable newly developed roofing material, resulted in serious problems with leaks and seepage into the walls. Commandeered during the Second World War as a school, the castle together with 600 acres of grounds was bequeathed to the National Trust in 1974, and has provided an introduction to Dartmoor for many thousands of visitors since then. At present extensive and expensive renovations are in progress, to prevent water ingress and, it is hoped, to prevent further deterioration.

At Venton, near Widecombe, a few miles from Drewsteignton, another residence that would attract crowds was refurbished to suit the genteel needs of Olive Katharine Parr, better known as Beatrice Chase, and her mother.

Born in Harrow-on-the-Hill and engaged in social work among the poor in London at the turn of the century, Beatrice Chase (1874-1955), a Roman Catholic tertiary, 'discovered' Widecombe-in-the-Moor in 1901 while recuperating from a bout of ill health. By 1908 she and her mother had bought a farm at Venton. They rented out the farm and its outbuildings, retaining a cottage and having a chapel built nearby where, between 1910-20, the Blessed Sacrament was reserved.

Writing as Olive Katharine Parr, Chase had been producing pieces for magazines, relating to her work in London and Devon. Then a friend – probably the writer, John Oxenham – suggested that Chase should abandon attempts at the romantic novel and concentrate on creating pictures in words:

> Write of the moor folk as you know them. Paint them as they are. There is no other writer with your splendid chances, your wealth of matter. None other is a landowner, living year after year on his own freehold, among his own tenants, out in the heart of the hills.[1]

The Heart of the Moor, published within a year of Eden Phillpotts' *Widecombe Fair*, was Chase's response to that advice and, like all her Dartmoor works issued during

101 *Becka Pond, a remote spot on the river Becky near Widecombe.*

and just after the First World War, proved extremely popular, for she conjures visions of peace and a stable social order during a period of uncertainty. Through her eyes the area around Widecombe and Venton corresponds in a number of respects to an archetypical image of England, and to the image of the Dartmoor fringes perpetuated in tourist writings.[2] Encircled by winding, hedged lanes and cultivated land, the village clusters around the tall towered church, the inn, and the village green. There is a row of quaint old almshouses, and a blacksmith's forge.

For Chase, a sense of well-being infuses the initial view of Venton:

> The farm hamlet lay sound asleep, with the thatched hood of every building pulled down to its very eyebrows. Our house, the farm house, the cottages, the farm buildings, even the humble linhays – each and all sheltered some warm, happy, well-fed form of life. Half-consumed ricks of bracken, hay, and oats gave silent pledge of plenty still to come before next harvest time. [...] Around all stood the sable hills, encircling us on every side from the invasions of civilisation.[3]

Around the village the placid animals, and the fields, are 'working out their allotted destiny, untroubled by the passions that ravage humanity'.[4] The peacefulness of the community seems to be signalled by the constable's 'guileless old thatched cottage with Madonna lilies growing under its windows and a cage of doves hanging in its porch'.[5]

Considering the date of its publication, 1914, the notion of protection from invasion, and of continuity of an established way of life must have given these images an added poignancy, and her remarks referring to the 'healing' silence obtained on returning to the village from the 'dead-cold' draughts of city streets, which induce the 'dust-irritated throat',[6] hint at a soldier's return from the front-line trenches of France to the comparative respite behind the lines.

Where Chase relates the environment to the development of the individual, she reaches rather different conclusions from her contemporaries, John Trevena and Eden Phillpotts, and her predecessor Anna Caldwell Marsh. Chase asserts that 'this perpetual feast of colour in which we moor people live has a great effect on our mental atmosphere. It produces a warm-hearted, buoyant, refined race'.[7] The old, she maintains, are full of wisdom, the young respect their parents and go gladly to school, wives are cherished, and their husbands, devoted to their offspring, work tirelessly. Locals trust one another, tend lovingly to their beasts and are charitable: the reception accorded to Preacher John, who 'wanders erratically about the moor', could not be in greater contrast to the casual cruelty meted out to the inoffensive Brightly, in *Furze the Cruel*, for John is provided with shelter in farms and cottages, and locals seek his blessing.[8] These qualities in the men lead Chase to wonder 'if they are descended from some old gentle race [...] I wonder', she ponders, 'if all these things are innate within them.'[9]

102   *Kitty Jay's Grave, near Hound Tor.*

Even the local dialect seems to mimic the moorland rivulets:

> Get a couple of moormen, too far from you to distinguish words, and listen only
> to the notes in their liquid voices. You will find precisely similar notes in the rapid
> purling of the little streams.[10]

This observation represents a change from the usual reaction to the local dialect as incomprehensible or the subject of mirth.

Not wholly mawkish, Chase is sensitive to the organic connection between house and environment. Her cottage

> is formed throughout of Dartmoor granite, [...]. The Dart herself has mingled her
> being with Mother Earth's, for the sand used in the foundations of the house and
> in the cement floors was water sand brought from the bed of the Dart. [...] Half the
> material of the great square of cement [...] on which the first floor stones rest came,
> dripping, from the Dart.[11]

Her 'stories' might seem to be trite and include much musing over trivia, a list of each object on every shelf of her dressers, or the number of snails she had picked out of her garden that morning, but she gave her readers what, for a short period, they wanted, explaining that 'it would be ungracious and ungrateful' to ignore requests for more of the same stories.[12] A technique she employs to great advantage is to personalise and present as new, incidents that might be well-known, as for example with the story of Jay's Grave, where below Hound Tor she 'walked straight into death', in the semblance of a grave by the roadside.

> Going nearer I found that unknown hands had placed upon it a rough cross of ducky flowers, which lay limp and dying in the sunshine [...] With a sense of tragedy I turned away at last, came home and peppered everyone with questions.[13]

After vainly searching through books and maps, Chase visits an old lady who solemnly announces, ''Tis a suicide's grave, miss', and relates the unhappy tale. In reality, it was patently untrue that the story was nowhere to be found, for besides appearing in guidebooks, it was, as guidebook writer Beatrix Cresswell mentions in 1905, 'pointed out by coach drivers'.[14]

Chase might assiduously foster an image of a fragile female, but she knew her market and wrote for it, and like her contemporaries she effectively mines the moor to supply a commodity. In her books, the labouring classes always 'know their place', her works are infused with her firm belief that Dartmorians, 'salt of the earth', of course, are nevertheless, inferior beings:

> I have often said in fun, when we were returning to London for the winter, 'Now you can all behave as you choose; fight like cats, break every rule, be as dirty and noisy as you like. How happy you will be till we come back again' and they were always genuinely furious at the remark, protesting again and again that it was so nice to have gentry who *cared*.[15]

As Trevena had bluntly stated, and Beatrice Chase implies, Dartmorians needed help and guidance from persons like herself. This assumption concurs with the view expressed by Watson in *The Hound of the Baskervilles*, of a need for intervention from 'outsiders' who will free the indigenous dwellers from the bondage of superstition, through benevolent leadership. Presenting herself as 'gentry', as 'the lady of the moor',[16] Chase fancies herself as an indispensable moral arbiter, her prestige symbolised by her possession of the only accurate clock and the only doorbell in the little community. In her telling of tenants hesitantly offering little gifts of food to her as a person 'of superior rank',[17] and of a grateful young woman kissing her hands, her rings, portions of her dress, 'anything she could catch hold of',[18] the writing may be self indulgent, but the public loved it.

Towards the close of *The Heart of the Moor*, Chase describes a strange sunset as which seems to foreshadow the First World War.

> Earth and sky were heavy, sombre, opaque, infernal. Behind Longaford it looked as if Hell had been recently stirred to emit a solid smoke which was too thick for even the fire to penetrate except in one place. It was as though the whole world were burning pitch. [...] It was desolation, despair, finality.[19]

Crowds of another kind were obliged to discover Dartmoor during the 1914-18 conflict. In the first war, people who had never given the region a thought settled there for the duration, as hospitals for war casualties and refugee centres were set up. After the armistice, when Dartmoor was left to its own devices, Chase passionately hoped readers might share her peaceful world:

> I am thinking, to-night, of all you who are on the wrong side of my hills. I ache with
> a longing which is absolute pain, to draw you all to this old-world haven of peace.[20]

Her devotees responded, large numbers travelled to Venton to see 'my lady of the moor' so dubbed by a fellow writer, John Oxenham, to gaze at her home, surroundings, and catch glimpses of the people she so lovingly described. At first 'pilgrims' were made welcome, but Chase's attitude changed and peremptory notices appeared around her property ordering 'trippers' not on any account to call. But, years after she had tired of visitors, eulogistic news items still encouraged her devotees to travel to Venton:

> At Widecombe-in-the-Moor, where she lives, she is as much at home as Uncle
> Tom Cobleigh himself.[21] No wise visitor to that charming rural retreat misses the
> opportunity, if it presents itself, of making her acquaintance and seeing something
> of the treasures she had gathered about her in Venton House.[22]

Around the time Chase was preparing her sentimental evocations of moorland life, Eden Phillpotts was planning an adaptation of his 1905 novel, *The Secret Woman*, in which his theatre audiences would wrestle with moral problems concerning adultery, revenge, and guilt. However, the Lord Chamberlain refused the play a licence unless certain sentences were deleted. This Phillpotts refused to do, receiving hearty support from other writers who objected to the fact that the moment Phillpotts had 'the ambition to write a play in the same spirit which inspired his novels' he was at the mercy of an official's decision. *Punch*, in 'The Guarding of Eden',[23] joined in the argument, friends rallied around, and a question about the matter in the House of Commons elicited the reply that the 'public passages of so objectionable a character', would not be read aloud but could be shown to any Member of the House privately.[24]

In order to circumvent the Lord Chamberlain's ruling, six free performances were organised. Before discussing the play's reception it might be timely to reveal what could not be heard by members of parliament, but had been available in print for several years:[25] the first passage is spoken by Joshua Bloom who, nearing retirement, works in the granite quarry near Belstone:

> Nature tickles us humans into breeding afore we've got the sense to keep away from
> it–that's her craft. But she didn't get over me.   Act 2, p. 28

Ann Redvers is the 'wronged wife', who is speaking of the incident that sparked her murderous attack on her husband after she had watched him with his mistress. Ann is 39, healthy, strong and imperious:

> And he spread the fern and made a soft couch of it. Presently he laughed – he
> laughed; and his laughter touched something deep down in me. 'Twas that laugh
> that always goes before a drink of cider with him, and the Sunday dinner, and such
> good things, and I said, 'What feast be coming to Anthony Redvers here?' And
> suddenly I guessed [...] I saw the two of them thicken into one.
>   Act 2, p. 32

103 *Cottage interior, postcard, early 20th century.*

Anthony Redvers, Ann's husband, too taken aback by learning his wife had seen him with Salome, explains that his actions were simply:

> The way of a man's body [...]. My flesh and blood's a bit too much for you and always was. And a bit too much for me sometimes.
>
> Act 2, p. 36

The final objection comes towards the play's close, when Salome, grief stricken, confronts Ann Redvers and, speaking of her passion for Anthony, says, 'I only nursed my flesh to keep it plump and sweet for him'. (Act 4, p. 72.)[26]

Fornication on the high moor was, as Phillpotts so often stressed in his novels, part of the natural order of things. But, in the play, without the dense descriptions and philosophical justification of such an action, that rural characters should joyfully gratify raw desire was not only an offence against decency, it undermined the national construct of rural life. Village life implied conformity, self-discipline, and adherence to the prevailing moral code.

As it turned out, paying playgoers were never to see high moorlanders' primitive passions enacted. A crass error in casting resulting in Ann's depiction as a bent, unattractive aged crone rather than a feisty woman undermined the point of the play, an unmitigated disaster, which 'lumbered and dawdled' along into obscurity.[27] There was some consolation for the author because the furore created a rush to buy the novel, presumably on account of the salacious bits.

Turning away from the seamy side of moorland life, we find consonance between paintings, postcards and Chase's work.

Popular paintings and postcards of the moor depicted images of quaint villages, with thatched cottages, or variations of high windswept hills. The village images are carefully crafted to offer the dream of rural living. But, we may wonder, do rugged steep hills and wild places fit into the national construct? The answer is a firm 'yes'. Paintings and postcards of Dartmoor hills belong, culturally, with popular books and magazines crammed with stories located in jungles, the outback, and on the prairies. Such material conveys a message – that places beyond managed lands may be reached and conquered by men of strength and fortitude, qualities held dear by the English.

Artists whose work was reproduced in postcard format include Edmund Morison Wimperis (1835-1900), Andrew Beer (1862-1954), George Henry Jenkins (1866-1937), William Henry Dyer (fl. *c*.1890-1930), and Charles E. Brittan (1870-1949). Regarded as one of the finest moorland water-colourists, Brittan's work, ranging over the whole of the area, was noted for its 'needlepoint acuity, its fine and lovely detail'.[28] Like Brittan, Eustace Tozer (fl. 1892-1940) was also commissioned to illustrate books, several examples of his drawings appearing in Sabine Baring-Gould's *A Book of Dartmoor*, 1900. Tozer's speciality was sunrise and early morning mists, a lively example seen in his water-colour 'On the Tavy at Gur Tor', a location close to his Lydford home, where Frederick John Widgery had his second home. Generally their paintings portray wide upland, heather-clad areas backed by tors, Wimperis' and Beer's often suggesting closing mists and lowering clouds so characteristic of the area.

Being lost in lowering cloud cover, or lost in any conditions, was just one of the moorland hazards William Crossing hoped readers of his *Guide to Dartmoor* would be able to avoid or cope with, once they had learned from him. By encouraging readers to explore, and by presenting the challenge of the long, tiring excursion, Crossing's work, like that of the local artists, suggests that the heights are where character may be tested.

As he had observed in 1903, 'all the existing Dartmoor guide-books are guides only in name. They are really brief descriptions of the moor, and generally interesting, but are unfortunately full of mistakes'. Visitors, he explains, armed with map and compass but unused to Dartmoor's terrain, would quickly become tired and confused, when confronted with a situation where walking was out of the question, where

> rains have laid the peat bare, and the surface of the hill presents the appearance of a vast sheet of black mud studded with innumerable small islands covered with bog grass [...] It is when you attempt to cross it that you become aware of the difficulties. This can only be done by leaping from tuft to tuft, and as it almost invariably happens that after a few minutes of this exercise you reach a part of the sea of soft peat that it is impossible to leap across, and have to return and make a fresh attempt. [29]

104   *Phillpotts' peat pass, Whitehorse Hill.*

But, as Crossing explains, had the weary ramblers only known, had they with them clear, unambiguous instructions they would have found a sound path, in fact, they may well have found a new path, one not primarily intended for walkers, but to facilitate the passage of stock and huntsmen. Knowing the place well, Frank Phillpotts (1837-1909), a keen huntsman, organised the cutting of several passages across boggy ground between 1895 and 1905. These 'cuts' provided a continuous sound route across the north moor.

To obviate visitors finding themselves misled by unreliable instructions, Crossing decided to produce a work that 'would inform the reader how to reach any given point on the moor from any town or village on its borders'.[30] Published in 1909, his *Guide* was instantly acclaimed as the 'Dartmoor Bible', and so it remains.[31] From one point of view Crossing cartographically regains control of the moor from Doyle and from the domination of the ordnance survey map. He fills in gaps left by the map makers, reinstates the shape of the moor as defined by its criss-cross of ancient tracks, and reminds his readers of place names that existed before map-makers imposed their linguistic authority on the moor. From

105   *From Gibbet Hill, sketch by P.G. Stevens, c.1909.*

another viewpoint, though, Crossing, like his friend Eden Phillpotts, makes the moor seem knowable, convincing potential walkers:

> The few inconveniences inseparable from a long ramble in a hilly region that gives
> birth to many rivers are as nothing. They have been magnified into dangers by those
> whose knowledge of the moor is slight; when one becomes familiar with it they take
> their proper place, and are unheeded.[32]

A great success, the *Guide* was reorganised into five parts in 1914 remaining in print in this format until 1939. It proved a far better arrangement for walkers always looking for ways to save weight – the earlier editions had run to around 500 pages. In 1964 a new edition was called for, since when the *Guide* has remained in print.

Philip Guy Stevens (1883-1944), who had spent much of his youth in Princetown, was working as a clerk at the prison when he agreed to provide illustrations Crossing needed for the proposed guide. Stevens would receive precise instructions as to the viewpoint from which a drawing should be made, whereon he would trek to the location, often some miles from home, and make his sketch before or after his normal duties. Stevens painted in oil and watercolour, and a selection of his moorland works, on public view for the first time, is included in the 1990 edition of the guide.

Although Crossings *Guide* is without doubt his outstanding work, no one interested in the discovery of the moor should fail to look at his descriptions of ancient crosses, collection of folk rhymes, his accounts of wanderings in *Amid Devonia's Alps*,[33] and especially his *Gems in a Granite Setting*, where he allows himself the luxury of lingering at his favoured haunts of beauty.[34]

16

DEWER RIDES

This chapter will touch on moorland developments between the 1920s and '40s, comment on *The Farmer's Wife*, a play by Eden Phillpotts, and *Dewer's Ride* by L.A.G. Strong, before drawing to a close soon after Dartmoor is assigned its role as a national park.

Moorland mining continued to decline during the 20th century. Golden Dagger remained operational until 1914, with intermittent surface activities during the 1920s and 1930s. Birch Tor, Vitifer and Hexworthy mines followed a similar pattern. China clay quarrying continued to expand around the upper valley of the Torry brook, the 40-acre pit at Lee Moor representing only the beginning of continuing ingress on the moor's south-west slopes. Just as unsightly as the clay waste and as detrimental to the flora and fauna, in 1919 an extensive programme of tree planting began to change the face of the moor. Former landmarks, homes, and ancient monuments would gradually be submerged by the unremitting green of conifer plantations at Fernworthy, Bair Down, Bellever, Soussons, Burrator and Brimpts. Less obtrusive, Venford reservoir supplemented by water from the River Swincombe provided additional supplies for the developing seaside resort of Paignton, and the dam across the Meavy at Burrator was heightened in 1928, the year Torquay, another holiday town on the south coast, began to take water from the South Teign at Fernworthy.

One outcome of the democratisation of the moor was deprecated in *Punch*:

> They come by wagonette, a vandal brood;
> They sprawl at leisure – 'a great herd of swine
> Feeding'; and having fed they strew around
> Paper, smashed glass and cardboard on the ground,
> Leaving, where none but the gods might meetly dine,
> Foul wrappings and the relics of their food.[1]

Military roads leading deep into the moor allowing easy access to Cranmere Pool contributed to reports of unsocial behaviour: in 1928, visitors were being warned to 'turn away from the orange peel and broken bottles to some spot less obviously bearing evidence of popularity'.[2] A few years later, the site was said to resemble 'a sordid village fair'.[3]

Ponderous, pinguedinous, or indolent, all moorland excursionists congregated at Princetown, 'one of the strangest towns in England'. Every day charabancs crowded into the square – by the war memorial designed by Philip Guy Stevens. For some reason

> a morbid curiosity draws thousands of people to the melancholy Town of the Broad Arrow. Old women, small shopkeepers, young girls, troop down towards the nearest work-gang and stand, very solemn, and awed watching the men whom society has removed for its own safety.[4]

A strangely paradoxical situation when you come to think of it: people escaping from the towns to enjoy the freedom of the moor, watching people confined there and longing to escape to civilisation.

The prison hit the headlines on Monday 25 January 1932 with sensational reports of the previous day's riot and fire. Mass escapes, it was rumoured, had

106 *Burrator Dam, enlarged in 1928.*

107   *Prisoners emerging from the main gate, postcard, early 20th century.*

108   *Chain Room at the prison, postcard, early 20th century.*

been planned to take place under cover of the disturbance. Members of the London underworld, it was said, had high-powered cars in the vicinity ready to whisk the convicts off the moor. Locals recalled having recently seen strange flickering lights –now assumed to have been signals passing between convicts and their would-be rescuers. The media swung into action, an aircraft was hired to photograph the devastated buildings, and 'kinamatograph operators hovered round for several days'.[5] Predictably, Princetown's trade was boosted by an extra influx of sightseers, who were out of luck because the convicts were confined to base.

Away from the 'honey-pot' of Princetown, artists continued to derive their inspiration from the untouched spaces. There is one notable exception: a painting by Henry Lamb (1883-

109 *Fire after the prison mutiny, aerial view, January 1932.*

1960), *Military Exercises, Devonshire*, in which from a distance groups of soldiers appear as scatterings of granite outcrops.

Hugh Breton, vicar of Sheepstor, published a series of guidebooks in aid of church funds. He includes a number of interesting biographies of moorlanders, and various collections of records relating to miners, and to church accounts. He also mentions the discovery of concentric circles on Yellowmead Down, the prone stones spotted during a period of drought when the furze was less rampant than usual.[6] A number of Breton's guide books were illustrated by Charles E. Brittan who for some years lived at Burrator, near Sheepstor. Brittan's ability to vary his style is apparent when his cover for *Beautiful Dartmoor; the Northern Quarter* showing the majesty of 'Tavy Cleave'[7] is compared with that for *The Heart of Dartmoor*, a jolly drawing – except for the poor old horse – of Uncle Tom Cobley and his pals off to the fair at Widecombe.

Twelve years after *The Secret Woman* debacle, *The Farmer's Wife*, a play based on Phillpotts' novel *Widecombe Fair*, brought Dartmoor into the heart of London. The play, part of the Birmingham Theatre's repertoire since 1914, opened at London's Court Theatre in March 1924 and, billed as 'the laugh of your life', after a shaky start ran for more than 1,300 performances.[8] For years afterwards it was a popular choice for amateur players, remaining in print until the end of the 20th century.

Widecombe Fair confronts some of the problems arising in an enclosed society with gentle humour and insight. *The Farmer's Wife*, billed as a comedy, is a farce. The actor Cedric Hardwick played Churdles Ash a servant – a character not in the novel – 'gnarled, nubbly, whiskered, apparently a composition of granite, peat and moss', who seemed the personification of Dartmoor. With his rural aphorisms and famed thumb-twitch over his shoulder, Hardwick, the star of the show, would 'bring the house down', and in so doing invented a definitive type of local yokel whose descendants still flourish in the media.

The Farmer's Wife was directed for the screen by Alfred Hitchcock in 1926 – before the advent of 'talkies'. The farmer, Samuel Sweetland, was played by matinée idol Jameson Thomas. The emphasis in this production is on romance, with the heroine never admitting her love for Samuel, but resolutely helping him select a mate, before a happy resolution is achieved – unlike the conclusions in most of Phillpotts' novels. There is little in the film, with the emphasis on people rather than place to indicate the unique qualities of the location.[9]

Between 1920-23 Phillpotts added three novels to his original Dartmoor series of 14, then, in acknowledgement of his position as the region's foremost writer, a celebratory Widecombe Edition of 20 works was mooted. Publishing was complete by 1928, comprising the 17 moorland novels, one partly set on the moor, together with two collections of short stories.[10] Although this edition is highly prized by collectors, the heavily abridged novels lose much of their shape, rhythm and ideological content in order to increase the pace of the narrative. But still, the characters in the novels, wrestling with the conflict between desire and duty, will be found to bear little resemblance to the caricatures in Phillpotts' most popular drama.

Leonard Strong (1896-1958), who wrote the introduction to Phillpotts' Widecombe Edition, emulated his friend by producing his own moorland novel *Dewer Rides*,[11] set around Dousland, Meavy and the Dewerstone. Strong, born in Plympton, knew these places well, and he had stayed at the *Burrator Hotel* where crucial incidents in the novel take place, and where, as mentioned in chapter 14, on several occasions Phillpotts had been refused a room. Through the life of David Brendon, the central character of *Dewer Rides*, the communion between place and persons is examined in a way reminiscent of both Phillpotts' and Trevena's novels. Speaking in half sentences, the men in the bar of the *Manor Inn* confirm that, having noticed certain portents, each of them 'here-born and here-bred' is aware of 'some confusion in nature', when the dark powers are made manifest. Dick learns that the Dewer Stone would shudder, and 'black gnarly roots come out of the ground, and couple like worms'.(114) Then, Dewer, the Demon Hunter of the Moor, would ride from the 'far end of Wigford Down, up along past Brisworthy and Ringmoor, in a great curve eastward and then north'. Years later, when in a highly emotional state after a failed sexual encounter, Dick plunges towards the Dewerstone through wild weather. He becomes aware of tremors in the earth:

> And now, when his spirit was wrought up to such a pitch of vision that he might have seen the primal error of his being towering above him in the clouds, or the course of his wild life racing by him in the wind, he saw nothing but the phantasmagoria of the countryside, the figures predetermined by centuries of superstition: the silent shape of a hunter and horse toad-coloured in the moonlight, with a pack of little leaden hounds that ran like pigs. (308)

Dick, we know, is aware of the predicted outcome of such an experience – that those who see the spectral huntsman will become profligate and meet an unhappy end. The author leaves us to decide the extent to which he unconsciously fulfils the prophecy, as a serial philanderer and, unwittingly, as the seducer of a woman he had no idea he had fathered.

At the inn, as tongues loosen over their drinks, we hear of a dead baby's ghost, of a local werewolf, of the voices of long-dead French prisoners heard near Yelverton, and of witchery on the moor. ''Tis my belief,' says one of the locals, 'this new learning have driven out such things. But where will you learn them in a book?'(117) Strong, obviously enjoying his little joke, knows that one answer could be 'in books like his, for example', for, as we have seen, for many years there had been ever increasing interest in recording village customs and folklore for posterity. Like his fellow moorland writers, Strong is playing his part in capturing legends and fragments of bar room chatter in order to preserve knowledge of moorland culture.

Towards the close of the novel, a couple of tourists – representatives of the 'outsiders' – listen with interest and amusement to the local gossip, before going off happily to bed, unaware of the ugly ramifications of that talk. But, to the locals, learning of Dick Brendon's *ménage a trois*, the gossip was not a juicy bit of local scandal. They perceived what they had heard as an offence against their community, and between themselves had decided that, according to tradition, members of the community would mete out Brendon's punishment. The presence of the visitors, extraneous to the narrative, serves to remind us that, while 'outsiders' might hear or read about customs and traditions, there is a level of significance beyond what they hear, to which they are not privy. They would never have connected the bar room chatter to an incident in Tavistock six weeks' later when a crowd gather around Dick and, goaded by his arrogant attitude, attack him, inflicting injuries that would prove fatal.

In the introduction to this work, I suggested that the representation of moorlanders does not change radically over the centuries. For Trevena there is no doubt – moorlanders are a race apart; Chase implies the same. Setting aside Phillpotts' *Farmer's Wife* 'twaddle', characters in his Dartmoor series generally accept change with equanimity, and, like Strong's people, have the skills to function in an urban environment when necessary. Yet, just as in Phillpotts' tales, Strong's *Dewer Rides* reveals how, in times of crisis, social skills are dispensed with, and behaviour patterns rooted in long traditions re-emerge. True or not, from a literary point of view this is important; it allows moorlanders to be different, to remain 'other'.

But, how about perceptions of the landscape, lauded by writers since the early 19th century, and interpreted as picturesque and sublime by artists? Books, illustrations, plays and films led to a widening knowledge of the moor in the 1930s, so much so that, in 1935, R.A.J. Walling, one time editor of the *Western Morning News*, concluded that no tract of country of its size had been more 'written up'.[12] He warned readers to be on guard against the temptation to take their imaginative conception of Dartmoor from writers who had taken no more than 'fugitive glimpses' of the regions. On the other hand, it was partly these glimpses, hints, and suggestions that attracted visitors, to 'get in touch with the early Celts', be 'pixy-led', or to discover why horses and dogs 'have trembled and sweated with fear in the neighbourhood of Cranmere'.[13]

It was not in the hope of discovering a mystical moor that strangers found themselves there between 1939-45. It was not by choice that they were there at all. They were evacuees, fleeing from bombing raids to the safety of moorland border villages and towns. Plymothians, too, discovered some relief in night-rest centres, a world away from the siren's wail – the naval dockyard was a prime target. At some time during the period of hostilities, representatives from many, if not all of the allied countries found themselves stationed at a number of hastily constructed camps. The sheer number of persons who spent some time on the moor is quite amazing – between July and December 1943, for example, more than 10,000 patients passed through the United States 115th Station hospital at Plaister Down, near Tavistock.[14] When an officer at the camp vented his feelings about Dartmoor: 'Brother r r r! the only spot in the world with horizontal rain', [15] we hear echoes of 17th-century historian John Hooker's observation that 'All the yere through out commonly it rayneth or it is fowle wether'.

Between 1939-45 the face of the moor changed as never before. Airfields, prisoner-of-war camps, tank traps, underground bunkers, food-stores, were hastily built. On the most remote parts defences were set up to deter gliders carrying invading troops. After this temporary set-back, the notion that the moor should be placed in public ownership, raised on a number of occasions since the late 19th century, was resurrected. Proposed in 1945, Dartmoor was finally designated as a National Park on 30 October 1951. All the researches, speeches, articles, books, field-work, and law-suits had finally come to fruition. Officially Dartmoor was discovered, conserved for posterity.

17

A National Park

Suddenly there was a great clearing up. Industrial buildings were razed, machinery was cleared away; unoccupied isolated dwellings were rendered unfit for use. Some of the abandoned industrial buildings in the Vitifer Mine complex had been destroyed a few years earlier when, as an outcome of the Second World War, unexploded bombs were taken into the valley and detonated. A water-colour of the Vitifer carpenter's shop and chimney of the dry, painted by Edward Neatby (1888-1949) around 1929, indicates that the buildings were quite sound, but by 1950 – before the National Park was formed – the area was in much the same condition as it is today.

The Princetown railway was closed in 1956, and the tracks were torn up. The now redundant railway bridge across the road at the bottom of Peek Hill was demolished, the stone used to improve the bends at Devil's Elbow near Princetown. Mineral mining ceased; small-scale granite quarrying continued. However, the price of Dartmoor's freedom from further industrial or commercial ventures and from military needs is eternal vigilance. At present the Ministry of Defence leases some 33,350 acres of the National Park – including about half of the high moor. Marker posts mark the limits of the ranges and red flags warn that firing is in progress.[1]

Fortunately there are around 40 interested organisations keeping a watchful over this 'wild and wondrous region'. Softening with time, traces of the past are fast becoming part of the multi-layered palimpsest of the moor. There are sites where Time and man's hand have effaced all but mere intimations that such places were once homes, yet they live on as such in memory: Brown's House, left unfinished and never lived in; Hillson's House, built and occupied by a clock maker; Snaily House where two sisters lived, subsisting on black slugs. There are newer memorials, too, commemorating individuals and groups, and there are sites designated as war graves. All are beginning to merge into the patina of the moor.

A new generation of writers has produced influential general works ranging over moorland history and culture: Douglas St Leger-Gordon followed his *Dartmoor in all its Moods* (1931) with *Devonshire* (1950), and there is Crispin Gill's *Dartmoor: A New Study* (1970); L.A. Harvey and D. St Leger Gordon's *Dartmoor* (1953), and E. Hemery's *High Dartmoor: Land and People* (1983). Brian Le Messurier's more recent *Dartmoor Artists* (2002) is a reminder of the wealth and range of art-work based on the region. Representative of contemporary

110   *Former Second World War RAF control tower at Harrowbeer, Yelverton.*

111   *Memorial to W. Crossing at Duck's Pool, near the source of the river Plym.*

112   *Letter box cairn at Cranmere Pool.*

artists, Ray Balkwill (1948-), is captivated by the unpredictability of the moorland landscape, always searching to capture the essence of its elemental force and to convey a sense of a unique place.

An estimated 10-11 million day visits are made to the moor each year. Locations identified over two hundred years ago as picturesque, remain firm favourites – 67,000 persons visited Lydford Gorge, now managed by the National Trust, in 2005. Apart from the usual outdoor pursuits, two activities have become part of the moorland tradition: letter boxing and the Ten Tors challenge. John Laskey's party initiated the custom of leaving messages on the moor in the late 18th century, a practice formalised over half a century later when James Perrott placed a receptacle at Cranmere and, in 1905, when the visitors' book was placed there. In 1938 a letterbox cairn was erected at Duck's Pool, the centre of the south moor, in memory of William Crossing, and since then the practice of placing boxes containing a die has proliferated, and the hunt to locate them has developed into a popular leisure activity.

The Ten Tors Expedition, inaugurated in 1960, with a 55-mile walk over one weekend, has evolved over time to include a variety of challenging treks. Annually over one weekend in May, young persons – under 19 – gather at the Okehampton military camp before setting off on their hike. Though it is only human nature to try to be first back, it is neither a race nor an individual effort. Only groups who complete the course together are deemed wholly successful. Why is Dartmoor a venue for this event? Because even on its benign days it poses a challenge to the mind, body and spirit. H.V. Morton sums up what most writers and artists through the ages have, in their disparate ways, expressed about the region's landscape:

> Here are no cosy acres, but miles that have never known the plough [...] miles that are as remote from humanity as the craters of the moon; that seem to say, 'I care not for man whether he lives or dies, and though you try to the end of time you shall not tame me'. The cruelty of desert and ocean is on Dartmoor.[18]

NOTES

Introduction, pp.xi-xii.

1. P. Hamilton-Leggett, *The Dartmoor Bibliography 1554-1991: Including a 1992 supplement, Non Fiction* (1992).
2. 'The Hound of the Baskervilles', *Strand*, 22 (1901) and 23 (1902).
3. *The Regional Novel in Britain and Ireland: 1800–1990*, ed. by K.D.M. Snell (1998), p.1.

Chapter 1 – Early Times, pp.1-13.

1. T. Risdon, *The Chorographical Description; or, Survey of the County of Devon, Printed From a Genuine Copy of the Original Manuscript; With Considerable Additions* (1811), p.1. Risdon (1580?-1640) completed his survey around 1630. As far as possible – there are pages missing – quotations from the 1811 edition have been compared with The Decimes; or, A Chorographicall Description of the County of Devon – 1650, PWDRO, MS, 74/287, mf 1-3.
2. M. Drayton, *Poly-Olbion*, ed. by J.W.Hebel, 4 vols (1613-1622; 1933), iv, p.290. A topographical poem, completed in 1622, which describes the beauties of Britain in a series of 30 'songs'.
3. Risdon, p.2.
4. S. Baring-Gould, *A Book of Dartmoor* (1907), p.3.
5. R.N. Worth, '"William of Worcester," Devon's Earliest Topographer', *Transactions of the Devonshire Association* (hereafter *TDA*) 18 (1886), pp.473-5.
6. J. Leland, *The Itinerary of John Leland the Antiquary, Published From the Original Manuscript in the Bodleian Library by Thomas Hearne, to Which is Added Antoninus's Itinerary Through Britain, With Various Readings and Dr Robert Talbot's Annotation Upon it*, 3rd edn 3 vols (1769), iii, p.49.
7. This is Richard Gough's assessment of Hooker's work as expressed in *British Topography; or, An Historical Survey of What Has Been Done for Illustrating the Topographical Antiquities of Great Britain and Ireland*, 2 vols (1780), i, p.299.
8. W.J. Blake, 'Hooker's Synopsis Chorographical of Devonshire', *TDA* 47 (1915), p.345.
9. R. Pococke, *The Travels Through England of Dr Richard Pococke, Successively Bishop of Meath and of Osborn During 1750, 1751, and Later Years*, ed. by J.J. Cartwright, Camden New Series 42 (1888), p.138.
10. R. Fraser, *General View of the County of Devon: With Observations on the Means of its Improvement* (1794; 1970), p.48.
11. W. Marshall, *The Rural Economy of the West of England Including Devonshire and Parts of Somersetshire, Dorsetshire, and Cornwall, Together with the Minutes in Practice*, 2 vols (1796; repr. 1970), ii, pp.20-1.
12. C. Vancouver, *General View of the Agriculture of the County of Devon, With Observations on the Means of its Improvement: A Report of the Work Drawn up for the Consideration of the Board of Agriculture and Internal Improvement*, 1808; (1969), p.271.
13. S. Rowe, *A Perambulation of the Antient and Royal Forest of Dartmoor, and the Venville Precincts; or, A Topographical Survey of the Antiquities and Scenery; With Notices of the Natural History, Climate, and Agricultural Capabilities, and a Valuable Collection of Antient Documents* (1848), p.2.
14. In the 'Selected Minutes of Council, Appointing Committees', *TDA* 11 (1879), 27. The parishes are listed as: Ashburton, Belstone, Bovey Tracey, Bridestowe, Bridford, Buckfastleigh, Buckland-in-the-Moor, Buckland Monachorum, Chagford, Cornwood, Dean Prior, Drewsteignton, Gidleigh, Harford, Holne, Islington, Lamerton, Lustleigh, Lydford, Manaton, Mary Tavy, Meavy, Moretonhampstead, North Bovey, Okehampton, Peter Tavy, Sampford Spiney, Shaugh Prior, Sheepstor, Sourton, South Brent, South Tawton, Tavistock, Throwleigh, Ugborough, Walkhampton, Whithurch and Widecombe-in-the-Moor. Twenty-two of these parishes were, at that time, in Venville.
15. A.B. Prowse, 'An Index of References to Dartmoor and its Borders Contained in the Transactions, vols. I to XXX', *TDA* 37 (1905), p.482. Prowse added Hennock, Brent Tor and Plympton to the Devonshire Association's 1879 list.
16. R.H. Worth, 'Address of the President', *TDA* 62 (1930), p.52. The substance of the 'Address' is also to be found in *Worth's Dartmoor, Compiled from the Published Works of the late R. Hansford*

Worth, ed. by G.M. Spooner and F.S. Russell (1981), pp.3-46. The metamorphic aureole refers to the band of rocks surrounding the granite area. The boundary between granite and slate is particularly dramatic above High Down Ford – on the river Lyd.

17. S.A. Moore and P. Birkett, *A Short History: the Rights of Common Upon the Forest of Dartmoor and the Commons of Devon. Report of Mr Stuart A. Moore to the Committee, and Appendix of Documents* (1890), p.48. The map was said to be at the foot of an undated document titled 'Instructions for my Lorde Prynces to the Kyngs moost Honorable Counsell concyning my said Lord Prynces Forrest of Dartmore in the Countye of Devonshire and in the mores and wasts of the same belongyn'.

18. *Manwood's Treatise of the Forest Laws: Shewing Not Only the Laws Now in Force, but the Original Forests, What They Are, and How They Differ From Chase, Parks, and Warrens, With Such Things as are Incident to Either*, 4th edn, rev. by W. Nelson (1717).

19. Totnes and Barnstaple had never been afforested.

20. Blake, p.336.

21. D. St Leger-Gordon, *Devonshire* (1950), p.217.

22. 'Forest' properly refers to an area of land possessed by the monarch as a hunting ground. That same stretch of land in the possession of any other person is designated a Chase.

23. R.N. Worth, *The West Country Garland: Selected From the Writings of the Poets of Devon and Cornwall, From the Fifteenth Century to the Nineteenth Century, With Folk Songs and Traditional Verses* (1875) John Johns fictionalises Gaveston's final dilemma in 'Gaveston on Dartmoor', pp.122-7. The poem was first published in the 1820s. See chapter 7.

24. P. Birkett, 'A Short History of the Rights of Common Upon the Forest of Dartmoor and the Commons of Devonshire', a Paper read in Plymouth on 26 October 1885 and printed in The Dartmoor Preservation Association's *A Short History: The Rights of Common*, p.xvi.

25. W. Chapple, *A Review of Part of Risdon's Survey of Devon; Containing the General Description of That County; With Corrections, Annotations, and Additions* (1785), p.91.

26. Of course the area would revert to its status as a Forest if there were no Duke of Cornwall.

27. J.L.W. Page, 'The Names of the Dartmoor Tors', *Western Antiquary* (hereafter *WA*) 7 (1888), p.107.

28. F. Pollock, *A Short History of the Rights of Common Upon the Forest of Dartmoor and the Commons of Devon* (1890), p.41.

29. The Forest Men were automatically considered to be 'in venville'.

30. The parish boundaries of Tavistock, Meavy, Whitchurch and Sampford Spiney do not meet the Forest, *Worth's Dartmoor*, p.347.

31. For further information on parishes in and out of venville see E.G. Fogwill, 'Pastoralism on Dartmoor', *TDA* 86 (1954), pp.98-9.

32. There were originally three Stannary towns; Plympton was designated as such in 1328.

33. E. Clarendon, Earl of, *The History of the Rebellion & Civil Wars in England, Begun in the Year 1641*, 2nd edn, 3 vols (1704), ii, p.103.

34. W. Camden, *Camden's Britannia, Newly Translated into English, With Large Additions and Improvements*, trans. and ed. by Edmund Gibson (1695), p.35.

CHAPTER 2 – 'A SCYTHIA WITHIN ENGLAND', pp.14-28.

1. Risdon, p.225.

2. T. Westcote, *A View of Devonshire in MDCXXX: With a Pedigree of its Gentry*, ed. by G. Oliver and P. Jones (1845), p.355.

3. T.H. Williams, *Picturesque Excursions in Devon and Cornwall, 1, Devonshire* (hereafter *PE*) (1804) p.86.

4. W. Browne, 'Lydford Journey' (1643?).

5. *Devonshire Doomsday and Geld Inquest: Extensions, Translations, and Indices*, 2 vols (1884-92), i, pp.4-5.

6. Summary execution is remembered in various parts of Britain: as Jeddart Justice, Jedburgh Justice, Jedwood Justice, Halifax Law, Caspar Justice or Abingdon Law. According to J.H. Harris, *My Devonshire Book: 'In the Land of Junket and Cream'* (1907), p.137.

7. There are several versions of the poem. That quoted here is given by Samuel Rowe in *A Perambulation of the Antient and Royal Forest of Dartmoor and the Venville Precincts: or a Topographical Survey of the Antiquities and Scenery*, ed. by J. Brooking Rowe, 3rd edn (1895), pp.425-8.

8. Risdon, p.12.

9. Baring-Gould, *Dartmoor*, p.109.

10. Risdon, p.6.

11. Westcote, p.53.

12. Anno quartio Henrici Octavi, Cap. 8: 'An acte concernying Richard Strode', Rowe, pp.326-8.

13. *Ibid.*, p.326.

14. The act confirmed the right of every man to dig for tin in the county without let or hindrance. There are conflicting opinions as to whether Strode's bill did enshrine the right of parliamentary free speech. R.N. Worth believes it did: *A History of Devonshire* (1895), p.177. While H.P.R. Finberg is adamant that the bill referred solely to Richard Strode, in *Tavistock Abbey: A Study in the Social and Economic History of Devon* (1951), p.177.

15. Stannary courts were finally abolished in 1896.

16. Rowe, p.316.

17. The Mariner's Way follows the route sailors

might have taken after leaving a port on the Devon coast to walk across the county.

18. Chapple, p.22.
19. Leland, iii, p.49.
20. W. Camden, *Britannia: Siva Florentiss Imorum Regnorum Angliae, Scotiae, Hiberniae, et Insularum Adiacentium Exintima Antiquitate* (1586; 1594), p.135.
21. Gibson, p.201.
22. T. Read, *The English Traveller: Giving a Description of Those Parts of Great Britain Called England and Wales*, 2 vols (1746), i, p.303.
23. *Britannia; or, A Chorographical Description of the Flourishing Kingdoms of England, Scotland, Ireland, and the Islands Adjacent, From Earliest Antiquity*, by W. Camden, trans. and ed. by R. Gough, 3 vols, 1607; (1789), i, p.26. Gough writes, 'Bishop Gibson translates squallida, dirty, and seems to derive the name from the tract thence, whereas it is from the river Dert. Mr Camden would not have been guilty of such a pun', i, p.26.
24. *Ibid.*
25. Blake, p.345.
26. Westcote, p.429.
27. Westcote, p.89.
28. Risdon, p.6.
29. Risdon, p.222. The writer was referring to the words of a grant made to the holders of the ancient Tenements of Balbery and Pushill, in 1280, that they should be allowed to attend services at Widecombe rather than travel to their parish church at Lydford.
30. Risdon, p.222.
31. The 'centre' is reckoned to be an undistinguished spot to the north of Wistman's Wood, called Horse Hole.
32. A. Brice, *The Grand Gazetteer: or, Topographical Dictionary, Both General and Special and Ancient as Well as Modern* (1759-74), p.419.
33. Risdon, p.198; Westcote, p.386.
34. Childe was 'supposed to have lived during the reign of Edward III', J. Prince, *Danmonii Orientales Illustres or The Worthies of Devon* (1791), pp.143-4.
35. 'Monks or Friars' from Tavistock according to Prince, p.144.
36. Edwin (Eadwig or Edwy), 'a youth of amiable disposition was driven from England by Edric (Eadric), at the command of Canute. [...] He lay concealed after a clandestine return, and lies buried at Tavistock'. J.A. Giles, *William of Malmesbury's Chronicle of the Kings of England* (1911), p.196. William of Malmesbury also relates the story of Edulfus, or Ordulf, who had instructed that he should be buried at Horton in Dorset, but dying on Dartmoor was buried in Tavistock. William of Malmesbury, *The Deeds of the Bishops of England: Gesta Pontificum Anglorum*, trans. by D. Preest (2000), pp.135-6.

37. Risdon, p.223.
38. Prince, p.144.
39. Risdon, p.130.
40. See R. Polwhele, *A History of Devonshire*, hereafter *HD*, 3 vols (1797-1806), i, pp.10-13.
41. *A True Relation of Those Sad and Lamentable Accidents, Which Happened in and About the Parish Church of Withycombe in the Dartmoores in Devonshire on Sunday the 21st of October Last, 1638* (1638), repr. in *The Harleian Miscellany: or a Collection of Scarce, Curious, and Entertaining Pamphlets and Tracts as Well in Manuscript as in Print, Found in the Late Earl of Oxford's Library, Interspersed With Historical, Political, and Critical Notes*, 12 vols (1809), iv, 286-96. The Harleian tracts were reprinted in full in *Things New and Old' concerning the Parish of Widecombe-in-the-Moor and Its Neighbourhood*, ed. by R. Dymond (1876), pp.88-109.
42. The account of the storm was included in Prince's *Worthies*, pp.447-9; and in Polwhele's *HD*, i, p.10.
43. Risdon, p.218.
44. Risdon, p 225.
45. This is a reference to an area near Ross in Pembrokeshire, settled by Flemish immigrants in the reign of Henry I, 'called by the Britans Little England Beyond Wales', Gough, ii, p.514.
46. 'Scythia' is a loose term, referring to northern Europe and beyond; Scythians were generally regarded as uncivilised.
47. T. Fuller, *The History of the Worthies of England*, 2 vols, 1662; (1811), i, p.273.
48. Gibson, p.27.
49. T. Cox, *A Topographical, Ecclesiastical, and Natural History of Devon* (1700), p.466.
50. Verses from Browne's 'Lydford Journey' in Brice's *Grand Gazetteer*, pp.828-9.
51. Westcote, p.359.
52. Various versions of this extract are given by Camden's translators. A modern version of the extract can be found in J. De Hauvilla's *Architrenius*, trans. and ed. by W. Wetherbee (1994).
53. L.C. Martin, ed., *The Poems of Robert Herrick* (1956), p.29.
54. Prince, p.4. Prince goes on to say that the assumption was 'a gross calumny'.
55. Brice, p.419. Whether he is referring specifically to the small group of professional Moormen, or to the inhabitants of the ancient tenements in general, is not clear.
56. Brice, p.440.
57. Brice, p.440.

CHAPTER 3 – SURVEYORS AND ENTREPRENEURS, pp.**29-38.**
1. Westcote, p.378.

2. Fraser, p.56.
3. W. Crossing, A *Hundred Years on Dartmoor*, 5th edn (1902), pp. 32-3. According to Crossing, one wretch lived in the cage for some time, 'the country people supplying him with food', p.33.
4. Blake, p.336.
5. Chapple, p.14.
6. K.G., 'An Essay on English Roads', *Gentleman's Magazine* (hereafter *GM*), 22 (1752), pp.517-20 (518).
7. K.G., p.552.
8. PWDRO, 1/133.
9. B. Donn, *A Map of the County of Devon, 1765*, intro. by W.L.D. Ravenhill (1965).
10. Notices were placed in local papers.
11. This was not an original idea; plans for enclosure had been set out in 1666.
12. In 1796 the Duchy rescinded the privilege of ancient tenement holders to 'newtake'.
13. He represented Okehampton from 1796-1802, Portarlington 1802-06, and Plymouth 1806-12, when he was knighted and assumed the role of Gentleman Usher of the Black Rod.
14. A. Smith, *An Inquiry into the Nature and the Causes of the Wealth of Nations*, 2 vols (1776, 1909), i, p.261.
15. Fraser, p.49.
16. *Ibid.*, p.55.
17. *Ibid.*, p.57.
18. *Ibid.*, p.58.
19. *Ibid.*, p.59.
20. *Ibid.*, p.29.
21. J. Laskey, 'Three Days Excursion on Dartmoor', *GM* 66 (1796), 729-30 (p.729).
22. *GM*, 66, p.729.
23. *GM*, 66, p.730. When granted municipal status in 1824 Plymouth Dock was renamed Devonport.
24. *GM*, 66, p.729.
25. Wordsworth's comment appears in 'A Description of the Scenery of the Lakes in the North of England', his introduction to T. Wilkinson's *Select Views in Cumberland*, by T. Wilkinson (1810).
26. Letter to Richard Gray, 28 February 1795. PWDRO, 51/7/11/3.
27. *The Letters of Thomas Gray: Including the Correspondence of Gray and Mason*, ed. by D.C. Tovey, 2nd rev. edn, 2 vols (1909), i, p.45.
28. *Johnson's Journey to the Western Isles of Scotland, and Boswell's Journey of a Tour to the Hebrides with Samuel Johnson, LLD*, ed by R.W. Chapman (1965), p.37.
29. G. Lipscomb, *A Journey into Cornwall Through the Counties of Southampton, Wilts, Dorset, Somerset, and Devon: Interspersed with Remarks Moral, Historical, Literary, and Political* (1799), p.163.
30. Lipscomb, p.181.
31. *Travels in Georgian Devon: The Illustrated Journals of John Swete*, ed. by T. Gray, 4 vols (1997-2000), i, p.121.
32. John Swete was born John Tripe, but changed his name as a condition of his inheritance.
33. Williams, T.H., *Picturesque Excursions in Devon and Cornwall, 1 Devonshire* (1804), hereafter *PE*, p.52.
34. *PE*, p.54.
35. Fraser, p.55.
36. Vancouver, pp.468-9.
37. W. Marshall, *A Review; or Complete Abstract of the Reports to the Board of Agriculture*, 5 vols (1808-17), v, p.575.
38. Fraser, p.63.

CHAPTER 4 – TOURISM AND TASTE, pp.39-54.

1. D. Defoe, *A Tour Through the Whole Island of Great Britain*, ed. by P. Rogers (1988), p.43.
2. S. & N. Buck, *Antiquities, or Venerable Remains of Above Four Hundred Castles, Monasteries, Palaces etc. in England and Wales*, 5 vols (1726-52).
3. Gough, in his Preface to Camden's *Britannia*, i, p.vi.
4. E. Burke, *A Philosophical Enquiry into Our Ideas of the Sublime and Beautiful* (1756). The second edn published 1757 included *A Discourse on Taste*.
5. Tovey, i, p.38. The letter, dated 13 October 1739, was from Gray to his mother. Travellers such as Gray, on the Grand Tour, would find visual reminders reinforcing memories of their scenic encounters, when confronted with the intense, dramatic mountainous landscape paintings of Salvator Rosa and his followers.
6. *Johnson's Journey*, pp.35-6.
7. W. Gilpin, *Observations on the River Wye, and Several Parts of South Wales, etc: Relative Chiefly to Picturesque Beauty, Made in the Summer of 1782* (1991), pp.1-2.
8. W. Gilpin, *Three Essays on Picturesque Beauty; on Picturesque Travel; and on Sketching Landscape: to Which is Added a Poem, on Landscape Painting*, 2nd edn (1794), p.42. Having made this pronouncement Gilpin warns, at length, against being too prescriptive.
9. Gilpin, *Three Essays*, p.iii.
10. *Three Essays*, p.ii.
11. Chapple, p.14.
12. *The European Magazine and London Review*, 7 (1785).
13. *Ibid.*, 'Lidford Waterfall: Illustrated by an Engraving', p.288.
14. *Ibid.*, 'The Bridge Over Lidford River: with a View of it', p.381.
15. *Ibid.*, p.381.
16. Swete's *Travels*, i, p.117.
17. *Ibid.*, i, p.116.
18. W. Gilpin, *Observations on the Western Parts of England: Relative Chiefly to Picturesque Beauty, to Which Are Added, a Few Remarks on the Picturesque Beauties of the Isle of Wight*, 2nd edn (1808), p.180.

19. *Ibid.*, p.185. This is Kitt's Steps, now in private property.
20. *Ibid.*, p.186.
21. *PE*, pp.97-8.
22. *Ibid.*, p.ix.
23. *Ibid.*, p.80.
24. *Ibid.*, pp.94-5.
25. J. Farington, *The Farington Diary*, 8 vols (1926), vi, p.168.
26. Marshall, *Rural Economy*, ii, p.44.
27. W.G. Maton, *Observations Relative Chiefly to the Natural History, Picturesque Scenery, and Antiquities of the Western Counties of England Made in the Years 1794, and 1796* (1797), p.306.
28. Picture at the National Trust's Stourhead property.
29. H.R. Hicks, 'William Payne: Painter in Oils and Water Colours', *TDA*, 75 (1943), p.137.
30. N. Howard, *Bickleigh Vale, With Other Poems* (1804), preface, n/p.
31. Swete's words, quoted in *PE*, p.99.
32. *HD*, i, p.24.
33. Maton, pp.300-01.
34. Antiquarius Secundus, 'Letter from Plymouth', *GM* 62 (1792), p.891.
35. *PE*, p.76.
36. Quoted in G. Pycroft, 'Art in Devonshire', *TDA* 13 (1881), p.235.
37. Line number/s follow quotations in the text.
38. Apparently topographically convincing, in reality the poem compounds the indeterminacy of place so typical of the moor. At the confluence of the Mew and the Plym, above Bickleigh, Howard referred to the left hand branch, the Mew or Meavy, as the Plym. The misnaming would be accepted as fact by at least two writers of guidebooks. H. Carrington, in *The Plymouth and Devonport Guide: With Sketches of the Surrounding Scenery* (1828), commented that 'the united waters of the Mew and Cad form the Plym. The Mew is sometimes improperly termed the Plym', p.222. Controversy occasionally erupted in local journals.
39. A dark hand-mirror used to concentrate features of landscape.

CHAPTER 5 – A RELICT LANDSCAPE, pp.55-68.
1. J. Laskey, 'Excursion on Dartmoor, July 21, 22, 23, and 24', *GM* 65 (1795), pp.910-11; 1008-09; 1080-82; and 'Three Days Excursion on Dartmoor', *GM* 66 (17960, pp.34-6; 194-6; 275-6; 393-4; 545-7, 729-30.
2. *GM* 65, p.910. Laskey reveals no personal details except that he was living at Blackawton, some miles to the south of the moor, and that one of his party was a servant.
3. *GM*, 65, p.910.
4. *Ibid.*
5. *Ibid.*
6. *GM* 66, p.393.

7. Laskey, *GM* 66, p.34.
8. *Ibid.*
9. Brice, T., in *The History and Description Ancient and Modern of the City of Exeter* (1802), writes that it was 'a vigorous fantasy' to see tables and chairs 'in this rude assemblage', p. 179.
10. *GM* 66, p.394.
11. DRO, 51/7/7/1-16, John Andrews' papers.
12. W. Chapple, *Description and Exegesis of the Drew's Teignton Cromlech: With Some Previous Particulars Relative to that Parish, and the Farm Whereon the Cromlech Stands*, n.p.1779?
13. *Ibid.*, p.1.
14. *Ibid.*, p.30. Using Donn's map, Chapple says, with reference to the cromlech, that its position was of significance only 'if the present county limits obtained'; p.30.
15. *Ibid.*, p.33.
16. Warner, p.172.
17. *Exegesis*, p.138.
18. *Ibid.*, p.149.
19. R. Polwhele, *Traditions and Recollections; Domestic, Clerical and Literary: in Which Are Included Letters of Charles II, Cromwell, Fairfax, Edgecumbe, Macaulay, Wolcot, Opie, Whitaker, Gibbon, Buller, Courtenay, Moore, Downman, Drewe, Seward, Darwin, Cowper, Hayley, Hardinge, Sir Walter Scott, and other Distinguished Characters*, 2 vols (1826), i, p.148.
20. 'Mr. Polwhele's Circular Letter to His Subscribers', *GM* 59 (1789), p.411.
21. Polwhele accused Sir John Pole, a local antiquarian, of reneging on a promise of assistance with the work, and said of John Swete, formerly his friend, 'I scarcely imagined that Mr S. professing that to facilitate my researches was his principal object, was secretly laying in materials for a little essay', *HD*, i, Postscript, p.2. Further references to this edn are given after quotations in the text. Apart from brief geological and geographical observations, most of Polwhele's comments on the Dartmoor relics derive from his earlier *Historical Views of Devonshire in Five Volumes* (1793), of which only one volume was published.
22. W. Browne, *The Works of William Browne: Containing Britannia's Pastorals With Notes and Observations by the Rev. W. Thompson. The Shepherd's Pipes, Consisting of Pastorals. The Inner Temple Masques Never Published Before; and Other Poems With the Life of the Author*, ed. by W. Thompson (1772).
23. *HD*, i, pp.40-6.
24. A belief that is quoted in several early writings.
25. *HD*, i, p.146.
26. *Ibid.*, p.151.
27. *Ibid.*, p.148.
28. *Ibid.* Other monuments Polwhele identifies are the single Stone-Pillar; two, three, or more Stone-

Pillars; Circular Stone-Pillars; and Inscribed Stone-Pillars.

29. *HD*, i, pp.149-50.
30. *Ibid.*, pp. 53-4.
31. J. Swete, 'On Some of the More Remarkable British Monuments in Devon', *Essays by a Society of Gentlemen of Exeter* (1796), p.106.
32. 'Preface', *Topographer*, i (1789), p.ii.
33. Gough, i, p.ix.

Chapter 6 – A Great Work, pp.69-80.

1. Risdon, p.407.
2. *PE*, pp.52-3.
3. *PE* p.97.
4. Basil Thomson, *The Story of Dartmoor Prison* (1907), p.86.
5. Risdon, p.410.
6. In 1813, during the 1812-14 war with The United States, the French were joined by 700 American captives. According to B. Thomson in *The Story of Dartmoor Prison* (1907), p.121, 24 Americans had been incarcerated there since 1810, having been 'taken under the French flag'.
7. 'Spare the humbled'.
8. D. and S. Lysons, *Magna Britannia: Being a Concise Topographical Account of the Several Counties of Great Britain*, 6 vols (1822), vi, p.315.
9. Alternatively, the name might have developed from the settlement's proximity to the Prince Hall estate. The place was, also, sometimes called Princes Town.
10. Between 1801 and 1831 the figures for the forest were included with those of Lydford village or Widecombe, and were extracted through estimation. Vancouver used the 1801 census, but seems to have omitted the Forest figures, in spite of a note that the numbers had been included with Lydford, p.423.
11. *Independent Whig*, 28 July 1811, qtd by Thomson, pp.80-1.
12. Regulations Article VII, Thomson, pp.21-6.
13. J.P. Jones, *Observations on the Scenery and Antiquities in the Neighbourhood of Moreton-Hampstead, and on the Forest of Dartmoor, Devon* (1823), p.47 (hereafter Moreton). Certain of Jones's notes had appeared some years earlier, in *The Devon Freeholder*.
14. *Moreton*, p.48.
15. *Examiner*, 28 July 1811, qtd by Thomson, p.80.
16. Thomson, pp.45-58.
17. 'Dartmoor: A Prize Poem', in *The Works of Mrs Hemans With a Memoir of her Life by her Sister*, 7 vols (1839), iv, pp.204-18.
18. N.T. Carrington, *Dartmoor: A Descriptive Poem* (1826).
19. R. Evans, *Home Scenes: Tavistock and its Vicinity* (1846), pp.141-2.
20. *Home Scenes*, p.143.
21. At present – 2006 – the church is closed.

22. For an account of prison life see C. Andrews, *The Prisoner's Memoirs etc; or, Dartmoor Prison, Containing a Complete and Impartial History of the Entire Captivity of the American in England* (1815).
23. *Moreton*, p.61.
24. Tyrwhitt was, of necessity, often absent from Tor Royal. His return in April 1818 was welcomed, as raising hopes that 'the plan so long talked of, for converting the great war prison thereon into a depot for Convicts, was to be carried into execution immediately', *Western Luminary*, 28 April 1818, p.2.
25. *Moreton*, p.59.
26. *Ibid.*, pp.59-60.
27. During its first year 21,000 tons of extracted materials and sundries was carried off the moor and around 10,000 tons of limestone brought up from Plymouth, quarried from the limestone ridge that extends some six miles along the town's coastline.
28. Except for removal of a small quantity of stone for his own house at Stover, the quarry had not been exploited.
29. *Substance of a Statement Made to the Chamber of Commerce, Plymouth, on Tuesday 3rd Day of November, 1818 Concerning the Formation of a Railroad From the Forest of Dartmoor to the Plymouth Lime-Quarries: With Additional Observations and a Plan of the Intended Line* (1819), p.4.
30. *Statement*, p.22.
31. The prospectus issued 24 March 1819 stated 'there are no buildings to be demolished, [...] no machinery is requisite in any part of the line, nor are any bridges necessary'. *In Parliament: Plymouth and Dartmoor Railroad Prospectus* (1819).
32. As money had run out, the line terminated at the quarries. A new company was formed and another mortgage was arranged to enable the line's completion.
33. 'Sheepstor' refers to the village, 'Sheeps Tor' to the rocky outcrop above the village.
34. *The Diocese of Exeter in 1821: Bishop Carey's Replies to Queries before Visitation, vol 2. Devon*, ed. by Michael Cooke, Devon and Cornwall Record Society New Series 4 (1960), p.19.
35. The quarry was sometimes referred to as Royal Oak.
36. *Flying Post* (hereafter *FP*), 7 March 1833, p.2.
37. *TDA* 18, 1886, p.477.
38. *HD*, i, p.24.
39. *Ibid.*
40. T. Brice, *The History and Description Ancient and Modern of the City of Exeter* (1802), 'Since the account and origin of the Dart given in page 119 was printed, we have received the very particular description now presented to the public. It is taken from memoranda, lately made in an actual survey, and may serve to correct the inaccuracies and supply the defects, which are very considerable in this part of Donn's large map of Devon', p.177.

41. Mrs Bray, *A Description of the Part of Devonshire Bordering on the Tamar and the Tavy: its Natural History, Manners, Customs, Superstitions, Scenery, Antiquities, Biography of Eminent Persons, Etc, Etc, in a Series of Letters to Robert Southey*, 3 vols (1836), i, pp.260-3 (hereafter *Borders*). From youth, Edward Atkyns Bray (1778-1857) had kept journals, intending to write a history of Tavistock. When his wife began her epistolary local history he gave her access to the journals. Mrs Bray includes extensive extracts from the journals in her topographical work.

42. J. Spry, 'Benjamin Gayer: An Okehampton Legend', *WA*, 3 (1884), p.190.

43. *Moreton*, p.54. Jones, sometimes known as Bovey Jones, was a man of varied interests, an expert on the botany of the moor, who had spent his early years in Chudleigh, within sight of the hills, before holding the curacy of a moorland village, North Bovey, between 1816 and 1831.

44. J.P. Jones, *Moreton*, already mentioned, and *Guide to the Scenery in the Neighbourhood of Ashburton, Devon* (1823). Further references will follow quotations in the text.

45. N.T. Carrington, *Dartmoor: A Descriptive Poem* (1826), p.21.

46. S. Dixon and J. Johns, both Dartmoor poets refer in their titles to Castaly, the fountain on Mount Parnassus whose waters inspired those who drank there with the gift of poetry; S. Dixon, *Castalian Hours* (1829); John Johns, *The Dews of Castalie: Poems on Various Subjects* (1828).

CHAPTER 7 – 'WILD SCENES AND ABUNDANT CURIOSITIES', pp.81-98.

1. Hemans had recently received an award from a literary panel in Scotland for a composition relating to Wallace and Bruce's meeting at the Carron.

2. Hemans, i, p.41.

3. Cottle had at various times included Coleridge, Southey, and Wordsworth on his lists. He had forged friendships with both Robert Southey and Samuel Coleridge, sharing their enthusiasm for 'pantisocratic' ideals.

4. J. Cottle, *Dartmoor and Other Poems* (1823), pp.1-33.

5. Cottle, line 2.

6. Cottle, line 178.

7. Carrington's *Dartmoor*. Where appropriate, references to this work follow quotations in the text.

8. N. Carrington, *The Collected Poems of the Late Nicholas Carrington*, ed. by H. E. Carrington, 2 vols (1834), i, pp.15-16.

9. Burt's introduction and notes comprise the larger part of the 1826 first edition. There is no acknowledgement of Burt's contribution on the title page.

10. Letter to the Editor of the *British Review*, March 1826, PWDRO, 522/1.

11. A.E. Polkinghorne, 'A Poet's Pride in Devon', *Western Morning News* (hereafter *WMN*), 2 September 1930, p.6.

12. Quoted by R.N. Worth in *A History of Plymouth from the Earliest Period to the Present Day* (1871), p.322.

13. *Oriental Herald*, 1826?, n.page.

14. *Monthly Magazine*, 1826?, n.page.

15. Yet, the poet was sadly in need of some financial support, for in spite of a deterioration in his health – he had developed 'consumption' – he was compelled to struggle on with his teaching duties, surviving just three months after relinquishing his teaching post, in 1830. He suffered the same eclipse as most local writers, since Plymouth Dock, where Carrington lived and worked, had no literary tradition; it was a relatively new town, a working-class development, existing and expanding in order to serve the armed forces bases.

16. Tenatus, 'The Author of "Dartmoor"', *South Devon Monthly Magazine* (hereafter *SDMM*) 2, 1833, p.140.

17. This recalls the similarity between his vision and Robert Fraser's, made 30 years earlier. And, of course, with the future as described by Cottle and Hemans.

18. Cottle, line 537.

19. Hemans, xviii, 10.

20. Census returns indicate that the population of several moorland villages rose and fell in response to the amount of local mining activity.

21. S. Dixon, *A Journal of Ten Days Excursion*. No publishing details. *A Journal of Eighteen Days Excursion on the Eastern and Southern Borders of Dartmoor* (1830). The second expedition began with four days' exploration from Chagford, the party then moving off the moor for north Devon.

22. *Castalian Hours*.

23. *Ten Days*, p.26.

24. *Ibid.*, p.26.

25. *Eighteen Days*, p.6.

26. *Ten Days*, p.27.

27. *Eighteen Days*, p.13.

28. Henry Woollcombe's Diaries, 3 September 1827, PWDRO, 710/397, mf 46-50. This more spectacular waterfall in the vicinity of Lustleigh had been off the route that topographers had traditionally followed – from Tavistock to Lydford – when they (usually with relief) left the vicinity of the moor at Okehampton. Lydford had, in effect, been visited by default, not because it represented the most beautiful scenery Dartmoor had to offer.

29. *Ten Days*, pp.17-20.

30. *Ibid.*, p.31.

31. *Ibid.*, p.32.
32. *Eighteen Days*, p.12.
33. *Moreton*, n/p.
34. A. Devonian, *Devonshire Scenery: or, Directions for Visiting the Most Picturesque Spots in the Eastern and Southern Coast, from Sidmouth to Plymouth* (1826), p.62.
35. Devonian, p.64.
36. George Pycroft, 'Art in Devonshire', *TDA* 14 (882), p.309.
37. Swete, iv, p.92.
38. J. Britton and E. W. Brayley, *Beauties of England and Wales: or Delineations Topographical, Historical, and Descriptions of Each County* (1803), iv, p.6. The extract was quoted as defining Dartmoor in W. White's *White's Devon: History Gazetteer and Directory of Devonshire* (1850; 1968).
39. *PE*, p.97.
40. *Ibid.*, p.47.
41. T.H. Williams, *A Guide to the Picturesque Scenery and Antiquities of Devonshire* 3rd edn (1830), pp.103-04.
42. Carrington, *Guide*, pp.202, 205, 258.
43. *Moreton*, pp.37-8.
44. C. Brooks, *The Gothic Revival* (1999), p.122.
45. S. Stokes, *The Lay of the Desert: A Poem in Two Cantos* (1830). Stokes said he had come across Carrington's 'Dartmoor' when his own composition was almost complete, and he had not read Hemans's verses, pp.iii-iv. He claimed his poem 'The Lay of the Desert' was 'not only designed, but in part executed on Dartmoor', and that he felt no anxiety that the work would be compared with that of either Carrington or Hemans.
46. *Ten Days*, p.29.
47. *Eighteen Days*, p.12.
48. Stories of a gambler's suicide and of a sick man drowning were included in Polwhele's *History*, both tales becoming standard items in local guidebooks.
49. There are various spellings; the ordnance survey map favours 'Crazy Well'.
50. *Westcountry Garland*, pp.122-7. The poem was first published in 1828.
51. Allegedly at one time the water rose and fell with the tide.
52. Called by Mrs Bray the 'Cowsick', *Borders*, i, p.70.
53. Edward Atkyns Bray was born at Bair-down, now known as Beardown. His father had leased the land, built a house, developed plantations and raised cattle.
54. *Borders*, i, p.74.
55. *Ibid.*, p.74.
56. *Ibid.*, p.77.
57. He includes in his journal the Bardic alphabet 'as it is given by the Rev. Edward Davies in his *Celtic Remains*', *Borders*, i, p.70. See also H. French, 'Sermons in Stones', *Dartmoor Magazine*, 20 (1990), pp.20-1.
58. Mona was an islet between mainland Britain and Ireland, reputedly inhabited by Druids. Some authorities think it was the Isle of Man, while others claim it was what is now Anglesey.
59. So Mrs Bray reports, *Borders*, i, p.70. However, even in the 21st century, it is possible to a find a number of the inscribed rocks.
60. Warner, pp.171-2.
61. *Ten Days*, p.19.
62. *Ibid.*, p.20.
63. *Borders*, vol. i, p.279.
64. *Ibid.*, p.282.
65. *Ibid.*, p.285.
66. *Ibid.*, pp.287-8.
67. *Ibid.*
68. Samuel Rowe, 'Antiquarian Investigations in the Forest of Dartmoor', *Transactions of the Plymouth Institution* (hereafter *TPI*), 1 (1828), pp.179-212.
69. *Ibid.*, p.180.
70. *Ibid.*, p.180.
71. Carrington, *Collected Poems*, i, p.267.

CHAPTER 8 – ENCROACHMENTS, pp.99-112.

1. 'Dartmoor', *Western Miscellany: A Journal of Literature, Science, Antiquities, and Art for the West of England 1849*, 1850, p.21.
2. Proh Pudor, 'Dartmoor', *FP*, 30 August 1849, p.7.
3. Small deposits of manganese, blende, and silver lead were also mined.
4. DRO, Courtney. 1508. M. Devon. 88. Mining 19.
5. In a letter from Samuel Rowe, 13 June 1836, Henry Woollconbe's papers, PWDRO, 710/608.
6. The word 'Carrington', with the date of his birth and of his death, is still to be found inscribed on the summit of the Dewerstone, a rocky outcrop above the confluence of the River Meavy and the River Plym.
7. H. Woollcombe, *To the Presidents, Officers and Members of the Several Literary and Philosophical Societies Established in the Counties of Cornwall and Devon* (1835).
8. *Address*, p.19.
9. *Address*, p.21.
10. *Western Counties*, p.160.
11. *Ibid.*, p.173.
12. *Ibid.*, pp.162-3. There is a hint, in this tale, reminiscent of Milton's lament in 'Lycidas' – see *The Oxford Book of English Verse: 1250-1918*, ed. by Arthur Quiller-Couch (1939), pp.345-51:
Who would not sing for Lycidas? [...]
He must not flote upon his water bear
Unwept and welter to the parching wind,
Without the meed of som melodious tear.

'Lycidas', 10, 12–14

13. It seems that a rung of the ladder on which he was standing collapsed.

14. Mrs Anna Eliza, *Autobiography of Anna Eliza Bray, 1789-1883*, ed. by John A. Kempe (1884), p.207.

15. *Autobiography*, pp.208-10.

16. 'On the 28th of August, 1828, I began in good earnest the composition of *Fitz of Fitzford* [...] and finished it by the 11th of October of the same year', *Ibid.*, p.207.

17. Mrs Bray, *Fitz of Fitzford: A Legend of Devon* (1830). In this section references to the novel will follow each quotation in the text.

18. *Autobiography*, p.208.

19. Prince, p.566.

20. *Borders*, ii, p.319.

21. 'Fitz of Fitzford', *Philo-Danmonian: A Western Magazine of Matters Chiefly Original*, 1 (1830), p.294.

22. *Autobiography*, p.211.

23. 'The Virtuous Lady Mine', *SDMM*, 2 (1833), pp.44-6.

24. Fuller, i, p.273.

25. *Autobiography*, pp.226-8. Letter from R. S. dated 26 February 1831.

26. This was *Borders*. Further references in this section will follow quotations in the text.

27. *FP*, 12 August 1883, p.5.

28. Detritus. A few years later it became profitable to sift over some of the spoil heaps.

29. This painting is held at Norwich Castle Museum and Art Gallery.

30. *Ten Days*, p.4, and in Jones' Accounts of Devon Villages, Bodleian Library, MS. Top. Devon e. 1-6.

31. J. Phillips, 'Arts and Crafts on Dartmoor in the Year when Queen Victoria was Crowned. Being Notes on the Narrative of Mrs Elizabeth Bidder, Daughter of William and Johanna Lillicrap, of the Parish of Sheepstor', *TDA*, 25 (1894), pp.535-40.

32. *Ibid.*, p.535. 'Bettermore' seems to be part of the careful gradation within the working class.

33. *Ibid.*, p.536.

34. 'I believe in no part of England has the march of intellect marched at a slower pace than on the moor', *Borders*, i, p.337. Bray concluded her comment by referring to the moorlanders as 'hardy as the aboriginal inhabitants of the soil'.

35. William, 'Chronicles of Dartmoor', *Exeter and Plymouth Gazette* (hereafter *EPG*), 24 December 1836, p.2. Four letters were published at weekly intervals. No other details of the writer's identity are known.

36. *EPG*, 7 January 1837, p.2.

37. Named in the letters as Jan Bellamy. Ale-house records show that a John Bellamy was innkeeper in 1811.

38. *EPG*, 31 December 1836, p.2.

39. Come to call muck 'dirt'.

CHAPTER 9 – 'PARCERE SUBJECTIS' AGAIN, pp.113-28.

1. 'Dartmoor Prisons', *FP*, 12 September 1850, p.5.

2. *A Handbook for Travellers in Devon and Cornwall*, 5th edn (1863), p.117.

3. Tickler, Elias Tozer (1825-73), was the proprietor of *Chambers Exeter Journal* and editor of the *Devon Weekly Times* (hereafter *DWT*), and the *Evening Gazette*. His reports of 'outings' appeared fortnightly at intervals in the *DWT* during the 1860s. A selection of pieces was revised and published in book form in 1869: Tickler (E. Tozer), *Devonshire Sketches: Dartmoor and its Borders* (1869), p.29. Further references to this edition are given after quotations in the text.

4. The prize was originally open only to members of the Devonport Mechanics Institute, but was extended. Candidates were instructed to consider five sections: products; means of employment within a 20-mile circuit; road and rail links needed; buildings for workers; individual enterprises that would result in colonisation.

5. H. Tanner, *The Cultivation of Dartmoor: A Prize Essay* (1854), pp.13-14.

6. Mrs Marsh, *Chronicles of Dartmoor* (1866). Anna Caldwell-Marsh, born in Newcastle-under-Lyme, succeeded to an estate in Staffordshire where she raised seven children. She published much of her work anonymously, though not *Chronicles*. Further references to this novel are given after quotations in the text.

7. S. Smiles, *Lives of the Engineers*, 5 vols (1874), v, pp.43-4.

8. Ten years later steam reached Tavistock, and by the 1870s Okehampton was linked to the national rail network.

9. C. Torr, *Small Talk at Wreyland* (1918), p.65.

10. 'The Moreton and South Devon Railway', *DWT*, 1 June 1866, p.7.

11. 'The Moreton Railway', *DWT*, 8 June 1866, p.6.

12. A recent invention, advertised in the local papers for £8.

13. Marsh names the place where the ducking will take place as 'Cranbourne Pool', vol. 3, p.216, acknowledging her debt to the description of Cranmere Pool in Moore's *History of Devonshire* (1829).

14. Quoted by Hugh Breton in *The Heart of Dartmoor* (1926), p.71.

15. 'Nooks and Corners', *FP*, 29 August 1850, p.7.

16. C. Kingsley, *Westward Ho!* (1855; 1961). Further references to this edition will follow quotations in the text.

17. *Charles Kingsley: His Letters and Memories of his Life*, ed. by his wife (1908), p.161.

18. This is the same image as Bray uses in *Warleigh*.

19. Meaning a 'hedge-priest'.

20. *Charles Kingsley: His letters and Memories of his Life*,

ed. by his wife (1908), p.18.

21. *Ibid.*, p.85.

22. *Ibid.*

23. *Handbook*, p.111.

24. W. Crossing, 'The Artist', *WMN*, 18 November 1903, p.5.

25. Colonel Hamilton Smith's notebooks were destroyed during the Second World War.

26. R.N. Worth, *A History of Plymouth: from the Earliest Period to the Present Time* (1877), p.341.

27. *Western Times* (hereafter *WT*), 16 April 1853, p.5.

28. Pycroft, *TDA*, 14 (1882), p.315.

29. Crossing, 'The Artist', *WMN*, 18 November 1903, p.5.

30. In 1897, the Forest dwellers commemorated Queen Victoria's Diamond Jubilee by a cross, erected near *The Forest Inn* at Hexworthy.

31. Ó. Véos, 'Dartmoor', *FP*, 17 October 1850, p.6.

32. J. Poulain, *Les Deux Soeurs* trans. by J.E.R.W as *The Two Sisters: A Dartmoor Story* (1891?). Further references to this novel are given after quotations in the text.

33. E.W.L. Davies, *Dartmoor Days or Scenes in the Forest, A Poem* (1862). Further references to this poem are given after quotations in the text.

34. Just above the Dart at Dartmeet. House party members were verifiable persons.

35. 'Ah! Postumus, Postumus, fast fly the years', *The Complete Works of Horace: Translated by Various Hands*, ed. by Dr John Marshall, 1911; (1927), book 2, xiv, l.

36. G. Hamlyn, *Rustic Poems by George Hamlyn, the Dartmoor Bloomfield* (1869?)

37. Robert Bloomfield (1766-1823) was the author of the popular song 'The Farmer's Boy'.

38. James Perrott of Chagford was a well known and respected moorland guide who kept a stable of horses for hire.

39. *Handbook*, p.80.

CHAPTER 10 – MILITARY MANOEUVRES, pp.129-38.

1. W.F. Collier, 'Dartmoor', *TDA*, 8 (1876), p.370.

2. *Ibid.*, p.375.

3. Details of the work of the Society are documented by G.A.S. Lefevre, Baron Eversley, in *English Commons and Forests: The Story of the Battle During the Last Thirty Years for the Public Rights over the Commons and Forests of England and Wales* (1894). The society's aim was 'to secure for the use and enjoyment of the public open spaces situate in the neighbourhood of towns and especially London', p.360.

4. In what would become a cause célèbre, the Commons Preservation Society lent its support to an Epping forester, Willingale, who continued to protest his rights of common after being jailed for defying an order prohibiting the gathering of kindling from within the forest bounds. The Commons Preservation Society began an examination of those rights that resulted by July 1874 in an order to remove all fences erected since 1851 in the Epping Forests.

5. W. F. Collier, 'First Report of Committee on Dartmoor', *TDA*, 9 (1877), p.120.

6. 21 October 1794, as John Andrews notes.

7. 'Dartmoor Manoeuvres: With the Enemy', *Western Daily Mercury* (hereafter *WDM*), 13 August 1873, p.3.

8. 'The Autumn Manoeuvres: With the First Division', *WDM*, 31 July 1873, p.5.

9. 'The Autumn Campaign on Dartmoor', *Illustrated London News* (hereafter *ILN*), 9 August 1873, pp.123-5.

10. 'The Autumn Manoeuvres: With the First Division', *WDM*, 31 July 1873, p.5.

11. *ILN*, 9 August, p.123.

12. 'Dartmoor Manoeuvres: With the Enemy', *WDM*, 13 August, p.3.

13. 'Ingzdon', *WT*, 22 August 1873, p.6.

14. 'Dartmoor Manoeuvres: With the First Division', *WDM*, 20 August, p.4.

15. R. Evans in her *Home Scenes*, p.146, uses this now so familiar phrase.

16. R.J. King, 'The Forest of the Dartmoors', in *The West Country Garland*, pp.234-6.

17. F. Adye, *Queen of the Moor*, 3 vols (1883?). Further references to this work are given after quotations in the text.

18. E. Lyall, *Donovan: A Modern Englishman* (1882) 10th edn (1888).

19. R.D. Blackmore, *Christowell: A Dartmoor Tale* (1880). Further references to *Christowell* are included after quotations in the text. The novel was serialised in *Good Words* during 1881.

20. M.S. Gibbons, *'We Donkeys' on Dartmoor* (1886) p.25.

21. W.H. Dunn, *R.D. Blackmore* (1956) in a letter to F. Armstrong, quoted by Dunn, p.225.

22. The Newton Abbot–Moretonhampstead branch, previously mentioned, that opened in July 1866.

23. There are similarities with Carver Doone's fate in chapter 74 of *Lorna Doone* (1869): 'the black bog had him by the feet; the sucking of the ground drew upon him'.

CHAPTER 11 – MOVES TOWARDS PRESERVATION, pp.139-52.

1. E.F. Tanner, 'Dartmoor Encroachments', *WA*, 2 (1883), p.78.

2. It had been estimated that about 15,000 acres of the Forest were enclosed during the 19th century.

3. Birkett, p. xxix.

4. W. Crossing, 'Tales of the Dartmoor Pixies', *WA* 7 (1888), p.173.
5. Crossing, 'The Moorland Haunts of the Pixies', *WA*, 5 (1886), p.11.
6. Page, *WA*, 7, p.107.
7. Carrington's *Dartmoor*, xxxviii, pp.48-9.
8. R. Burnard, *Dartmoor Pictorial Records*, 4 vols (1890-94), iv, p.53.
9. W. Crossing, *Gems in a Granite Setting: Beauties of the Lone Land of Dartmoor* 1905; (1986), p.164.
10. S. Baring-Gould (hereafter SBG), *Dartmoor*, p.74.
11. *Ibid.*, p.76. Baring-Gould's interpretation of folk songs was, by his own admission, 'creative'. Baring-Gould and antiquarian Robert Burnard were friends; one of Baring-Gould's daughters married Robert Burnard's son. Both SBG and Burnard were friends with William Crossing.
12. *A Book of Dartmoor*, p.xi.
13. Anecdotal information is to be found in SBG's *Early Reminiscences: 1834–64* (1903) and *Further Reminiscences: 1864-94* (1925).
14. Baring-Gould, S., *John Herring* (1883; 1898). References to this novel are given after quotations in the text.
15. SBG refers to 'salting' in *A Book of Devon* (1909), pp.222-3.
16. SBG's remarks after his reference to Fuller and Browne's description of the Gubbins: 'It cannot be said that the race is altogether extinct. The magistrates have had much trouble with certain persons living in hovels on the outskirts of the moor who subsist in the same manner', *A Book of Dartmoor*, p.136. This concurs with Harris's observation, mentioned above.
17. *Urith: A Tale of Dartmoor*, 3 vols (1891). Further references to this edition are given after quotations in the text. *Urith* followed the publication of the folk songs, the novel having been preceded by other works located just beyond the periphery of the area. *Red Spider* (1887) was intended to preserve memories of village life, *Margery of Quether and Other Stories* (1891) is concerned with isolated, brooding rural characters enchained by superstition, one tale based on witch burning in the neighbourhood of Brent Tor. *Kitty Alone* (1895) moves occasionally from Devon's south coast to the vicinity of Dartmeet, and *Eve* (1898) makes reference to the legend of the Whist Hounds and introduces an escaped convict. From the author's regional fictions only those in which aspects of Dartmoor life are central themes have been selected for comment.
18. SBG, *Guavas the Tinner* (1897). Further references to this edn are given after quotations in the text.
19. R. Burnard, 'Dartmoor Preservation', *WA*, 9 (1890), p.vi.
20. Fuller states that Derbyshire miners were subject to a similar form of this punishment: 'He that

stealeth Oar twice is fined; and the third time struck through his hand with a Knife unto the haft into the Stone, and is there to stand until death , or loose himself by cutting off his hand', *Worthies*, i, p.251.
21. The bargemaster or bailiff of the Stannaries was a Duchy appointee, in charge of the mining operations and of ascertaining that the monarch received his portion of tin and gold.
22. From its topographical description and in relation to other places described, this would seem to be Swincombe.
23. A number of these aspects of the moor are discussed in *A Book of Dartmoor*, pp.243-7.
24. SBG adds a footnote in *Urith*, i, p.120, referring readers to his and H. Fleetwood Sheppard's *Songs of the West: Traditional Songs and Ballads of the West of England* (1889). 'The Lady's Coach' is also included in a manuscript donated by Baring-Gould to Plymouth Library: MS, 'Songs of the West: Devon and Cornwall as Taken Down, Words and Melodies, From the Mouths of the People', 2 vols (1892), vol. i, p.xxx.
25. The author relates this anecdote in several publications.
26. *Further Reminiscences*, pp.184-5.
27. SBG, 'Folk Songs and Melodies of the West', *WA*, 8 (1889), p.105.
28. SBG, 'Ballads in the West', *WA* 8 (1889), p.x.
29. SBG, *Old Country Life* (1890), p.260.
30. SBG donated his original torn and water-stained collection of songs, together with the fair copy, referred to earlier, to the Plymouth Public Library.
31. 'Widecombe Fair' MSS i, 16, is the best-known Dartmoor song, telling the story of a group·of men who borrowed a horse to visit the Fair. The grey mare died, and was said to haunt the vicinity on cold, windy nights.
32. *Red Spider*, preface, p.6.
33. SBG, *A Book of the West: Being an Introduction to Devon and Cornwall, Devon*, 2 vols (1899), i, p.12.
34. B. Le Messurier, *Dartmoor Artists* (2002), p.51.
35. S. Rowe, *A Perambulation of the Antient and Royal Forest of Dartmoor and the Venville Precincts*, 3rd edn, rev. by J. Brooking Rowe (1985), p.219.
36. *Ibid.*, p.211.

Chapter 12 – The Hound of the Baskervilles, pp.153-60.

1. *The Hound of the Baskervilles* appeared in *Strand Magazine*, 22 (1901), and 23 (1902), concluding in April 1902. The edition used here is based on the first English edition of the novel, published in March 1902. A.C. Doyle, *The Hound of the Baskervilles: Another Adventure of Sherlock Holmes*, ed. by C. Frayling (2001). Further references are given after quotations in the text.

2. A.C. Doyle, 'Dry Plates on a Wet Moor', *British Journal of Photography*, 29 (1882), pp.627-9.
3. *Ibid.*, p.628.
4. *Ibid.*, p.628.
5. *Ibid.*, p.629.
6. 'A.C. Doyle (unsigned), 'The Winning Shot', *Bow Bells*, 39 (1883), pp.301-6.
7. *Ibid.*, p.62. Not an original image, for it occurs in Davies's 'Dartmoor Days'.
8. *Hound*, p.97.
9. A.C. Doyle, 'Silver Blaze', *Strand*, 4 (1892), pp.645-60.
10. A.C. Doyle, 'Silver Blaze', *The Adventures of Sherlock Holmes and The Memoirs of Sherlock Holmes*, intro. by Iain Pears (2001), p.285. Tavistock lies between the western heights of Dartmoor and the eastern heights of the Cornish moors.
11. A.C. Doyle, 'How the King Held the Brigadier', *The Exploits of Brigadier Gerard*, 1896, in *The Conan Doyle Historical Romances* (1932), pp.507-32.
12. In a letter from Doyle to his mother: R.L. Green and J.M. Gibson, *A Bibliography of A. Conan Doyle* (1983), p.129.
13. Letter from Doyle to his mother, 2 April 1901, qtd. Green, p.129.
14. E. Wheeler, '"Rescuer" of Sherlock Holmes', *WMN*, 24 October 1969, p.6, says that 'from all accounts [Harry Baskerville] was a most genial lovable man, extremely talkative and very proud of his connection with the great Conan Doyle, who had given him a proof copy of the book called after him'. Christopher Frayling in his introduction to the Penguin edition states the inscription in Baskerville's copy was signed by Robinson, p.xxviii.
15. *The Hound of the Baskervilles* predates Holmes's supposed 'death'. His survival was not revealed until October 1903.
16. A. Marshall, *Out and About: Random Reminiscences* (1933). Marshall says that Doyle intended the novel should appear under their joint names, but Doyle's 'name alone was wanted because it was worth so much more', p.5.
17. *Ibid.*, p.5.
18. *Fitz of Fitzford*, iii, p.20.
19. Poulain, p.20.
20. The allusion in her *Borders* to the sighting by a Tavistock resident of a 'hound start' as the clock struck midnight, she dismisses as the appearance of a living animal that had slipped away from its kennel. *Borders*, ii, p.320.
21. Crossing tells 'how a single black hound roams constantly over the Moor', and of Lady Howard travelling nightly between Tavistock and Okehampton 'in the form of a spectral hound'. *One Hundred Years on Dartmoor, Historical Notices of the Forest and its Purlieus*, 5th edn (1902), p.84. A Lydford sighting of a black dog was reported in 'The Fifth Report of the Exploration Committee on Devonshire Folklore', *TDA*, 12 (1880), p.100. The Dean Burn incident was included in various guide books from the late 19th century. By the 1960s about 170 black dog stories had been collected from all over Britain; see Theo Brown, 'The Black Dog in Devon', *TDA*, 91 (1959), pp.38-44.
22. S. Baring-Gould recounts a version of the Cabell legend in *Devon*, 6th edn (1922), p.126.
23. *Guavas*, p.157.
24. *Ibid.*, p.271.
25. *TLS*, 11 April 1902, p.101.
26. A.C. Doyle, *Micah Clarke: His Statement* (1892), p.87.
27. Thomson, p.255.
28. The only date mentioned in the novel is that inscribed on Dr Mortimer's walking stick: 1884. However, from a painstaking analysis of Holmes's life and work W. Baring-Gould has compiled the detective's chronology and places the events of *The Hound of the Baskervilles* between Tuesday 25 September and Saturday 20 October 1888. *Sherlock Holmes: A Biography of the World's First Consulting Detective* (1962), pp.257-8.
29. H.Greenhough Smith, ed., *What I Think – A Symposium on Books and Other Things by Famous Writers of Today* (1927), p.40.
30. This was the opinion of the Prison Commandant in *Queen of the Moor*.
31. *Hound*, p.75.
32. J.H. Speke, *Journal of the Discovery of the Sources of the Nile* (1863), p.xxviii.
33. 'Arthur Conan Doyle', *Book and Magazine Collector*, Feb 2006, p.58.

CHAPTER 13 – 'STARK STARING REALISM', pp.161-71.

1. H.R. Haggard, *Rural England: Being an Account of Agricultural and Social Researches Carried out in the Years of 1901 and 1902*, 2 vols (1902), i, p.185. Rowe was well known to Crossing and Phillpotts.
2. *Ibid.*, i, p.185.
3. W. Crossing, *A Hundred Years on Dartmoor*, 5th edn (1902).
4. There were six coach excursions to the moor each week from Bovey Tracey in 1889, expanding to two trips each day from 1891. Tours also operated in conjunction with rail services from Newton Abbot, Okehampton, and Moretonhampstead.
5. B.F. Cresswell, *Dartmoor and its Surroundings*, 4th edn (1905), p.121.
6. *Ibid.*, p.114.
7. In an hotel advertisement, *ibid.*, p.xii.
8. A.B. Collier's remark, quoted in *A Book of Dartmoor*, p.7.
9. There was rarely a day between July 2004 and

July 2005 without at least one signature in the book.

10. Location of Trevena's cottage and house in MS, John Trevena, Mémoire Présenté pour le Diplôme d' Etudes Supérieures, by Théophile, Tanguy, Université de Rennes, 1961. Private Collection.

11. At this time there was a sanatorium at Didsworthy on the southern slope of the moor above South Brent, and at Tawcroft, in Belstone.

12. Chapman & Son of Dawlish was foremost among firms responding to the challenge; their cards, instantly recognisable by the backward-sloping writing style of the captions, covered practically every aspect of moorland life and were on sale in practically every settlement in the region. Their photographs are included as illustrations in numerous books and, when, in 1967, the firm closed down, many of the negatives were placed in the County archive, a valuable resource for posterity.

13. J. Trevena, *Pixy in Petticoats* (1906), p.122. The first edition was published anonymously.

14. J. Trevena, *Heather* (1908), p.154.

15. *Pixy*, p.65.

16. *The Dartmoor House That Jack Built* (1909).

17. *Furze the Cruel* (1907).

18. *Heather* (1908).

19. *Granite* (1909).

20. *Pixy*, p.38.

21. *Ibid.*, p.39.

22. *Heather*, p.29.

23. In some editions the note is omitted.

24. *Heather*, p.7.

25. *Ibid.*, p.22.

26. *Furze*, p.174.

27. 'Granite', *Bookman*, 37 (1909), p.159.

28. *Furze*, pp..35-6. Further references to this novel will follow quotations in the text.

29. A fictitious name-place, in reality most probably Belstone, where there was a sanatorium, and was the village in which the author first lived when he moved to the area.

30. *Heather*, p.453.

31. *The Westminster Gazette*, u/d, pre-1912.

32. *Bookman*, 37 (1909), p.159. How times change: critic Mark Beeson believes *Granite* to be 'the nearest we have to Dartmoor literature of the highest order': Bob Mann, 'John Trevena', *Dartmoor Country Magazine*, 14 (2001), 22-4 (p.24).

33. *Granite*, pp.52-3.

34. *Ibid.*, p.58.

35. *Ibid.*, p.63.

36. There is, in Trevena's expression of this sentiment, an echo of Gray's 'Elegy Written in a Country Churchyard' (1750).

37. *Granite*, p.233.

38. 'Granite', *Bookman*, 37 (1909), p.159.

39. *Heather*, p.357.

40. As in Dante Alighieri's *The New Life (La Vita Nuova)*, trans. by Dante Gabriel Rossetti (1903).

41. *Pixy*, p.147.

42. *Ibid.*

43. *Pixy*, p.321.

44. *Ibid.*, pp.320-3.

45. *Ibid.*, p.134.

46. *Heather*, p.164.

47. *Dartmoor House*, pp.394-5.

48. *Ibid.*, p.401.

CHAPTER 14 – THE EPIC OF DARTMOOR, pp.172-88.

1. A phrase used by reviewer C.S. Evans, in 'Eden Phillpotts and the Epic of Dartmoor', *Bookman*, 49 (1916), p.115.

2. E. Phillpotts, *Widecombe Fair* (1913), p.vii. Unless stated all works cited in this chapter are by Phillpotts.

3. W.H.K. Wright, 'Eden Phillpotts, Poet and Novelist', *Devonian Year Book, 1912*, pp.43-68.

4. *The Journals of Arnold Bennett*, ed. by N. Flower (1932); *Letters of Arnold Bennett*, ed. by James Hepburn (1966).

5. W. Girvan, ed., *Eden Phillpotts: An Assessment and a Tribute* (1953).

6. A. Ross in *Reverie* (1981) suggests that her father was a serial adulterer – in the interests, or so he claimed, of his work. With regard to women and the 'love of women' Bennett quotes Phillpotts as writing: 'Some natures are self-contained and don't want it – some can't do without it. Golden Rule in the matter: *To keep the mouth shut and go one's own way*', Bennett, *Journals*, i, p.126.

7. J.Y. Dayananda, ed., *Eden Phillpotts (1862–1960), Selected Letters* (1984) (hereafter *Letters*).

8. That novel was *Children of the Mist* (1898).

9. *From the Angle of 88* (1951), p.119.

10. *Letters*, p.47.

11. 'Trash', in a letter to W.M. Colles, 3 February 1906, *Letters*, p.150; 'potboilers' and 'twaddle' when writing to R.A. Scott-James, 11 February 1908, *ibid.*, p. 56. There were detective stories; observations on nature; fairy tales; volumes of short stories; poetry; more than forty plays; and over ninety novels, some set in exotic locations, others in various parts of Britain.

12. Letter to R.A. Scott-James, 4 February 1908, *ibid.*, p.55.

13. Letter to R.A. Scott-James, 4 February 1908, *Letters*, p.55. Expressing ideas fashionable at the time, in the works of H. G. Wells and George Bernard Shaw, for example.

14. Sir A. Quiller-Couch, *Adventures in Criticism* (1924), pp.111-12.

15. *Letters*, p.54.

16. In a review of *The Mother* (1908). 'Mother and

Son', unsigned, in *Bookman*, 33 (1908), p 253.

17. *The Whirlwind* (1907). By 1916 this novel was acclaimed a 'masterpiece', with especial praise for the 'sheer tragic power' of the penultimate chapter in which the heroine kills herself as an act of reparation. C.S. Evans, 'Eden Phillpotts and the Epic of Dartmoor', *Bookman*, 49 (1916), pp. 115-21.

18. *Children of the Mist* (1898).

19. *Sons of the Morning* (1900).

20. 'Sons of the Morning', *Bookman*, 19 (1901), p.60.

21. *Letters*, p.138.

22. *Ibid.*, p.56.

23. *Ibid.*, p.142.

24. *Ibid.*, p.90; *The Secret Woman* (1905).

25. *The Portreeve* (1906).

26. *The Whirlwind* (1907).

27. William Barry, 'A Cruel Story', *Bookman*, 31 (1907), pp.261-2.

28. *Letters*, p.151.

29. *Ibid.*, p.62.

30. *The Virgin in Judgment* (1908).

31. A.G., 'The Virgin in Judgment', *Bookman*, 35 (1908), p 54.

32. *The Three Brothers* (1909).

33. Then the *Dousland Barn Hotel*, and known as Wonnacots. Quoted by L.A.G Strong, in 'The Dartmoor Novels', *Eden Phillpotts, An Assessment and a Tribute* (1953) p.33.

34. Keighley Snowden, 'Mr Phillpotts's New Novel', *Bookman*, 38 (1910), pp.42-3. This was *The Thief of Virtue* (1910).

35. *Letters*, p. 270.

36. *Demeter's Daughter* (1911).

37. *Letters*, p.264.

38. *The Forest on the Hill* (1912).

39. 'Mr Eden Phillpotts' Novel', *Bookman*, 42 (1912), p.38.

40. Evans, p.119. Phillpotts' scrupulous attention to detail is evident in the sketch of Widecombe included in his manuscript: Plymouth Local Studies Library, MS, Widecombe Fair.

41. *Widecombe Fair*, p.vii. The author uses a similar image in *Whirlwind*: Dartmoor was 'a hypaethral temple [...] where Nature rolls her endless frieze along entablature of Time', p.284.

42. Charles Darwin, *The Origin of Species*, ed. by J. W. Burrow (1966) p.119.

43. *The Portreeve* (1906), p.199.

44. *The Beacon* (1911), p.10.

45. *The River* (1902; 1965), p.6.

46. *The Forest on the Hill* (1912), pp.5-9.

47. *River*, p.112.

48. *Whirlwind*, p.17.

49. *Children*, pp.148-9.

50. *Portreeve*, pp.3-4.

51. *Children*, pp.99-100.

52. *Secret Woman*, p.4.

53. *Ibid.*, p.3.

54. *Angle*, p.125.

55. *Whirlwind*, p.6.

56. *Ibid.*, p.330.

57. *Ibid.*, pp.1-3.

58. E. Phillpotts, *The Thief of Virtue* (1910), pp.9-11.

59. *River*, p.221.

60. *Whirlwind*, pp.87-8.

61. *Ibid.*, p.88.

62. *Ibid.*, p.125.

63. *Ibid.*, pp.330-2.

64. *Ibid.*, p.323. 'Regression' was an important element of Darwinian theory and a late-Victorian anxiety.

65. *Ibid.*, p.331.

66. *Ibid.*, p.334.

67. *Virgin*, p.2.

68. *Sons*, p. 53.

69. *Sons*, p.58.

70. *Children*, p.284.

71. Most of the land had been farmed previously, then abandoned, but Will Blanchard does filch some additional pasture.

72. *Ibid.*, p.288.

73. *Ibid.*, pp.289-90.

74. *Ibid.*, pp. 281-2. Again that sense of the continuum of history.

75. *Ibid.*, p.82.

76. *Ibid.*, pp.114-15.

77. For a discussion on the demerits of popular 'blotterature', see Queenie Leavis, *Fiction and the Reading Public* (1932).

78. *Thief*, p.75.

79. *Letters*, p.54. There are over 460 characters in the 18 novels of the Dartmoor cycle according to Kenneth F. Day in *Eden Phillpotts on Dartmoor* (1981), pp.232-48.

80. *Portreeve*, p.54. The military authorities were expanding their leases on the moor.

81. *Thief*, p.186.

82. *Portreeve*, p.18. The viaduct across the West Okement was on the main railway route between Plymouth and Okehampton.

83. There were weekly markets in a number of moorland towns and an annual pattern of fairs and various gatherings.

84. *Three Brothers*, pp.229-33.

85. *Virgin*, p.2.

86. *Mother*, p.205.

87. *Sons*, p.157.

88. *Ibid.*, p.161.

89. *Children*, pp.60-1.

90. *Virgin*, p.128.

91. *Children*, p.60.

92. *River*, p.36.

93. *Ibid.*, p.366.

94. *Widecombe Fair*, p.495.

95. M.P. Willcocks, 'Mr Eden Phillpotts's New Novel', *Bookman*, 38 (1910), p.42.

CHAPTER 15 – SENSIBILITY AND SENSE, pp.189-99.

1. B. Chase, *The Heart of the Moor* (1914), pp.4-5. The giver of this advice quoted by Chase may well be John Oxenham, a popular author who wrote an effusive novel with Chase as its heroine, entitled *My Lady of the Moor* (1916).
2. Chase calls Widecombe-in-the-Moor Graystone. Some places she describes retain their identity.
3. *Heart of the Moor*, p.22.
4. *Ibid.*, p.117.
5. *Ibid.*, p.74.
6. *Ibid.*, p.1.
7. *Ibid.*, p.199.
8. Preacher John is similar to the stranger in Davies's *Dartmoor Days*, both almost Lob-like characters, personifications of the moor.
9. *Heart*, p.187.
10. *Ibid.*, p.27.
11. B. Chase, *Through a Dartmoor Window* (1915; 1917), pp.11-12.
12. *Ibid.*, p.v.
13. *Heart*, pp.85-94.
14. Cresswell, p.29.
15. B. Chase, *The Dartmoor Window Again* (1918), p.107.
16. A title probably coined by her friend, John Oxenham.
17. *Heart*, p.189.
18. *Ibid.*, p.166.
19. *Ibid.*, p.238.
20. *Window Again*, p 1.
21. Just to set the record straight, Tom Cobley was a native of Spreyton, and it was from that village he and his friends set out on the horse's fateful journey.
22. 'A Silver Jubilee', *WMN*, 2 February 1934.
23. *Punch*, 142 (1912), p.132.
24. The Parliamentary Debate, 5th series, vol 34, First volume of Session 1912, p 286.
25. E. Phillpotts, *The Secret Woman: A Play in Five Acts* (1912).
26. C. Meadowcroft says, in *The Place of Eden Phillpotts in English Peasant Drama: A Thesis* (1924), pp.30-1, that he wrote to Phillpotts who supplied details of the sentences, now quoted above.
27. *Angle*, p.81.
28. *WMN*, 19 December 1949. p.4.
29. W. Crossing, 'Present Day Life on Dartmoor: The Guide', *WMN*, 9 December 1903, p.5.
30. *Ibid.*
31. William Crossing, *Guide to Dartmoor: A Topographical Description of the Forest and Commons* (1909). A second edition appeared in 1912, the third in five parts between April and July 1914.
32. W. Crossing, *Crossing's Guide to Dartmoor: The 1912 Edition Reprinted With New Introduction*, intro. by Brian Le Messurier (1965), p.8.
33. W. Crossing, *Amid Devonia's Alps, or Wandering and Adventures on Dartmoor* (1888).
34. W. Crossing, *Gems in a Granite Setting* (1905). First published as a series, in the *WMN*, starting in August 1902.

CHAPTER 16 – DEWER RIDES, pp.200-6.

1. From *Punch*, quoted by Breton in *Heart of Dartmoor*, p.15.
2. S.P.B. Mais, *Glorious Devon* (1928), p.84.
3. D. St.Leger-Gordon, *Devonshire* (1950), p. 240.
4. H.V. Morton, *In Search of England* (1932), p.105.
5. *WMN*, 26 January 1932, p.5.
6. H. Breton, *The Forest of Dartmoor, 2: South-West* (1932), pp.55-6.
7. H. Breton, *Beautiful Dartmoor, 2 The Northern Quarter* (1912).
8. Eden Phillpotts, *The Farmer's Wife: A Comedy* (1914).
9. *The Farmer's Wife*, directed by Alfred Hitchcock (1926).
10. The Widecombe Edition in 20 volumes (1927-8), now a collector's edition.
11. L.A. G. Strong, *Dewer Rides* (1949), p.110. Further references to this edition are given after quotations in the text.
12. R.A.J. Walling, *The West Country* (1935), p.80.
13. *Glorious Devon*, pp.86-7.
14. A.J. Riedesel, *A New History of the 115th Station Hospital, United States Army WW2* (n.p).
15. *115 Station Hospital. Birth and Life of O115-7, England 1943-1945?* intro. by Robert E. McMahon (n.p).

CHAPTER 17 – A NATIONAL PARK, pp.207-10.

1. See various web sites and notices in car parks and villages for dates ranges are closed to the public.
2. *In Search of England*, p.111.

Select Bibliography

Adye, F., *Queen of the Moor*, 3 vols (1883)

Andrews, C., *The Prisoner's Memoirs etc; or, Dartmoor Prison, Containing a Complete and Impartial History of the Entire Captivity of the American in England* (1815)

'Arthur Conan Doyle', *Book and Magazine Collector*, Feb 2006

Autumn Campaign on Dartmoor', *ILN*, 9 August 1873

Autumn Manoeuvres: With the First Division', *WDM*, 31 July 1873

A-Z (Mrs Prior), Dartmoor Sketches

Baring-Gould, S., *John Herring* (1882)

Baring-Gould S., *Red Spider* (1887)

Baring-Gould S., 'Ballads in the West', *WA*, 8 (1889)

Baring-Gould S., 'Folk Songs and Melodies of the West', *WA*, 8 (1889)

Baring-Gould S., *Old Country Life* (1890)

Baring-Gould S., *Margery of Quether and Other Stories* (1891)

Baring-Gould S., *Urith: A Tale of Dartmoor*, 3 vols (1891)

Baring-Gould S., *Kitty Alone* (1895)

Baring-Gould S., *Guavas the Tinner* (1897)

Baring-Gould S., *Eve* (1898)

Baring-Gould S., *A Book of the West: Being an Introduction to Devon and Cornwall, Devon*, 2 vols (1899)

Baring-Gould S., *Early Reminiscences: 1834–64* (1903)

Baring-Gould S., *A Book of Dartmoor*, 2nd edn (1907)

Baring-Gould S., *A Book of Devon* (1909)

Baring-Gould S., *Devon*, 6th edn (1922)

Baring-Gould S., *Further Reminiscences: 1864-94* (1925)

Baring-Gould, Sabine, and H. Fleetwood Sheppard, *Songs of the West: Traditional Sons and Ballads of the West of the West of England* (1889)

Baring-Gould, W., *Sherlock Holmes: A Biography of the World's First Consulting Detective* (1962)

Barry, W., 'A Cruel Story', *Bookman*, 31 (1907)

Bate, C.S., 'On the Original Map of the Royal Forest, Illustrating the Perambulation of Henry III, 1240', *TDA*, 5 (1872)

Birkett, P., 'A Short History of the Rights of Common Upon the Forest of Dartmoor and the Commons of Devonshire', a Paper read in Plymouth on 26 October 1885 and printed in The Dartmoor Preservation Association's *A Short History: The Rights of Common*

Blackmore, R.D., *Lorna Doone* (1869)

Blackmore, R.D., *Christowell: A Dartmoor Tale* [1880]

Blackmore, R.D., *Good Words* (1881)

Blake, W.J., 'Hooker's Synopsis Chorographical of Devonshire', *TDA*, 47 (1915)

Bloomfield, R. 'The Farmer's Boy', *Bookman*, 37 (1909)

Bray, Mrxs, *Fitz of Fitzford: A Legend of Devon* (1830)

Bray, Mrs, *Warleigh or the Fatal Oak* (1834)

Bray, Mrs, *A Description of the Part of Devonshire Bordering on the Tamar and the Tavy: its Natural History, Manners, Customs, Superstitions, Scenery, Antiquities, Biography of Eminent Persons, Etc, Etc, in a Series of Letters to Robert Southey* (1836)

Breton, H., *Beautiful Dartmoor, 2 The Northern Quarter* (1912)

Breton, H., *The Heart of Dartmoor* (1926)

Breton, H., *The Forest of Dartmoor, 2: South-West* (1932)

Brice, A., *The Grand Gazetteer: or, Topographical Dictionary, Both General and Special and Ancient as Well as Modern* (1759-74)

Brice, T., *The History and Description Ancient and Modern of the City of Exeter* (1802)

Britton, J. and E.W. Brayley, *Beauties of England and Wales: or Delineations Topographical, Historical, and Descriptions of Each County*, 18 vols (1803)

Brooke, R., *Collected Poems* (1918)

Brooks, C., *The Gothic Revival* (1999)

Brown, T., 'The Black Dog in Devon', *TDA*, 91 (1959)

Buck, N. & S., *Antiquities, or Venerable Remains of Above Four Hundred Castles, Monasteries, Palaces etc. in England and Wales* (1726-52)

Burke, E., *A Philosophical Enquiry into Our Ideas of the Sublime and Beautiful*, 2nd edn (1757)

Burnard, R., *Dartmoor Pictorial Records*, 4 vols (1890-94)

Burnard, R., 'Dartmoor Preservation', *WA*, 9 (1890)

Camden, W., *Britannia: Siva Florentiss Imorum Regnorum Angliae, Scotiae, Hiberniae, et Insularum Adiacentium Exintima Antiquitate 1586*; (1594)

Camden, W., *Camden's Britannia, Newly Translated into English, With Large Additions and Improvements*, trans. and ed. by Edmund Gibson (1695)

Camden, William, *Britannia; or, A Chorographical Description of the Flourishing Kingdoms of England, Scotland, Ireland, and the Islands Adjacent From Earliest Antiquity*, trans. and ed. by Richard Gough, 3 vols 1607 (1789)

Carrington, H., *The Plymouth and Devonport Guide: With Sketches of the Surrounding Scenery* (1828)

Carrington, H.E., ed., *The Collected Poems of the Late Nicholas Carrington*, 2 vols (1834)

Carrington, N. *Dartmoor, A Descriptive Poem* (1826)

Chapman, R.W., ed., *Johnson's Journey to the Western Isles of Scotland, and Boswell's Journey of a Tour to the Hebrides With Samuel Johnson*, LL.D. (1965)

Chapple, W., *A Review of Part of Risdon's Survey of Devon; Containing the General Description of That County; With Corrections, Annotations, and Additions* (1785)

Chapple, W., *Description and Exegesis of the Drew's Teignton Cromlech: With Some Previous Particulars Relative to that Parish, and the Farm Whereon the Cromlech Stands* (1779?)

Chase B., *The Heart of the Moor* (1914)

Chase B., *Through a Dartmoor Window* (1917)

Chase B., *The Dartmoor Window Again* (1918)

Clarendon, E., Earl of, *The History of the Rebellion and Civil Wars in England, Begun in the Year 1641*, 3 vols 2nd ed. (1704)

Collier, W.F., 'Dartmoor', *TDA*, 8 (1876)

Collier, W.F., 'First Report of Committee on Dartmoor', *TDA*, 9 (1877)

Cooke, M., ed., *The Diocese of Exeter in 1821: Bishop Carey's Replies to Queries before Visitation*, vol 2. Devon (1960)

Cottle, J., *Dartmoor and Other Poems* (1823)

Cox, T., *A Topographical, Ecclesiastical, and Natural History of Devon* (1700)

Cresswell, B.F., *Dartmoor and its Surroundings*, 4th edn (1905)

Crossing, W., 'The Moorland Haunts of the Pixies', *WA*, 5 (1886)

Crossing, W., *Amid Devonia's Alps, or Wandering and Adventures on Dartmoor* (1888)

Crossing, W., 'Tales of the Dartmoor Pixies', *WA*, 7 (1888)

Crossing, W., *A Hundred Years on Dartmoor*, 5th edn (1902)

Crossing, W., 'The Artist', *WMN*, 18 November 1903

Crossing, W., 'Present Day Life on Dartmoor: The Guide', *WMN*, 9 December 1903

Crossing, W., *Gems in a Granite Setting: Beauties of the Lone Land of Dartmoor*, (1905)

Crossing, W., *Guide to Dartmoor: A Topographical Description of the Forest and Commons* (1909)

Crossing, W., *Crossing's Guide to Dartmoor: The 1912 Edition Reprinted With New Introduction*, ed. by B. Le Messurier (1965)

'Dartmoor Manoeuvres: With the Enemy', *WDM*, 13 August 1873

'Dartmoor Manoeuvres: With the First Division', *WDM*, 20 August 1873

'Dartmoor Prisons', *FP*, 12 September 1850

'Dartmoor', *Western Miscellany: A Journal of Literature, Science, Antiquities, and Art for the West of England 1849* (1850)

Darwin, C., *The Origin of Species*, ed. by J.W. Burrow (1966)

Davidson, J.R. 'Some Anglo-Saxon Boundaries, Now Deposited at the Albert Museum, Exeter', *TDA*, 8 (1887)

Davies, E., *Celtic Remains* (n.d.)

Davies, E. W. L., *Dartmoor Days; or, Scenes in the Forest. A Poem* (1862)

Day, K.F., *Eden Phillpotts on Dartmoor* (1981)

Dayananda, J.Y., ed., *Eden Phillpotts (1862–1960), Selected Letters* (1984)

Defoe, D., *A Tour Through the Whole Island of Great Britain*, ed. by P. Rogers (1988)

Devonian, A., *Devonshire Scenery: or, Directions for Visiting the Most Picturesque Spots in the Eastern and Southern Coast, from Sidmouth to Plymouth (1826) Devonshire Doomsday and Geld Inquest: Extensions, Translations, and Indices*, 2 vols (1884-1892)

Dixon, S., *Castalian Hours* (1829)

Dixon, S., *A Journal of Ten Days Excursion* (1829?)

Dixon, S., *A Journal of Eighteen Days Excursion on the Eastern and Southern Borders of Dartmoor* (1830)

Donn, B., *A Map of the County of Devon, 1765* (1965)

Doyle, A.C., 'Dry Plates on a Wet Moor', *British Journal of Photography*, 29 (1882)

Doyle, A.C. (unsigned), 'The Winning Shot', *Bow Bells*, 39 (1883)

Doyle, A.C., *Micah Clarke: His Statement* (1892)

Doyle, A.C., 'Silver Blaze', *Strand*, 4 (1892)

Doyle, A.C., 'How the King Held the Brigadier', *The Exploits of Brigadier Gerard*, 1896 (1932)

Doyle, A.C., 'The Hound of the Baskervilles', *Strand Magazine*, 22 (1901), and 23 (1902)

Doyle, A.C., *The Hound of the Baskervilles: Another Adventure of Sherlock Holmes*, ed. by C. Frayling (2001)

Doyle, A.C., 'Silver Blaze', *The Adventures of Sherlock Holmes and The Memoirs of Sherlock Holmes*, intro. by Iain Pears (2001)

Drayton, M., *Poly-Olbion*, ed. by J. William Hebel, 4 vols (1933)

Dunn W.H., *R.D. Blackmore*, London (1956)

Dymond, R., ed., *'Things New and Old' concerning the Parish of Widecombe-in-the-Moor and Its Neighbourhood* (1876)

European Magazine and London Review, 7 (1785)

Evans, C.S., 'Eden Phillpotts and the Epic of Dartmoor', *Bookman*, 49 (1916)

Evans, R., *Home Scenes: Tavistock and its Vicinity* (1846)

Examiner, 28 July 1811

J. Farington, *The Farington Diary*, 8 vols (1926)

The Farmer's Wife, directed by Alfred Hitchcock (1926)

'Fifth Report of the Exploration Committee on Devonshire Folklore', *TDA*, 12 (1880)

Finberg H.P.R., *Tavistock Abbey: A Study in the Social and Economic History of Devon* (1951)

Fitz of Fitzford, *Philo-Danmonian: A Western Magazine of Matters Chiefly Original*, 1 (1830)

Flower N., ed., *The Journals of Arnold Bennett* (1932)

Flying Post, 7 March 1833

Fogwill, E.G., 'Pastoralism on Dartmoor', *TDA*, 86 (1954)

Fraser, R., *General View of the County of Devon: With Observations on the Means of its Improvement*, London, 1794 (1970)

French, H., 'Sermons in Stones', *Dartmoor Magazine*, 20 (1990)

Fuller, T., *The History of the Worthies of England*, 1662, rev. by J. Nicholls, 2 vols (1811)

G. A. 'The Virgin in Judgment', *Bookman*, 35 (1908)

G. K., 'An Essay on English Roads', *GM*, 22 (1752)

Gibbons, M.S., *'We Donkeys' on Dartmoor* (1886)

Giles, J.A., *William of Malmesbury's Chronicle of the Kings of England* (1911)

Gill, C., ed., *Dartmoor: A New Study* (1970)

Gilpin, G., *Three Essays on Picturesque Beauty; on Picturesque Travel; and on Sketching Landscape: to Which is Added a Poem, on Landscape Painting*, 2nd edn (1794)

Gilpin, W., *Observations on the River Wye, and Several Parts of South Wales, etc: Relative Chiefly to Picturesque Beauty, Made in the Summer of 1782* (1991)

Gilpin, W., *Observations on the Western Parts of England: Relative Chiefly to Picturesque Beauty, to Which Are Added, a Few Remarks on the Picturesque Beauties of the Isle of Wight*, 2nd edn (1808)

Girvan W., ed., *Eden Phillpotts: An Assessment and a Tribute* (1953)

Gordon, D., St Leger-, *Dartmoor in all its Moods* (1931)

Gordon, D., St Leger-, *Devonshire* (1950)

Gough, R., *British Topography; or, An Historical Survey of What Has Been Done for Illustrating the Topographical Antiquities of Great Britain and Ireland*, 2 vols (1780)

Gray, T., ed., *Travels in Georgian Devon: The Illustrated Journals of John Swete*, 4 vols (1997-2000)

Green, R.L. and J.M. Gibson, *A Bibliography of A. Conan Doyle* (1983)

'The Guarding of Eden', *Punch* (1912)

Haggard, H.R., *Rural England: Being an Account of Agricultural and Social Researches Carried Out in the Years of 1901 and 1902*, 2 vols (1902)

Hamilton-Leggett, P., *The Dartmoor Bibliography 1534-1991 Including a 1992 supplement, Non Fiction* (1992).

Hamlyn, G., *Rustic Poems by George Hamlyn, the Dartmoor Bloomfield* (1869?)

Harleian Miscellany, 'A True Relation of Those Sad and Lamentable Accidents, Which Happened in and About the Parish Church of Withycombe in the Dartmoores in Devonshire on Sunday the 21st of October Last, 1638' (1638); repr. *Harleian Miscellany: or a Collection of Scarce, Curious, and Entertaining Pamphlets and Tracts as Well in Manuscript as in Print, Found in the Late Earl of Oxford's Library, Interspersed With Historical, Political, and Critical Notes*, 12 vols (1809)

Harris, J.H., *My Devonshire Book: 'In the Land of Junket and Cream'* (1907)

Harvey, L.A. and D. St Leger-Gordon's *Dartmoor* (1953)

Hemans, F., *The Works of Mrs Hemans With a Memoir of her Life by her Sister*, 7 vols (1839)

Hemery, E., *High Dartmoor: Land and People* (1983)

Hepburn, J., ed., *Letters of Arnold Bennett* (1966)

Hicks, H. R., 'William Payne: Painter in Oils and Water Colours', *TDA*, 75 (1943)

'Hound of the Baskervilles', *Times Literary Supplement*, 11 April 1902

Howard, N., *Bickleigh Vale, With Other Poems* (1804)

In Parliament: Plymouth and Dartmoor Railroad Prospectus (1819)

Independent Whig, 28 July 1811

Ingzdon', *WT*, 22 August 1873

'John Trevena', *American Bookman*, 28 (1908)

Johns, J., *The Dews of Castalie: Poems on Various Subjects* (1828)

Jones, J.P., *Guide to the Scenery in the Neighbourhood of Ashburton, Devon* (1823)

Jones, J.P., *Observations on the Scenery and Antiquities in the Neighbourhood of Moreton-Hampstead, and on the Forest of Dartmoor, Devon* (1823)

Kempe, J.A. ed., *Autobiography of Anna Eliza Bray, 1789-1883* (1884)

King, R.J. 'The Forest of the Dartmoors', *The West Country Garland* (1873)

Kingsley, C., *Westward Ho!* (1855; 1961)

Kingsley, Mrs, ed., *Charles Kingsley: His Letters and Memories of his Life* (1908)

Laskey, J., 'Excursion on Dartmoor, July 21, 22, 23, and 24', *GM*, 65 (1795)

Laskey, J., 'Three Days Excursion on Dartmoor', *GM*, 66 (1796)

Le Messurier, B., *Dartmoor Artists* (2002)

Leavis, Q., *Fiction and the Reading Public* (1932)

Lefevre, G.A.S., Baron Eversley, *English Commons and Forests: The Story of the Battle During the Last Thirty Years for the Public Rights over the Commons and Forests of England and Wales* (1894)

Leland, J., *The Itinerary of John Leland the Antiquary, Published From the Original Manuscript in the Bodleian Library by Thomas Hearne, to Which is Added Antoninus's Itinerary Through Britain, With Various Readings and Dr Robert Talbot's Annotation Upon it*, 3rd edn, 3 vols (1769)

Lipscomb, G., *A Journey into Cornwall Through the Counties of Southampton, Wilts, Dorset, Somerset, and Devon: Interspersed with Remarks Moral, Historical, Literary, and Political* (1799)

Lyall, E., *Donovan: A Modern Englishman* (1822; 1888)

Lysons, D. and S., *Magna Britannia: Being a Concise Topographical Account of the Several Counties of Great Britain*, 6 vols (1822)

Mais, S.P.B., *Glorious Devon* (1928)

Mann, B., 'John Trevena', *Dartmoor Country Magazine*, 14 (2001)

Manwood's Treatise of the Forest Laws: Shewing Not Only the Laws Now in Force, but the Original Forests, What They Are, and How They Differ From Chase, Parks, and Warrens, With Such Things as are Incident to Either, 4th edn, rev. by W. Nelson (1717)

Marsh, Mrs, *Chronicles of Dartmoor* (1866)

Marshall, A., *Out and About: Random Reminiscences* (1933)

Marshall, J., *The Complete Works of Horace: Translated by Various Hands* (1927)

Marshall, W., *Rural Economy*, 2 vols (1796)

Marshall, W., *The Rural Economy of the West of England Including Devonshire and Parts of Somersetshire, Dorsetshire, and Cornwall, Together with the Minutes in Practice*, 2 vols, London, 1796 (1970)

Marshall, W., *A Review; or Complete Abstract of the Reports to the Board of Agriculture* (1808-17)

Martin, L.C., ed., *The Poems of Robert Herrick* (1956)

Maton, W.G., *Observations Relative Chiefly to the Natural History, Picturesque Scenery, and Antiquities of the Western Counties of England Made in the Years 1794, and 1796* (1797)

McMahon, Robert E., *115 Station Hospital. Birth and Life of O115-7, England 1943-1945?* (n.p)

Meadowcroft, C., *The Place of Eden Phillpotts in English Peasant Drama: A Thesis* (1924)

Monthly Magazine (1826)

Moore, S.A. and P. Birkett, *A Short History: the Rights of Common Upon the Forest of Dartmoor and the Commons of Devon. Report of Mr Stuart A. Moore to the Committee, and Appendix of Documents* (1890)

Moore, T., *The History of Devonshire: From the Earliest Period to the Present*, 2 vols (1829)

'The Morton and South Devon Railway', *DWT*, 1 June 1866

'The Morton Railway', *DWT*, 8 June 1866

Moreton, H.V., *In Search of England* (1932)

'Mother and Son', unsigned, in *Bookman*, 33 (1908)

'Mr Eden Phillpotts' Novel', *Bookman*, 42 (1912)

'Mr. Polwhele's Circular Letter to His Subscribers', *GM*, 59 (1789)

Murray, *Handbook for Travellers in Devon and Cornwall*, 5th edn (1863)

'Nooks and Corners', *FP*, 29 August 1850

Oriental Herald, 1826?

Oxenham, J., *My Lady of the Moor* (1916)

Page, John Ll.W., 'The Names of the Dartmoor Tors', *WA*, 7 (1888)

Parliamentary Debate, 5th series, vol 34, First volume of Session 1912

Phillips, J., 'Arts and Crafts on Dartmoor in the Year when Queen Victoria was Crowned. Being Notes on the Narrative of Mrs Elizabeth Bidder, Daughter of William and Johanna Lillicrap, of the Parish of Sheepstor', *TDA*, 25 (1894)

Phillpotts E., *Children of the Mist* (1898)

Phillpotts E., *Sons of the Morning* (1900)

Phillpotts E., *The River* (1902; 1965)

Phillpotts E., *The Secret Woman* (1905)

Phillpotts E., *The Portreeve* (1906)

Phillpotts E., *The Whirlwind* (1907)

Phillpotts E., *The Mother* (1908)

Phillpotts E., *The Virgin in Judgment* (1908)

Phillpotts E., *The Three Brothers* (1909)

Phillpotts E., *The Thief of Virtue* (1910)

Phillpotts E., *Demeter's Daughter* (1911)

Phillpotts E., *The Beacon* (1911)

Phillpotts E., *The Forest on the Hill* (1912)

Phillpotts E., *The Secret Woman: A Play in Five Acts* (1912)

Phillpotts E., *Widecombe Fair* (1913)

Phillpotts E., *The Farmer's Wife* (1914)

Phillpotts E., *From the Angle of 88* (1951)

Pococke, R., *The Travels Through England of Dr Richard Pococke, Successively Bishop of Meath and of Osborn During 1750, 1751, and Later Years*, ed. by James Joel Cartwright (1888)

Polkinghorne, A.E., 'A Poet's Pride in Devon', *WMN*, 2 September 1930

Pollock, F., *A Short History of the Rights of Common Upon the Forest of Dartmoor and the Commons of Devon* (1890)

Polwhele, R., *Historical Views of Devonshire in Five Volumes* (1793)

Polwhele, R., *A History of Devonshire*, 3 vols (1797-1806)

Polwhele, R., *Traditions and Recollections; Domestic, Clerical and Literary: in Which Are Included Letters of Charles II, Cromwell, Fairfax, Edgecumbe, Macaulay, Wolcot, Opie, Whitaker, Gibbon, Buller, Courtenay, Moore, Downman, Drewe, Seward, Darwin, Cowper, Hayley, Hardinge, Sir Walter Scott, and other Distinguished Characters*, 2 vols (1826)

Poulain, J., *Les Deux Soeurs* (1852), trans as *The Two Sisters: A Dartmoor Story*, by J.E.R.W., ed. by W.H.K. Wright (1891-2)

Preest, D., trans., *The Deeds of the Bishops of England: Gesta Pontificum Anglorum* (2000)

'Preface', *Topographer*, 1 (1789)

Prince, J., *Danmonii Orientales Illustres: The Worthies of Devon* (1701)

Prowse, A.B., 'An Index of References to Dartmoor and its Borders Contained in the Transactions, vols I to XXX', *TDA*, 37 (1905)

Pudor, P., 'Dartmoor', *FP*, 30 August 1849

Pycroft, G., 'Art in Devonshire', *TDA*, 13 (1881)

Pycroft, G., 'Art in Devonshire', *TDA* 14 (1882)

Quiller-Couch, Sir A., *Adventures in Criticism* (1924)

Read, T., *The English Traveller: Giving a Description of Those Parts of Great Britain Called England and Wales*, 2 vols (1746)

Riedesel, A.J., *A New History of the 115th Station Hospital, United States Army WW2* (n.p)

Risdon, T., *The Chorographical Description; or, Survey of the County of Devon, Printed From a Genuine Copy of the Original Manuscript; With Considerable Additions* (1811)

Ross, A., *Reverie* (1981)

Rowe, S., 'Antiquarian Investigations in the Forest of Dartmoor', *TPI*, 1 (1828)

Rowe, S., *A Perambulation of the Antient and Royal Forest of Dartmoor, and the Venville Precincts; or, A Topographical Survey of the Antiquities and Scenery; With Notices of the Natural History, Climate, and Agricultural Capabilities, and a Valuable Collection of Antient Documents* (1848)

Rowe, Samuel, *A Perambulation of the Antient and Royal Forest of Dartmoor and the Venville Precincts; or, A Topographical Survey of Their Antiquities and Scenery*, 3rd edn revised and corrected by J.B. Rowe, 1896 (1985)

Secundus, A., 'Letter from Plymouth', *GM*, 62 (1792)

'Selected Minutes of Council, Appointing Committees', *TDA*, 11 (1879)

'Silver Jubilee', *WMN*, 2 February 1934

Smiles, S., *Lives of the Engineers*, 5 vols (1874)

Smith, H.G., ed., *What I Think – A Symposium on Books and Other Things by Famous Writers of Today* (1927)

Smith, A., *An Inquiry into the Nature and the Causes of the Wealth of Nations*, 1776, 2 vols, (1909)

Snell, K.D.M., ed., *The Regional Novel in Britain and Ireland: 1880-1900* (1998)

Snowden K., 'Mr Phillpotts's New Novel', *Bookman*, 38 (1910)

'Sons of the Morning', *Bookman*, 19 (1901)

Speke, J.H., *Journal of the Discovery of the Sources of the Nile* (1863)

Spooner, G.M. and F.S. Russell, eds, *Worth's Dartmoor, Compiled from the Published Works of the late R. Hansford Worth* (1981)

Spry, J., 'Benjamin Gayer: An Okehampton Legend', *WA*, 3 (1884)

Stokes, S., *The Lay of the Desert: A Poem in Two Cantos* (1830)

Strong, L.A.G., *Dewer Rides* (1949)

Strong, L.A.G., in 'The Dartmoor Novels', *Eden Phillpotts, An Assessment and a Tribute* (1953)

Swete, J., 'On Some of the More Remarkable British Monuments in Devon', *Essays by a Society of Gentlemen of Exeter* (1796)

Tanner, E.F., 'Dartmoor Encroachments', *WA*, 2 (1883)

Tanner, H., *The Cultivation of Dartmoor: A Prize Essay* (1854)

Tenatus, 'The Author of "Dartmoor"', *SDMM*, 2 (1833)

Thompson, W., *The Works of William Browne: Containing Britannia's Pastorals With Notes and Observations by the Rev. W. Thompson. The Shepherd's Pipes, Consisting of Pastorals. The Inner Temple Masques Never Published Before; and Other Poems With the Life of the Author* (1772)

Thomson, B., *The Story of Dartmoor Prison* (1907)

Torr, C., *Small Talk at Wreyland* (1918)

Tovey, D.C., ed., *The Letters of Thomas Gray: Including the Correspondence of Gray and Mason*, 2nd edn, 2 vols (1909)

Tozer, E. ('Tickler'), *Devonshire Sketches: Dartmoor and its Borders* (1869)

Trevena, J., *Pixy in Petticoats* (1906)

Trevena, J., *Furze the Cruel* (1907)

Trevena, J., *Heather* (1908)

Trevena, J., *The Dartmoor House That Jack Built* (1909)

Trevena, J., *Granite* (1909)

Tyrwhitt, T., Substance of a Statement Made to the Chamber of Commerce, Plymouth, on Tuesday, 3rd Day of November, 1818, Concerning the Formation of a Rail Road from the Forest of Dartmoor to the Plymouth Lime-Quarries, With Additional Observations and a Plan of the Intended Line (1819)

Vancouver, C., *General View of the Agriculture of the County of Devon, With Observations on the Means of its Improvement: A Report of the Work Drawn up for the Consideration of the Board of Agriculture and Internal Improvement*, 1808 (1969)

Véos, Ó., 'Dartmoor', *FP*, 17 October 1850

'The Virtuous Lady Mine', *SDMM*, 2 (1833)

Walling, R.A.J., *The West Country* (1935)

Warner, R., *A Walk Through Some of the Western Counties* (1800)

Westcote, T., *A View of Devonshire in MDCXXX: With a Pedigree of its Gentry*, ed. by G. Oliver and P. Jones (1845)

Western Luminary, 28 April 1818 [Sir T. Tyrwhitt Return]

Westminster Gazette, u/d, pre-1912

Wetherbee, W., trans. and ed., *Architrenius* (1994)

Wheeler, E., '"Rescuer" of Sherlock Holmes', *WMN*, 24 October 1969

White, W., *White's Devon: History Gazetteer and Directory of Devonshire*, 1850 (1968)

Willcocks, M.P., 'Mr Eden Phillpotts's New Novel', *Bookman*, 38 (1910)

William, 'Chronicles of Dartmoor', *EPG*, 24 December 1836

Williams, T.H., *Picturesque Excursions in Devon and Cornwall*, 1 Devonshire (1804)

Williams, T.H., *A Guide to the Picturesque Scenery and Antiquities of Devonshire*, 3rd edn (1830)

WMN, 26 January 1932, p.5

Woollcombe, H., *To the Presidents, Officers and Members of the Several Literary and Philosophical Societies Established in the Counties of Cornwall and Devon* (1835)

Wordsworth, W., 'A Description of the Scenery of the Lakes in the North of England', in T. Wilkinson's *Select Views of Cumberland* (1810)

Worth, R.H., 'Address of the President', *TDA*, 62 (1930)

Worth, R.H., *Worth's Dartmoor, Compiled from the Published Works of the late R. Hansford Worth*, ed. by G.M. Spooner and F.S. Russell (1891)

Worth, R.N., *The West Country Garland: Selected From the Writings of the Poets of Devon and Cornwall, From the Fifteenth Century to the Nineteenth Century, With Folk Songs and Traditional Verses* (1875)

Worth, R.N., *A History of Plymouth: from the Earliest Period to the Present Time* (1877)

Worth, R.N., '"William of Worcester," Devon's Earliest Topographer', *TDA*, 18 (1886)

Worth, R.N., *A History of Devonshire* (1895)

Wright, W.H.K., 'Eden Phillpotts, Poet and Novelist', *Devonian Year Book* (1912)

WT, 16 August 1873

Manuscripts

Bodleian Library, MS. Top. Devon b.1-2; d.1-2; e.1-6. Notes by J.P. Jones.

DRO, 51/7/7/1-16, John Andrews

DRO, Courtney. 1508. M. Devon. 88. Mining 19

MS, John Trevena, Mémoire Présenté pour le Diplôme d'Etudes Supérieures, by Théophile Tanguy, Université de Rennes, 1961. Private Collection.

MS Widecombe Fair Plymouth Local Studies Library

MS, Songs of the West: Devon and Cornwall as Taken Down, Words and Melodies, From the Mouths of the People, 2 vols (1892) Plymouth Local Studies Library

PWDRO, MS, 74/287, mf 1-3, The Decimes; or, A Chorographicall Description of the County of Devon – 1650

PWDRO, 51/7/11/3, Letter to Richard Gray, 28 February 1795

PWDRO, 1/133, Receiver's Book

PWDRO, 522/1, Letter to the Editor of the *British Review*, March 1826

PWDRO, 710/608, Woollcombe diaries

PWDRO, 710/397, mf 46-50, Woollcombe, diaries

INDEX

Numbers in **bold** refer to illustration page numbers
Roman numerals refer to colour plates

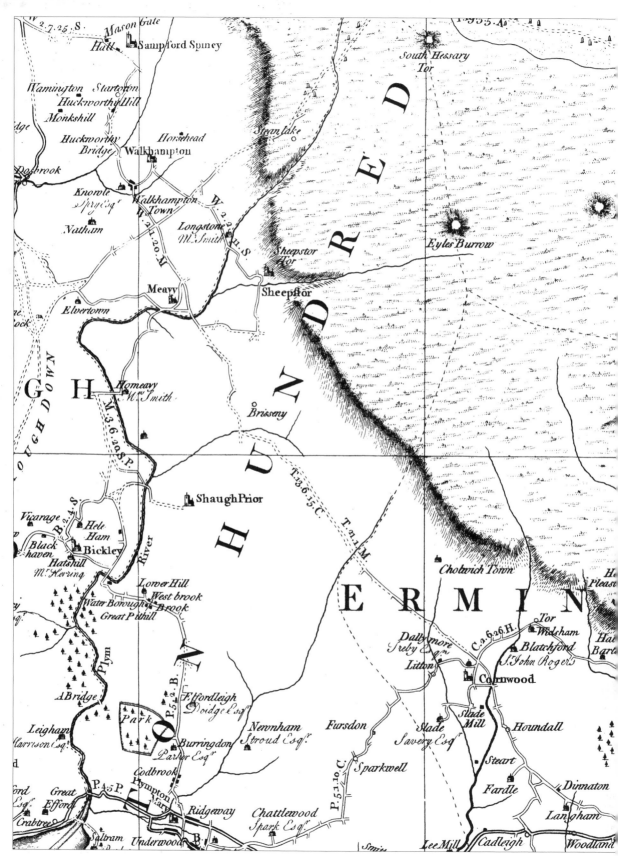

Dartmoor – from Donn's Map of Devon, 1765.